DEREK WALCOTT'S LOVE AFFAIR WITH FILM

Photograph of Derek Walcott courtesy of Sigrid Nama

DEREK WALCOTT'S LOVE AFFAIR WITH FILM

JEAN ANTOINE-DUNNE

PEEPAL TREE

First published in Great Britain in 2017
Peepal Tree Press Ltd
17 Kings Avenue
Leeds LS6 1QS

ISBN13: 9781845233655

Dedication

To: Senan, Lea, Ceola, Ava,
Danann & Freyja Mary-Jean
Dunne

ACKNOWLEDGEMENTS

First of all I wish to thank Professor Edward Baugh for reading and commenting on the manuscript at an early stage. Eddie, I deeply value your support and your encouragement. Thanks to Jeremy Poynting for his sensitive editing and careful scrutiny and Hannah Bannister for her help and generosity. Thank you to my students whose insights have enabled me to see this work in a new light. I am also grateful to all the film artists with whom I have worked for all their many lessons in seeing, listening and framing. In this regard Albert Bailey, sound editor, deserves particular mention. Thank you to the University of the West Indies Campus Research and Publications for three grants that have allowed the completion of this work. My thanks go also to Mrs Angela Harding and Ms Adel Bain for their administrative support.

A very special thanks to all the librarians with whom I have worked and who have been so helpful for more years than I can remember as I perused the Walcott collections at the Alma Jordan Library, the University of the West Indies and the University of Toronto. In particular, I am grateful to Mrs Lorraine Nero, Senior Librarian, for her help over an extended period. The illustrations in this book are there in the main because of the generosity of the Alma Jordan Library, the University of the West Indies and the Thomas Fisher Rare Book Library at the University of Toronto, where I undertook a considerable portion of my research, and for permissions to reproduce material. Thank you to Jennifer Toews in particular who is my main guide in the Walcott archives and whose warmth and support I deeply value. Thank you also to my sister, Professor Rose Marie Antoine who first insisted that I visit these archives when I lived in Ireland, and to Dr. Kenny Anthony for his guidance during filming and researching in St. Lucia and for his hospitality. In St Lucia, both Monsignor Patrick Anthony and Robert Lee have provided support and help as well as friendship.

The actors with whom Derek Walcott worked have been generous and sustaining. Particular mention should be made of Albert Laveau, Michael Cherrie, Nigel Scott and Wendell Manwarren. Christopher Laird of Banyan has been exceptionally generous during the research for this book and during the making of my documentary film, *Walcott as Poet and Seer*. He not only provided copies of video productions, but gave advice and material from the Gayelle/ Banyan archives. I also wish to thank Michael Gilkes.

I am deeply indebted to Sigrid Nama who has always been so kind, so generous and so willing to offer her friendship and hospitality, even as she cared for Derek during his final illness. My thanks are also due to the Literary Executors of Walcott's estate, his daughters Elizabeth and Anna, for permissions to quote from the Walcott archives and unpublished material.

My deepest gratitude is to Derek Walcott himself. Derek was courteous and generous both in his time and in making available material whenever I needed it, and the fact that he had been so since my undergraduate days is truly a sign of his extraordinary personality and depth of spirit. I recall in particular interviewing him in 2015 and his patience. My thanks are most particularly due for the permissions for the use of illustrations and manuscript material that he has granted over the years.

I wish to acknowledge the use of a photograph by Bruce Paddington, which he took during the filming of *The Rig*. The cover image for this book is a reproduction of one of Derek Walcott's recent paintings, based on his musical *Moon-Child* and the stage play, *Ti-Jean.* Derek very graciously allowed its use for this book.

CONTENTS

Prologue 11

Introduction
The Film Sense and the question of form 13

Chapter 1
Film and the attack on the Senses 24

Chapter 2
The Body as Instrument. Shock and Dissonance 39

Chapter 3.
Film and the True Light of the World 63

Chapter 4
Creating at the Interstices 80

Chapter 5
Lines of Sight and Sound and a Leap to the Sublime 102

Chapter 6
Revolution and Return 128

Chapter 7
The Rig and Omeros as Film 142

Chapter 8
Ghostly Echoes 159

Chapter 9
Making New 177

Conclusion 189

Works Cited 191

Index 203

ILLUSTRATIONS

Derek Walcott at home – frontispiece
Title page "Ti Jean" 19
Page from "Ti Jean Notebook" 21
Zora Dancing from *Steel* 54
"Omeros" Storyboard, page eight 84
"Omeros", Hector hurling his javelin 86
Design for "Marie Laveau": Overseer 98
Design for "Marie Laveau": Sam and Marie 99
Design for "Marie Laveau": Marie 100
Design for "Remembrance" 101
"Omeros" Storyboard, page one 106
"Omeros" Storyboard, page ten 111
Design for "The Haytian Earth" 115
Design for "The Haytian Earth" 116
Design for "Vangelo Nero" 119
Design for "Vangelo Nero" 121
Image from "To Die for Grenada" 129
Image from "To Die for Grenada" 130
Storyboard from "To Die for Grenada" 131
Filming *The Rig* 143
"Omeros" Storyboard 152
"Omeros" Storyboard: Helen in the bar 157
Storyboard for "Franklin" 183
Page from "Ti Jean Notebook" 184

PROLOGUE

Walcott wrote many film scripts and his deeply visual poetry moved into a form of film writing. Whether Walcott could ever have produced viable film works is not the point at issue. What is important is that film provided him with a way of thinking about art, and this includes poetry as well as painting, and a way of communicating directly into the mind and body of the audience and of using all the expressive means available to a Caribbean poet. Film, and the qualities specific to the camera, also allowed him to think through ideas of what constituted beauty and the Caribbean's image of itself as this has been shaped by the passage of time.

The question arises in this era of the digital whether film is relevant. I assert at the outset that we still use film montage as a structural principle in film's digital metamorphosis. This book is about montage and its relevance to poetry.

Interestingly, one of Walcott's most recent works is a mural-like painting of *Moon-Child*, a version of *Ti-Jean*, which is composed in a way that is quite similar to the ribbon of a film. The various characters are distributed in a flattened space throughout the canvas without use of perspective or any form of foregrounding of any individual character. This may, of course, be an influence of the art of Latin America. I choose to think that it is another way of Walcott working out the play *Ti-Jean* as a film script, and there are several versions of such attempts.

Ti-Jean represented for Walcott a classic folk figure and an image of resistance. The innocence of this character and its status in Walcott's *oeuvre* and the constant reworking of this early play suggest that Walcott may perhaps have yearned to be clear and to be accessible. Film provided the medium for this clarity and impact. According to Albert Laveau in a 1992 interview, film led Walcott to an increasing clarity in his stage plays.

> Laveau: I find that the plays have changed. All of them almost up to *O Babylon*, had that sort of symbolic quality, whereas in the newer plays, like *Steel*, *Viva Detroit*, to a lesser extent *Marie Laveau*, the themes, for one thing, have changed, and they are written in a less poetic manner. I'd ascribe this to his departure from the Caribbean, you know, his living in the States. They're more naturalistic as opposed to metaphorical, more filmic....[1]

He added that when he asked Walcott what new plays he had written, he answered, "What plays? Films boy. I want to do films." Walcott's desire to make films, a desire that is well recorded, led then to a change in style, content and structure of his literary works. In particular, his language and his forms seek clarity and effective communication. This, I argue, led Walcott to both the study and the application of very specific film techniques, gleaned from classical film theory and practice, and early theorised by the filmmaker and aesthetician, Sergei Eisenstein.

I specify Eisenstein in this study, despite the fact that Walcott was influenced by many other filmmakers, including Akira Kurosowa, whom he acknowledged. I speak specifically to Eisenstein's work in the first instance because he is the clearest articulator of problems of composition in film editing. He is also a philosopher of film and despite the fact that he worked in silent cinema, his published works remain the key classical texts for all film students. Walcott's poetry confronts many of the issues that Eisenstein sought to resolve in his writings and film-making, in particular film's capacity to create affect, its relation to time and its move to the poetic. Eisenstein's writings, and in particular his film, *The Battleship Potemkin*, are used throughout this book in a manner similar to the way that we think of Shakespeare when writing about literature: his presence hovers. But more specifically with Eisenstein, the body of his published work enables a theorisation of what I see as Walcott's desire to introduce film into writing. Finally, I argue that Gilles Deleuze in his thinking through of the image of cinema was deeply influenced by Eisenstein. While Dziga Vertov's mechanical Kino-Eye and indeed his *Man with A Movie Camera* (1929) provide a logical explanation for the creation of a virtual reality in Deleuze's work and his use of machine assemblages, it is to Eisenstein that Deleuze looks for his basic premises. Vertov's *cinéma vérité* style of documentary movie making still resonates today, but it is the Eisensteinian idea of shock and emotional and psychological impact that I see as directly important to Walcott's evolving film sense.

The use of film has a philosophical dimension and one that is related to Walcott's belief in the wonder, the awe and the newness of Caribbean life and culture. Film has the capacity to make new at each and every re-enactment. Unlike the stage, each projection of film is fashioned by a mind constructed and imbued with a particular world view, and is therefore a re-crafting of the work – not simply in the sense of any art's reformulation by a particular viewer or reader, but by the fact that film's movement in time triggers a response in body and mind that activates a new way of seeing. This idea leads us to encounter the philosopher Gilles Deleuze.

Endnote

1. "Derek Walcott poet and playwright", Wayne Brown interview with Albert Laveau, *Sunday Guardian Magazine*, 18 Oct. 1992 p. 8.

INTRODUCTION

THE FILM SENSE AND THE QUESTION OF FORM

> The essence of a thing never appears at the outset, but in the middle, in the course of its development, when its strength is assured. (Deleuze, *The Movement-Image*)

We all know Walcott as a poet. I see him as a film poet, although he made only a few films, because he appears to have been unable to generate the capital for realizing the many film scripts that he wrote. Another reason for the failure to complete films was Walcott's need to have control over the material and the reluctance of potential financiers to allow this. According to Dean Walton, with whom he worked on the filming of *Ti Jean*, at least one such meeting ended after six minutes when the producer suggested another director.[1] However, the evidence shows that he very obviously wanted to become a filmmaker. His attempts at film script writing and his several versions of film scripts for plays and poems demonstrate this.

Walcott made a number of attempts to produce his films. In 1972, he worked closely with director Ossie Maingot in the production of *Malcauchon*, which, was filmed for Trinidad and Tobago television in 1972. *Pantomime* was produced by Trinidad & Tobago Television and directed by Horace James in 1978. *Pantomime* was also filmed in 1982 at Gainsville, Florida, but there are no credits on the film. *Dream on Monkey Mountain* was filmed by Banyan for Carifesta 1981 in Barbados. There are also no credits on the Banyan footage. In 1979 Michael Gilkes adapted *Ti-Jean and His Brothers* for Stage One production under contract for the Ministry of Labour and Community Welfare Services in Barbados.[2] This was filmed by Banyan Productions, who filmed a number of Walcott's stage plays and also rehearsals for *The Last Carnival*. *Beef, No Chicken*, *A Branch of the Blue Nile* and others, with Derek directing them. This 1979 film version of *Ti-Jean* begins with a colourful prelude that includes drawings by Walcott of frog and landscape and one has the sense that this was conceived as an animated film. There are several film versions of this play, including an animation script and storyboards. Walcott seems to have been obsessed with *Ti Jean*. In 1970, a version of *Dream on Monkey Mountain* was aired on Trinidad and Tobago television, starring Errol Jones as Makak and directed by Hugh Robertson, who later directed the Trinidadian film *Bim* in 1974. It was shot at different locations in Trinidad and was cut from three hours to 52 minutes. After bad reviews, Walcott, according to Irma Rambaran, decided to make his own films.[3] *The Haytian Earth* was written initially as a five part television series. It was then adapted for stage and subsequently filmed and televised in St Lucia. Banyan Productions also filmed a version of *Marie Laveau*. There are many scripts for films that bear no relation to the stage plays or that began as film and ended as stage plays. "Voyage a Cythère" began as a film scenario, and then merged into a film script called *The Last Carnival* and then mutated into a stage drama, and bears some relation to the film script "To Die for Grenada." *The Rig* (1983) is Walcott's only completed feature film and was written and conceived as a film for television, initially as a television series. It was produced by Banyan Productions with Bruce Paddington as producer and Christopher Laird as editor. Walcott also wrote the script and developed storyboards for *Hart Crane*, directed by Lawrence Pitkethly, with Nigel Scott as Hart Crane. This was filmed in St. Lucia and screened in Trinidad in 1985. This film allowed Walcott to experiment with outdoor shots, in particular of the sea, which he saw as one of the great attributes of film-making. The 1980s appear to be years of intense film activity and this resonates in the poem "The Fortunate Traveller".

Walcott himself has stated in conversation that the non-production of his films was due to a lack of funding from a society that places little value on the arts. Film is expensive and in need of patronage.[4] He was unable to finance his film productions and this fact is recorded in his archive, which contains correspondence, and an agreement dated 1 April 1972, between Walcott and the Italian Dino deLaurentiis, which was later severed.[5] For Walcott, then, his love of film materialises as completed works, most often in his poetry.

This study, then, contains the premise that, for varying reasons, Walcott's desire to make films remained more a desire than a reality, but that desire nonetheless influenced the poetic works. It examines this impact on his writing through archival evidence from available papers at the West Indiana section of the University of the West Indies, St. Augustine, and the Thomas Fisher Library at the University of Toronto and through an examination of what cinema means in the Caribbean. By this I mean the very important fact of Caribbean writings' engagement with the oral traditions and ways of seeing, and equally the fact that the Caribbean has had to encounter images of itself in film. These images have pointed to, by and large, as in films such as *I Walked with a Zombie* and *Fire Down Below,* as well as the more recent exoticisation of this space in *Pirates of the Caribbean*, a clear need to confront the visual image in the desire to re-imagine the Caribbean's idea of itself.

This notion is already implicit in Walcott's use of the postcard image, which he has reworked constantly. The land is as "flat" as a postcard and this space, which is ripe for appropriation by the tourist and his camera, became the core figure that Walcott reworked and reinvented. I will look at Caribbean theory and literature and their correspondence with and influence on Walcott's work in this re-conceptualization of the visual and its ideological implications. In this sense, this work will also create a conversation between film theorists such as Sergei Eisenstein and film philosophers such as Gilles Deleuze and Walcott. It suggests a move towards an audiovisual "moving" image as a site of creativity and a way of generating thought and the new.

Derek Walcott's visual sense led to works such as *Tiepolo's Hound*, which incorporates his paintings, and to later poems, in particular *Omeros* and *The Prodigal*, in which the visual is an important part of the dynamic. He was a multifaceted artist and his stage plays and his post 1980 poems, in particular, point to significant attempts to use the many facets of his work and life to create a form of hybrid aesthetics. *Arkansas Testament*, *Omeros, The Prodigal* and *Tiepolo's Hound*[6] exemplify his desire to find a form through which the paradoxes of his chosen apprenticeship to a Western classical tradition and his simultaneous position as spokesperson for the Caribbean person, who is predominantly black, might achieve a harmonious marriage. The idea of blackness, later imaged in the black mongrel, already foregrounds the notions of sight and visibility. These core concerns led to a preoccupation with finding a mechanism to articulate his growing sense of relation to the experiences of the black Caribbean and the relevance of these experiences to the world at large. His later writings bring him in close proximity to Édouard Glissant's position as expressed and theorised in Glissant's *Poetics of Relation*.[7]

Glissant in *Poetics* is concerned with form and language and with the relationship between aesthetics and ethics. His reformulation of Deleuze and Guattari's theory of the rhizome and the vital transformative effect of the simulacrum as a site of difference, enabled Walcott to think the future through the potential of the flight of the imagination and to imagine art as a medium through which boundaries of time and territory are made fluid.[8] To be able to imagine and to re-invent through an imagined or simulated reality is at the very heart of Walcott's writing since "The Muse of History".

The potential of the imagination to create myths brings his thinking in line with filmmakers for whom cinema, or more properly, film, is the new myth-making art that has superseded oral narratives. It achieves its power because of its control of both time and space: film allows time and space to become both plastic and elastic. A film can condense time and it can stretch time. It can elide boundaries of space and make new connections through editing, and in this process of bringing together pieces to make a new and productive whole, film-making is an art that leaps from material to concept or moves from a concrete event to a process of conceptual transformation. However, film also brings different modes of existence into one frame and in this way gives new power to these images. As Walcott observed in a 1983 review, written probably while completing *The Rig*:

> The child's mind may be more capable of accepting, even of creating, its own fears than the adult's, just as it is more capable of making a world of inconceivable peace, or one of permanently possible delight. It is, in retrospect, a mind of fantastic strength in which fantasy can be controlled and directed. It is a mind that flies. (pp. 37 & 51) [9]

What is most significant in "Papa's Flying Machines" is the idea that the flight of fantasy and imagination with which a child endows experience is compared in filmic terms to what a film does through framing, so that, "images defined in the boundary of a frame can have all the terrors of authority". The word "terror" links the frame to the sublime, but it also creates a relation between the purity of a child's imagination and the enduring quality of the mythic as it shapes how the adult sees the world. This is one of the key themes and structures of *The Prodigal*.

In a peculiar way the art of film draws close to the philosophical insights of writers such as Édouard Glissant and Wilson Harris. The writings of Harris, specifically his theorising of art as a portal through which the past and present maintain a plastic relationship, because the limbo imagination forges a new architecture through body and word, are almost filmic in their conception. Harris's work as a whole is relevant for reading the new positions and techniques employed by Walcott post nineteen-eighty.[10]

In this book, I will focus on a selection of film scripts and scenarios to illustrate Walcott's theorising of the filmic and his incorporation of classical montage forms into both film and poetry. I use the word montage here in its widest sense and as used by classical film theorists for whom film *is* montage. Montage means editing or constructing by putting fragments together and the word comes from engineering. This means that film only becomes an art form when it uses the techniques of editing to place fragments or shots in a construction that is meaningful and powerful, and that takes account of film's capacity to stretch time and to condense time. Classical montage sees movement as giving a new dimension to the image, since movement provides psychological and emotional power. For Soviet artists, such as Sergei Eisenstein, who were schooled in the dialectic, montage also meant a form of opposition or putting conflict at the base of the shot, as in quick cutting dialectical montage. This conflict is also to be found within the *mise en scène* and the play of sound and image even when there are smooth transitions.[11]

Tracing the development of a film aesthetic in Walcott's later works also means pointing out how some motifs, such as that of the coral and the photograph, have undergone extensive changes. These transformations develop in tandem with his changing views of Western traditions, and his ideas of national as well as racial identity.

These mutations are particularly relevant to his use of the motif of the photograph and his increasing use of this figure in opposition to that of the cinematic. The poem *Omeros*, for example, contains several images of the camera. These include the photographic lens which Philoctete fears will steal his soul; the lens of the glasses of Ma Kilman; and the slit eyes of the iguana in lines such "The slit pods of its eyes/ ripened in a pause that lasted for centuries,/ that rose with the Aruacs' smoke till a new race/ unknown to the lizard stood measuring the trees" (*Omeros*, 4-5). In the latter image of the iguana, the camera signifies a witness that reinforces its nature as a tool for recording and as an extension of memory. The camera also signifies an immutable present or presence in the face of constant apparent change. The camera moves into the cinematographic in such instances, as in the use of montage technique in the word "cut", most specifically in the recounting of Hector's death. *Omeros* is a key text in my analysis of Walcott's use of the filmic because, of all of Walcott's work, it best expresses his familiarity with film and his experiments with filmic time and affect. I consider it the work that brings to fruition Walcott's concern and experimentation with the cinematic and its constant reference throughout this book is inevitable.

I use film as a vehicle of thought and affect throughout this analysis and engage Gilles Deleuze as a philosopher who has creatively appropriated and extended Eisenstein's conception of film montage as a vehicle of thought and as an art of time. The use of the word "affect" is specific to Eisenstein in this book. Film creates an affective response in the body and then the mind of the viewer. It does this through what Eisenstein calls "the attraction", which is any "available means" to strike a "hammer blow" on the psyche of the viewer.

Eisenstein "discovered" the "fourth dimension" of cinema on the cutting table and many of his writings attempt to push this new art of time and movement to its limit and to think cinema as a vehicle for shaping concepts and for raising consciousness. Deleuze developed theories of the movement-image and the time-image, which he saw as the images that give power to thought, or to the creation of the outside of thought. By this, he meant that cinema enables the viewer to think difference and beyond institutionalised ways of seeing and beyond incarcerating ideas.

The cinematic has power for Deleuze because it mirrors the brain.[12] The brain is a screen and processes thought and memory in specific ways. These ways are not static, but change with the passage of time and of circumstance and evolving events, including the effects of trauma. So that for Deleuze the brain thinks differently after World War Two, and the cinema of this period represents or images that new thought process. In his introduction to that important collection, *The Brain is the Screen. Deleuze and the Philosophy of Cinema*, Gregory Flaxman describes this idea in these words:

> Whatever their intricacies and digressions, *The Movement-Image* and *The Time-Image* fundamentally contend that, beyond all other arts, the cinema opens the possibility for deterritorializing the cogito, the rigid "image of thought" that in one form or another has dominated Western philosophy. The cinema provokes us to see, to feel, to sense, and finally to think *differently*, and while this induces Deleuze to write his two volumes, those volumes in turn compel us to return to the cinema, to see its images in the light of our own captivity to the rituals of representation, the philosophic-narrative program we have been running. [...] they constitute, to twist a phrase of Foucault's, an "introduction to non-fascist thinking".[13]

Philosophy for Deleuze consists of an act of construction and artists construct what he terms as "percepts" through which philosophy can engage on the level of concepts. There is no "always already given" thought or truth, but rather something that of necessity needs to be created. The project of film is one of hijacking the terrorism of systems that engage in official discourses and through this guerrilla warfare to "mobilize against the artillery of the powers of the false". This is exemplified in the cinema through its creation and construction of false images or simulacra. Thus Baudrillard's "demonic image" takes on a particular force here.[14] Cinema's capacity to generate the new and to enthral the viewer intrigues both Deleuze and Eisenstein. Film is a generator of illusions and thus is an art form that enables the triumph of the imagination as the creator of chimeras and fictions. This idea of the new and the possibilities of the imagination create an extraordinary connection between these thinkers and a writer such as Walcott. For Deleuze, cinema already introduces movement into thought,[15] so that the leap from cinema to philosophy is ready made and inevitable. For Walcott, and indeed for Kamau Brathwaite, movement is introduced into poetry to simulate the effect of the cinematic and to provoke new ways of seeing beyond received ideologies.

The capacity of film to insinuate an idea of reality that is in opposition to official records and versions is initially located for Walcott in the art of improvisation. The Caribbean as a place that is looked at and that generates voyeuristic photographs and postcards opens the possibility for the image of shipwreck. Those who are left with nothing, must make new. The Caribbean imagination shapes the possibility of a new aesthetic from the grit and guts of the sheer need to survive. The film script and stage play for *Pantomime* provide initial examples of the attempt by Walcott to marshal an idea of newness through ex-tempo language and improvisation in the Caribbean.

TI-JEAN AND HIS BROTHERS
Animated Film

Screen Play by:
DEREK WALCOTT

Songs and Music by:
ANDRE TANKER

Original Play by:
DEREK WALCOTT

Author's Agent:
Bridget Aschenberg
International Famous Agency Inc.
1301 Avenue of the Americas
New York, N.Y. 10019
U.S.A:

Title page for "Ti Jean"
Derek Walcott Collection, The Alma Jordan Library, UWI St Augustine, box 6 folder 27

The goat is a primary vehicle for this idea in *Pantomime* and is a first sally into a poetics of sense and body that culminates in *Omeros*.[16] It evokes the use of a limbo aesthetic or an aesthetic that remembers Africa and the gods of other cultures in spatialised form. Erna Brodber's kumbla metaphor[17] and the constant use of the Anansi figure throughout the Caribbean exemplify such usage and give concrete and sensuous expression to the relation between body, survival and craft, and creativity born of necessity on these islands.

The poem *Omeros* also foregrounds the idea of "endurance", both in terms of the lasting capacity of art, the will to survive, and the artist's ability to transform the relics of the past to make new forms, as exemplified in the "craft", "In God we Troust". There are, however, differences in the ways in which these ideas are articulated in the poem *Omeros* and the film script of that name, though there are differences between this and earlier storyboards for "Omeros". My analysis focuses on the dual conceptions of the poem and the film script written circa 1995.[18] The discussion uses both works as vehicles for examining earlier works such as *The Fortunate Traveller* and *The Arkansas Testament*, since these provide clues to the progression of Walcott's interest in film forms and ideas.

I am referring to film scripts throughout this book, but most of these scripts are in archival holdings or in personal collections and are not in the public domain. The Walcott archives, which are primarily lodged in the West Indiana section of the Alma Jordan library of the University of the West Indies in St. Augustine, Trinidad, and at The Thomas Fisher Rare Book Library at the University of Toronto, provide essential insights into the formative influence and relationship between his films, his stage plays and his poetry. The various film versions of several stage plays including *Ti Jean, O Babylon, Franklin, Pantomime, The Last Carnival*, *A Branch of the Blue Nile* and *Steel,* show that Walcott has either had a dual conception of film/stage productions for these plays, or has conceived of them, in some instances, as films.

Helen Camps, one of Walcott's close associates in the early years of the Trinidad Theatre Workshop, has suggested in conversation that Walcott's lack of success as a film producer/writer is related to his over-dependence on words which, in a film, hamper the visual impact of the production.[19] Many of the works for film have, nonetheless, influenced the formal structure and the visualisation of his later poetry. This is the core of my argument and I examine Walcott's use of contrapuntal montage, his use of the close-up, his creation of interstitial spaces that generate overtones, and his evocation of spectral presences through the facility of filmic devices.

The later works, in particular *Tiepolo's Hound* and *The Prodigal*, are read alongside earlier works specifically as they evoke metaphors, in particular light as figure and also as formal device, derived from Walcott's concern with film's effective transmission of ideas and the mechanisms through which these ideas enter into the body of the audience. Of course, poems are not films and their efficacy is, one might say, a simulation of a simulation. This is one of the primary issues this book seeks to address.

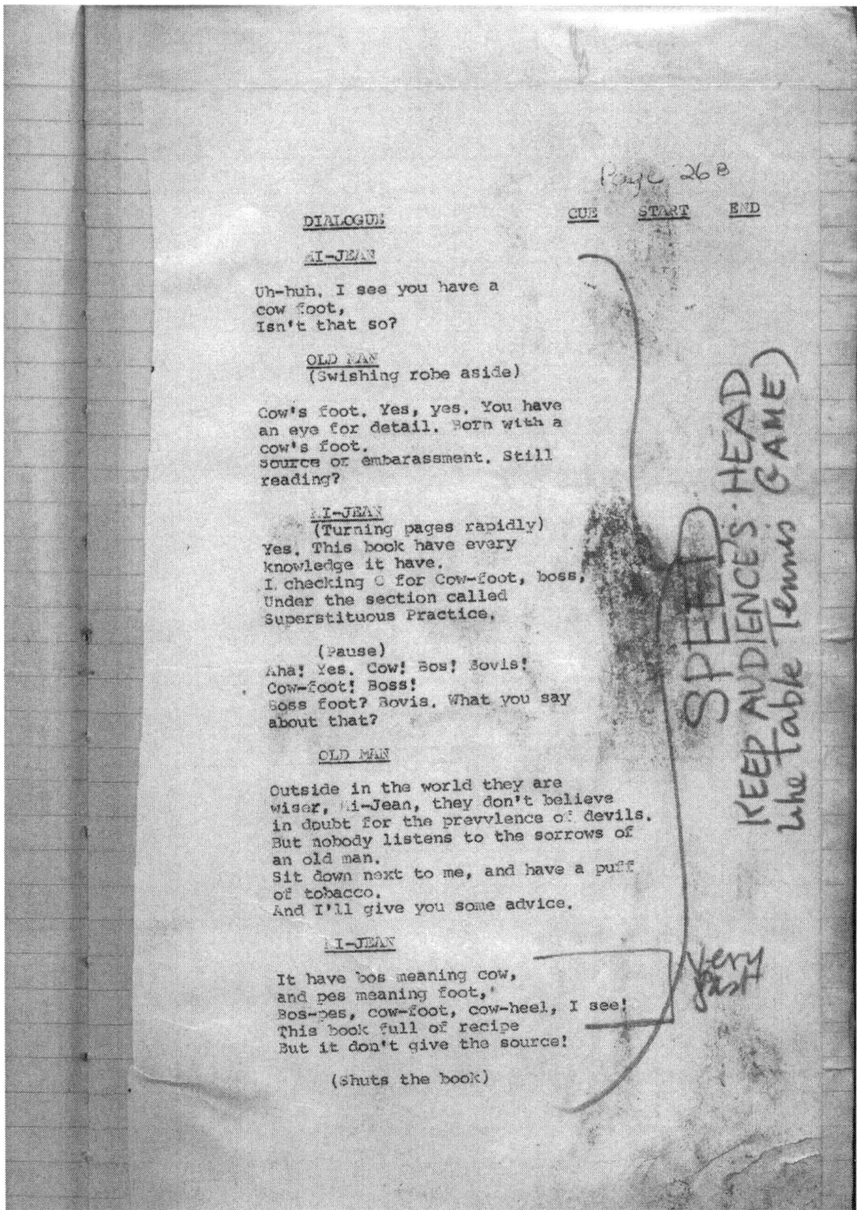

Page 26B

DIALOGUE | CUE | START | END

TI-JEAN

Uh-huh. I see you have a
cow foot,
Isn't that so?

OLD MAN
(Swishing robe aside)

Cow's foot. Yes, yes. You have
an eye for detail. Born with a
cow's foot.
Source of embarassment. Still
reading?

TI-JEAN
(Turning pages rapidly)
Yes. This book have every
knowledge it have.
I checking C for Cow-foot, boss,
Under the section called
Superstituous Practice.

(Pause)
Aha! Yes. Cow! Bos! Bovis!
Cow-foot! Boss!
Boss foot? Bovis. What you say
about that?

OLD MAN

Outside in the world they are
wiser, Ti-Jean, they don't believe
in doubt for the prevvlence of devils.
But nobody listens to the sorrows of
an old man.
Sit down next to me, and have a puff
of tobacco.
And I'll give you some advice.

TI-JEAN

It have bos meaning cow,
and pes meaning foot,'
Bos-pes, cow-foot, cow-heel, I see!
This book full of recipe
But it don't give the source!

(Shuts the book)

SPEED
KEEP AUDIENCES HEAD
like Table Tennis (GAME)
Very Fast

Page from "Ti Jean Notebook"
Derek Walcott Collection, The Alma Jordan Library, UWI St Augustine, box 10 folder 13

Endnotes

1. Conversation with Dean Walton in St Lucia on 25th April at his studio in Castries.
2. Irma Rambaran, "Reel Text: a comparative analysis of the filmic works of Derek Walcott", MPhil Thesis presented to the University of the West Indies, St Augustine, 2011.
3. See Irma Rambaran's MPhil Thesis.
4. Derek Walcott in conversation with Jean Antoine-Dunne, 14 October 2015, filmed at his home in Cap in St Lucia.
5. Letters and telegrams between Walcott and Dino deLaurentiis concerning "Vangelo Nero". No. 29. Box 7, Derek Walcott Collection, Alma Jordan Library, The University of the West Indies, St Augustine: "I think very highly of it, but it does not reflect the type of film I wanted to make." Final telegram 6 June 1972.
6. *The Fortunate Traveller* (New York: Farrar, Straus and Giroux, 1982); *The Arkansas Testament* (London: Faber and Faber, 1987); *The Prodigal* (New York: Farrar, Straus and Giroux, 2003); *Tiepolo's Hound* (New York: Farrar, Straus and Giroux, 2000).
7. Édouard Glissant, *Poetics of Relation*, trans., Betsy Wing (Michigan: University of Michigan Press, 1997).
8. I will be referring throughout this book to Gilles Deleuze's *Cinema 1. The Movement-Image*, trans., Tomlinson and Habberjam (London: Athlone Press, 1992) and *Cinema 2. The Time-Image*, trans. Tomlinson and Galeta (London: Athlone Press, 1989).
9. Derek Walcott, Review of *The Glorious Flight. Across the Channel with Louis Blériot*, July 25, 1909. Written and illustrated by Alice and Martin Provensen (NY, the Viking Press). In the *New York Times Book Review*, Nov. 13, 1983, p. 37.
10. I am using *The Fortunate Traveller* as a point of departure.
11. See the introduction to *The Montage Principle. Eisenstein in New Cultural and Critical Contexts*, eds. Jean Antoine-Dunne and Paula Quigley (Amsterdam: Rodopi, 2004).
12. See *The Brain is the Screen. Deleuze and the Philosophy of Cinema*, ed. Gregory Flaxman (Minneapolis and London: University of Minnesota Press, 2000), p. 254.
13. Gregory Flaxman, *The Brain is the Screen. Deleuze and the Philosophy of Cinema*, p. 3.
14. Jean Baudrillard, *The Evil Demon of Images* (Sydney: Power Institute Publications, 1987).
15. Gregory Flaxman, "The Brain is the Screen. An Interview with Gilles Deleuze", trans. Marie Therese Guirgis, *The Brain is the Screen*, pp. 365-373.

16. Derek Walcott, *Remembrance and Pantomime* (New York: Farrar, Straus and Giroux, 1980).
17. See Erna Brodber, *Jane and Louisa Will Soon Come Home* (London: New Beacon, 1983).
18. The script is at the Thomas Fisher Rare Books Library, The University of Toronto. There are other versions of this script. There are also storyboards that were completed before this 1995 version of the film script.
19. Helen Camps, telephone interview, 22 June 1993. Republic of Ireland.

CHAPTER 1

FILM AND THE ATTACK ON THE SENSES

As an art form, film challenges the supremacy of the written word, while extending the reach of the word, since in terms of its written script, it originates as written language, but as film it navigates into the spheres of both music and the visual arts. As such, the use of film techniques enables an attack on the senses and the direct projection of an idea. Film also has the technical ability to make shadows move, and through this give the illusion of the past as a ghostly presence existing in the present. In a real sense film allows the existence of spectres.

In this chapter I introduce an outline of the classic film theory of Sergei Eisenstein and its postmodernist revision by Gilles Deleuze. The pertinence of Deleuze's ideas to the Caribbean is noted in the work of the Martiniquan poet and theorist, Édouard Glissant. Ideas from these writers are used to begin the discussion of Walcott's poetics of the visual in time.

In Walcott's essay "Down the Coast",[1] it is film's capacity to engender a presence that is in part imagination and part mythic that makes the writer yearn to make a film of the play *Ti-Jean*. Thus, despite the fact that a "film falls short and even shrivels from poetry" and, "A film can be poetic but it cannot be poetry",[2] film remains a yearned-for product. As a writer and a poet and one invested in giving shape to the imagination of a particular people, Walcott states in the same breath in which he expresses the apparent limitations of film, that this desired project was "what I was determined to do."[3] "Down the Coast", as an essay, evokes all the senses, and further summons sight, smell and sound to create a medley of meaning, that is also aligned to memory.

But the essay also musters an argument about the "thereness" of simile as opposed to metaphor. According to Walcott, film cannot deal in metaphors because one frame follows the other and the meaning is always a result of one thing being "like" another. "Only simile can be filmed, not metaphor, the two halves of separate frames placed or run side by side or one after the other stops at *this is like that*, since metaphor has no conjunctions".

But film, he argues, nonetheless breeds a new way of seeing. Film in this sense is both concrete and ephemeral. Its origin is the "isness" of a thing and its "thereness". But as a projection it gives permission to the imagination to create fantasy, because of the very fact of placing one frame after the next. In other words, he refers us to the creation of a new concept through montage where the juxtaposition of two elements leads, not to the sum of the parts, but to a new idea-image.[4] This plasticity is the key to Walcott's enthralment. What is not visible offers an open ground of possibility, which is always amenable to transformation in this most pliable mechanical technological art – an art that is at heart based on tricks and illusions, but which, despite this, is able to seduce the viewer into belief. Film can do this because, as Eisenstein discovered, it plays on the senses, not the mind.

Laura Marks has pointed out in *The Skin of the Film. Intercultural Cinema, Embodiment and the Senses*,[5] that film can generate sensuous memories and that it penetrates the body through the activation of sense. Walcott notes in "Down the Coast" that the seduction of Soufriere and the tale of Ti-Jean and his brothers was stimulated by the memory both of wandering in the region and of his aunt Sidone telling tales to himself and his twin brother Roderick. "The landscape was already paradisal, but not to the labourer, only to two young boys, my twin brother and I, who drank in the stories and chants of Sidone, her head now heraldic and sibylline, her voice the guttural of a cave or of a blackbird possessed by its own chortling. A voice that was a landscape, an island in itself."[6]

Sound and sight combine to activate memory. For Marks, film has a key function in the stimulation of memory. This for her occurs through the senses, in particular the sense of touch. The importance of film's utilisation of the body and sense she derives from the writings of Gilles Deleuze. What for her is important in the writings of Deleuze is his recognition of the potency of film montage in its penetration of the body through a system of vibrations generated by movement. Marks and Deleuze use this image as a way of entering into those spaces that we now associate with migrants and refugees. These are dubbed "any spaces whatever" in that they are areas of transition with no connection to a homogeneous whole or nation or even community.[7] Sensory vehicles of affect enable the confrontation of the silences and erasures of the past, in particular where trauma has given rise to huge gaps of memory, where loss of history has led to what one might term cultural amnesia.

For Deleuze, those "any spaces whatever", which became visible post World War Two, led to a recognition of the interstitial spaces and extreme situations of migrant peoples for whom the past exists as "overwhelming erasures, silences and lies of official histories" (Marks, p. 45). The new cinema of post World War Two, which Deleuze calls the cinema of the "time-image", "confronts" this lack of history of diasporic communities by excavating the traces of memory that remain resident in the body. Deleuze, throughout his *Cinema 1. The Movement-Image*, takes Latvian filmmaker and theorist Sergei Eisenstein as a point of departure for his description of the movement-image, but differentiates in *Cinema 2* between Eisenstein's organicism, or a cinema that seeks unity and a raising of consciousness, and post-war cinema that ruptures that idea of unity and creates instead wide fissures between past and present, therefore enabling a pure image of time.[8]

For Eisenstein, montage, or the construction of a film through the editing together of disparate lines or images, often in opposition to each other, meant the creation of a system through which the viewer could be led from one state to another, higher state or consciousness. This was possible because film through its movement, and as an art of time and movement, acted on the nervous system of the viewer and triggered the generation of thought through the body. Eisenstein's many writings, in particular in *Film Sense*, *Film Form* and the posthumous work *Nonindifferent Nature*[9], describe this qualitative leap and its many stages and attempt to trace the processes through which this power of affective communication and transmission could be accomplished. Deleuze takes up what is in effect Eisenstein's theory of "the attraction" and the recognition of the fourth dimension of cinema, or the inclusion of time, and incorporates these theories into a philosophy of film.[10] While Deleuze's conception of a cinema of the time-image moves away from the organic whole of classical cinema and towards a cinema of disjunction or "irrational cuts", through which "pure time" gushes forth, it nonetheless uses Eisenstein's key ideas of "the attraction" and the "overtone".

The overtone is not the same as a musical overtone. The overtone of film is a resonance that emerges between the lines of images in movement. It is specifically a vibration caused by movement in time. Its closest analogy is to the effect of music as rhythms that are felt by the body, in the sense that when a body hears music, it moves with that music. The overtone of film generates a similar sensation to music felt in this way, and it is this sensation that a writer such as Walcott seeks to emulate through moving lines of poetry and through the use of montage in his film writings. Such an impact on the body activates primal sensations and memories.

Deleuze's conception of the thinking of the outside – that is the outside of the known and habitual – in terms of the importance of the virtual and its relation to thought, myth and imagination, is linked to his concept of deterritorialised space, or a space without borders, and to his figuration of "the body without organs" and the rhizome. These ideas that seek to move thought outside of a transcendental origin or an overarching ideology are, of course, the origins of Édouard Glissant's theorising of a poetics of relation,[11] in particular, his refutation of individualism and his move to a cross-cultural poetics. As Glissant writes:

> The root is unique, a stock taking all upon itself and killing all around it. In opposition to this they [Deleuze and Guattari] propose the rhizome, an enmeshed root system, a network spreading either in the ground or in

> the air, with no predatory rootstock taking over permanently. The notion of the rhizome maintains, therefore, the idea of rootedness but challenges that of a totalitarian root. Rhizomatic thought is the principle behind what I call the Poetics of Relation, in which each and every identity is extended through a relationship with the Other. [12]

The rhizome enables the touching on all sides of the new and the different. Since origins are no longer connected or traceable to one root or point of origin, but rather meet and connect through literally lines of flight, as peoples meet, disperse, separate and come together again, the idea of becoming is linked to unending possibility and to on-going difference and indeed differentiation.

In Deleuze's writings, cinema, as an art form, actively participates in and invites the process of becoming, and also enables the thinking of difference as a potent mechanism for enabling a multiplicity of connections both over time and with a non-subjected other. As such, cinema activates new ways of thinking. The ability to engage in different dimensions without the interference of an imperial, authoritative or hegemonic idea, is enabled by the processes through which cinema operates. Cinema generates a form of associative thinking whereby one image burgeons into the next. In this, one also recognises the aesthetic processes of Glissant's writing, in which there are eruptions within the text that remain "assertively subsisting through repetition".[13] In effect, this too is a principle of montage formation and is based on the creation of peaks or leaps, or what Deleuze calls "intensities". This "chiming" leads to the unity of the work and of the concept/ image, while yet asserting difference.

Deleuze's books on cinema derive from a clear rethinking, a thinking beyond thought, perhaps, of the elements that together constitute Eisenstein's aesthetic theory. Conflict is the foundational element of montage, and from this flows the other mechanisms through which the filmmaker shapes his film. Chief amongst these are structures which are vehicles of affect, such as "the attraction" and *pathos* structure. These theories and the discussion of the structures of montage are found in the first instance in Eisenstein's *The Film Sense* and in his early essays, but are most clearly articulated in the posthumous work *Nonindifferent Nature* and in those essays collected in *Towards a Theory of Montage*.[14] I am therefore doing a triple move in this book and thinking Eisenstein as an originator of film aesthetics and at the same time I am thinking of him as a point of departure for Deleuze and for Walcott. The idea that holds all together is the capacity of film montage to generate an image of becoming.

Both Deleuze, and Laura Marks in her interpretation of Deleuze, signal the core importance of theories of montage as these are based on systems of opposition leading to new explosions of idea/ images. What is new in Deleuze's work is the way thought itself manifests in certain types of late modernist cinema. As Deleuze asserts, "The fissure has become primary, and as such grows larger. It is not a matter of following a chain of images, even across voids, but of getting out of the chain or association."[15] Thought, post Second World War, now becomes the impossibility of thinking unity. It emerges as a thinking of the unthought. Eisenstein's theory of organic montage, a montage based on the structure of organic movement and mapped through the Golden section as a spiral, no longer provides the structural rationale. In fact the idea of organic unity becomes equated with hegemonic thought. Deleuze describes the spiral in two ways. The spiral in its large form is the universal or the outside; in its small form it speaks to the action that is a prelude to the development of a situation leading to a raising of consciousness or a leap from quantity to quality, or in artistic terms a leap to ex/ stasis.

Deleuze is able to go beyond Eisenstein's mapping of organic unity, which one might think of in terms of a whole that brings together all without allowing difference – or the subsuming of the many into the one, because he uses Eisenstein's theorising of the overtone in creative ways. The method of montage that Sergei Eisenstein called contrapuntal montage or dialectical montage causes a shock to the nervous system and gives rise to thought or to a concept. For Eisenstein, film created thought "through the body".[16] As Deleuze puts it, "from the image to thought there is shock or vibration, which must give rise to thought in thought; from thought to the image, there is the figure which must be realized in a kind of internal monologue (rather than in a dream), capable of giving us the shock again."[17] This shock is mediated through the body and caused by a break or caesura that is the beginning of a new transition from two separate states to a new state or quality of becoming. This transition or transformation occurs because two images are placed in opposition to each other. The break or gap between two non-identical images sets up a dynamic relationship in the movement of light through a projector.

This idea of shock that emerges at the interstices between two conflicting lines or images is the basis of Eisensteinian thought. However, in the cinema of the pure image of time, for Deleuze, there is a recognition of powerlessness, of a break down of connections and of the impossibility of wholly coherent or totalising thought: "it can only think one thing, *the fact that we're not yet thinking*, the powerlessness to think the whole and to think oneself, thought which is always fossilized, dislocated, collapsed."[18] In citing Artaud, Deleuze alludes to the "body without organs". For him the powerlessness to think the whole frees the individual and releases the power for self-actualisation.

The cinema of the new time-image quite literally disbands the traditional organic relationships between signs and images. What becomes important is not the relationships that set up a causal chain and that lead to a unified whole and idea, but that the interstice itself takes on the previous function of the combination of images in organic montage where the transition leads to a leap to a new dimension. "What counts is on the contrary the *interstice* between images, between two images: a spacing which means that each image is plucked from the void and falls back into it." He argues that what is important is the process of "differentiation" in choosing two different images, so that "a difference of potential is established between the two, which will be productive of a third or of something new".[19]

The space in-between or the idea of a gap between two images is consistently to be found in the later Walcott and is held as a contradictory idea in his work. The new image/idea is shaped or emerges within this space, often as a shadow or a trace. This interstitial space is to be found in the transition between action and reaction, or in the interval, that is the caesura or pause, only to begin again.

In "The Muse of History", Walcott broaches the concept of the acid/sweet history of the New World, and this recognition of both loss and potential enables a re-theorising of time as both return and newness. The void of history, or the gap between an ancestral past and a new aesthetic and a new people, provides that fissure through which the spectres and convergences of the varying pasts of Caribbean reality can meet, do battle and ignite. As his work and thinking progress, the gap widens to engender spectres or ghostly presences, which cannot be contained either through rational thought or an idea of wholeness.

According to Jason Skeet in his discussion of the generation of the power of the outside of thought, which is linked to Deleuze's theorising of the time-image, the concept is not to be seen in spatial terms, but rather as the generation of energy caused by the meeting of two forces that lead to an interval:

> [These] irrational intervals are not spatial, nor are they images in the usual sense. They open onto what is outside of space yet immanent to it: the anteriority of time to space, or virtuality, becoming, the fact of returning for that which differs."(22) [...] encountering the outside, disrupt [s] the flow of linear time and [creates] a break that makes possible the virtual, that "vast territory of potentialities in every present that passes." (23)The result is a virtual reality, a screen on the infinite possibilities beyond the self that accesses the atavistic past and the speculative future, but could also merely reinforce limitations and prejudices [...].

This "border crossing" in cinema is engineered by cinema. The cinema "liberates "the sequencing of images from a single, fixed point of view.[20]

The "space in between" makes consciousness possible because the brain is in itself the largest of the gaps. Within these gaps, the imagination as a mechanism for calling up presences, hallucinations, imaginings and illusions gives rise to an open potential, or an outside of thought.[21]

Through this opening the artist creates what Deleuze calls a crystalline conception of time. The past and the present are constituted together in a time-image or time machine, which is an accumulation of layers of experiences or moments of intensity that are produced in the present and exist in coalescence with that present. That crystalline form shapes a circuit that is open on both ends, past and present, and becomes a circuit of relations. In the cinema of the crystalline image "the actual and the virtual image coexist and crystallize; they enter into a circuit which brings us constantly back from one to the other".[22]

The crystalline form may be a prism or a cube, and for Skeet it is not montage because in the crystal there is a "'coexistence of non-chronological layers and incommensurable points', that is, the nomadic and rhizomatic image of thought".[23] Here, in discussing montage, Skeet is wrong, since he is thinking of montage only as a series of oppositions, whereas montage is the combination of any and all fragments in a film through editing, both within the shot and beyond the shot. What Deleuze does is to differentiate between organic montage or a montage based on causal relations and a form of montage that fully utilizes the interval or gap. This gap is the point of transition between action and reaction, or between one stage (quantity) to the other stage (quality), and is the cinema of the time-image or the cinema that emerges from a people who have lived with trauma and at the margins. The work of artists who represent such peoples is a manifestation of a wide fissure since reaction cannot follow action; and there are no longer logical connections, in particular there is no longer a rational link between the past and the present.

To put this in terms of Caribbean historiography, the time-image is the crystalline form that emerges when a film artist seeks to map the present as a concrete figural manifestation of the traumatic effects of time on body or event. The Caribbean's history cannot create a set of relationships in space or time that provides an idea or an image of continuity. Instead, the figure or the form in itself is a map of the impact of the past as a broken set of miles or as absence or as void. The actions of a character or an event are not therefore imaged as giving rise to a set of logical developments, but as a continuing encirclement whereby the figure, as in the combined crew of *Palace of the Peacock*,[24] is caught in a continuing circuit of relations that constantly re-members the past and reappraises and reinvents the future. The present is then always in process, and caught in the possibly unimaginable and irrational set of circumstances that has given birth to the present. For Deleuze, quoting Fellini, we are constructed in memory, "we are *simultaneously* childhood, adolescence, old age and maturity".[25] According to Lisa Åkervall, the transition from movement-image to time-image in Deleuzian terms marks the difference between seeing "behind" the image and enduring it. Cinema becomes an experience of endurance.[26] This idea of endurance may be seen to be the key theme of several of Walcott's works including *Omeros* and *Malcauchon*.

The brain is perceived by Deleuze as molecular and this provides a model for cinema. By the same token cinema presents a compelling paradigm for the brain, since:

> In the screen there can be a brain, as in Resnais or Syberberg's cinema. Cinema does not operate only with linkages by rational cuts, but by re-linkages on irrational cuts.[27]

The brain is a screen and can create an "image of thought" through "relinkage" of "irrational" cuts. Deleuze's "constructive pluralism"[28] derives from his meditation on cinema and on Eisenstein's writings. This pluralism is not simply associated with, but emerges from, acts of assemblage, as in montage. The contact between the brain and the "outside of thought" gives rise to the rhizome. Cinema traces the "circuits of the brain" because it adds motion to the image.[29]

For Gregg Lambert in *The Brain is the Screen. Deleuze and the Philosophy of Cinema*,[30] Deleuze's enquiry into Eisensteinian thought and its link to ideology has led to a crucial re-consideration of the ways in which an image creates thought or can generate thought and in the ways that one can "deduce" an image from thought.[31] The image is shaped through careful calculation of all the parts of an assemblage, what Eisenstein called throughout his writings a "monistic ensemble". The end result of this assemblage is not the sum of its parts, in other words, again, it does not flow from causal relationships, but as in a game of football (Eisenstein's analogy) and as a result of the careful putting into play of various strategies that would allow the final effect. There is a very apt analogy to be found here between Deleuzian ideas and Wilson Harris's quantum images that explode in the mind and that lead to an intuition that generates other intuitions.

Deleuze and Guattari see the arts as presenting ways in which thought can shatter and create flights that break down the walls of power. The "affect" is one primary mechanism for this. According to Deleuze and Guattari's translator:

> *L'affect* is an ability to affect and be affected. It is a prepersonal intensity corresponding to the passage from one experiential state of the body to another and implying an augmentation or diminution in that body's capacity to act. *L'affection* is each such state considered as an encounter between the affecting body and a second affecting body (with body taken in its broadest possible sense to include mental or "ideal" bodies)" (translator's foreword, xvi).[32]

The process that Deleuze seeks to map leads to a form of depersonalisation and a movement to community. It may even be seen as a process to death. He calls it "becoming imperceptible". This is in opposition to the modernist desire for individuation or the cult of the individual.

To become "imperceptible" is to be beyond subjectivity or to be subsumed within a crowd. According to Professor Rosi Braidotti in the article "The Ethics of Becoming Imperceptible",[33] ethics means "faithfulness" to the joy of the affirmation of the self through the "encounters and minglings" with other bodies and forces. Her focus is on activism and putting the active back into activism and the ushering in of change. "Becoming imperceptible" is therefore an encounter with the other in all the force of space and time as a body situated in a particular place and at a particular time. "Nomadic ethics" is therefore not about any master ideology or "master theory", but about the openness to encounter. Potential becomes the "affirmative aspect of power".

More specifically "becoming imperceptible" is to eschew the "I" again, as in Harris's *Palace of the Peacock*,[34] where the blind seeing eye is symbolic of the self and the journey across time and space which leads to new encounters and to an idea of a shared communality and common destiny. This is actualised through the explosive force of the image or through quantum leaps of the imagination. One finds in Harris the self-same refusal of law and institutions and thought as prison, more concretely expressed perhaps in the imprisonment of the woman in *The Mask of the Beggar*.[35] Here law equals institutions of power or in Althusserian terms, state apparatuses. Prisons, libraries, and religion as a fixed idea, are all subsumed in the image of a prison that none the less allows for the birth of a new child in *Mask*. Deleuze suggests that deterriorialisation inevitably recognises and precedes re-territorialisation in a perpetual circuit. *Palace of the Peacock* represents that circuit and moves the reader and crew to recognition of the unfinished genesis, or perpetual re-birthing through imagination of the human capacity for renewal, and equally the repeated forms of imprisonment.

This refusal of an identity that is focussed on self-identity or that is solipsistic to the point that it makes the other an object, is continued in Glissant's creative reinterpretation and appropriation of both the rhizome and the concept of "becoming imperceptible". For Édouard Glissant the Caribbean is forged from diverse factors, stories, histories and there is something beyond individual consciousness that the artist engenders and that he calls Antillianité. He acknowledges the roots of the Caribbean as rhizomatic and as such connected by different and multiple nodes to various cultures and races, and he simultaneously recognises the continuing flight or potential of Caribbean being and imagination in its constant movement beyond racial and territorial borders and beyond any attachment to an individual root.[36]

For Glissant, the Caribbean emerges from the sea which is conceived of as a womb, and hence the "unity is submarine". The very idea of the sea as subterranean space displaces any fixed notion of origin. As Kamau Brathwaite has also suggested in his theory of "tidalectics", Caribbean becoming is like the tides and not at all fixed as within the conception of the dialectic. Caribbean identity and culture emerge from all sides and move laterally, back to origins, hitting many points of origin in its travelling, but always moving forward as it gathers the material from the seabed. Becoming is accumulative and essentially always a movement to difference and deferral.

Walcott's works mediate between a search for organic unity and a sense of the void of history. What is set in play in his writings and in his film scripts is a dialogue between the recognition of the fact that the Caribbean is a place where people in one sense do not exist and are without true memory of origins, and are thus like shadows – a theme found in his early work – but also have the potential to recreate an idea of community by creative use of the void. His work is essentially rhizomatic in the Deleuzian sense, since he constantly sought forms to encounter the outside of experience and the outside of time. This led to his concept of simultaneity, or a tone felt and sounded in common by writers of the New World who share the "elation" of the openness to possibility that the Americas offer.

But his qualification is that this sense of openness is a circuit of encounters and relations that puts the writer in perpetual dialogue and movement with a past that is acidic. So, the image of the *pomme cythere* Walcott uses to describe Helen and her pregnancy in *Omeros*[37] is essentially a crystalline image or a crystal formed by the present, in a circuit of relations with images that flow into that present and that remain embedded, but yet in constant change with each moment. This prismatic form is also expressed in his metaphor of the prism which is "a crystal of ambiguities,"[38] used in *Another Life*, and which again sets up the contradictions of a present always in rhizomatic encounter with the past. The creative potential of the New World is forged by the shock of the encounter of traumatic experiences in manifold ways and between the meeting of languages and gods of different cultures.

There is integral to this encounter an idea of loss and plenitude: the loss occurring through forced meetings and the plenitude by virtue of the emptiness that presages the growth of something new, a process of creolisation or syncretism or art born of endurance and survival. This shock then foregrounds the role and function of the imagination in the act of re-making. The enslaved must create a virtual reality akin to a phantom limb that is not born of resemblance or mimesis, but is a copy of an idea or a memory (an image of the mind). Let me then creatively suggest that this shock of encounter fashions what Deleuze has called a crystalline image and what Glissant calls a rhizomatic cultural identity.

The various lines of flight and deterritorialisation in Deleuze and Guattari's thinking constitute an assemblage and in Deleuze's cinema books that assemblage is in reality a mirror of the assemblages of cinema, strictly speaking, montage. Cinema by its forms and its creation of virtual realities provides a paradigm, a method and a mirror of the process of becoming or the becoming of thought.

This book is a simple attempt to map Walcott's work onto this idea of cinema. The idea of assemblage is already contained in the notion of the hybrid. Gordon Rohlehr's theory of "aesthetic code-switching" in this regard is useful as a further entry point into this idea, since it foregrounds both contradiction and creative appropriation. Walcott's work, according to Rohlehr, participates in an aesthetic continuum, which moves between the angst of a modernist preoccupation with alienation and the opposite position of bardic voice, but is of neither pole. Rohlehr notes of Walcott in his "The Problem of the Problem of Form" that by the late sixties his work :

> was a synthesis of dead-end and green beginning, the opposite Legba poles of a Caribbean possibility. It gave Walcott a new freedom with language: the sealed-off crypt of the lyric began to yield to the pressure of narrative, and it became increasingly possible for Walcott to open himself up, not only to the immense achievements of Latin American prose, but also to the steady pressure of Caribbean orality.[39]

Edward Baugh has also noted Walcott's use of multiple modes and forms.[40] Walcott is seen then to be fashioning an aesthetic out of the legacies of fragments of traditions, none of which he can fully claim to be his own. His work becomes situated as a bridge between a modernist and grass roots culture, and begins to incorporate the oral and the literary, the filmic and the scribal, the painterly and the sonic. The availability of forms through which both the gestural and the tonal are given equal status with the word and the conceptual finds an eminent place in film.

"The dialectic between aesthetic possibilities" (Rohlehr), which continued to operate in Walcott's head would seem to have led to a work such as *The Star Apple Kingdom*[41] in which Walcott adopts as his "double", the figure of Shabine, who is given the function of the acerbic voice and the rhythmic beat of a calypsonian in the first truly sustained use of such forms in his poetry, while also deploying forms derived from Western satirists such as Pope. This combination comes to imaginative fruition in "The Spoiler's Return" of *The Fortunate Traveller*.[42] Here one sees the process of transformation through encounter and movement, as in Deleuze's use of the term "nomadic" to designate the fluidity of invention, imagination and what he called "deterritorialisation".

Deleuze continues his theorising of the rhizome in his analysis of cinema. For him cinema creates concepts through that process of deterritorialisation, or that flight from power structures. For Deleuze, the time-image entails a "new breed of signs", and refers above all to "subjective images, memories of childhood, sound and visual dreams or fantasies, where the character does not act without seeing himself acting".[43] There are hauntings because the world is out of joint. The present is obsessively in relation with the past.

These ideas of time as immanent in the image, and of an image as a circuit of relations, are very much to the fore in the later works by Walcott and culminate in the filmic structure of the poem *Omeros* and the film script of that name. But *Steel,*[44] as stage play and as film script, also uses a structure where lines converge, then diverge and where individuals trigger events that lead to inaction, reverie or a form of stasis that is mapped through the use of a filmic interlude in the stage version. In *Steel*, film is used to denote time as memory and the enthralment of the individual by the past. But that constriction of the past paradoxically gives birth to the only new musical instrument of the twentieth century. The structure of the play is shaped through systems derived from contrapuntal montage, where different lines are in counterpoint, but carry a similar idea/image. The multiplicity of lines has led to almost universal criticism of the play.

Endnotes

1. Derek Walcott, "Down the Coast" in *ep;phany. A literary journal* (Fall/winter 2007-2008), ed. Willard Cook.
2. Walcott, "Down the Coast," p. 165.
3. Walcott, "Down the Coast," p. 165.
4. The credit for this first discovery of the effects of cinematic montage goes to the Soviet film-maker, Lev Kuleshov (1899-1970) who pioneered the discovery that a cinematic image could change meaning for the viewer depending on the images that preceded or followed it. See YouTube to see the short film Kuleshov made to demonstrate the effect.
5. Laura Marks, *The Skin of the Film. Intercultural Cinema, Embodiment and the Senses* (Durham and London: Duke University Press, 2000).
6. Walcott, "Down the Coast," p. 164.
7. Marks, p. 24.
8. Gilles Deleuze's *Cinema 1.The Movement-Image*, trans. Tomlinson and Habberjam (London: Athlone Press, 1992) and *Cinema 2. The Time-Image*, trans. Tomlinson and Galeta (London: Athlone Press, 1989).
9. Sergei Eisenstein, *The Film Sense* (London: Faber and Faber, 1947); *Nonindifferent Nature*, ed. and trans. Herbert Marshall (Cambridge: Cambridge University Press, 1987).
10. The "attraction" is any method whereby an artist can "strike a hammer blow" on the psyche of viewer or auditor. It is the channelling of all available means in order to enthral an audience. But ultimately the creation of a tendentious line in film is possible only through its incorporation of time. So that film moves towards the art of music since it derives its "affect" through what Eisenstein called the overtone.
11. Édouard Glissant, *Caribbean Discourse. Selected Essays*, trans. J. Michael Dash (Charlottesville: University Press of Virginia, 1989) and *Poetics of Relation*, trans. Betsy Wing (Ann Arbor: University of Michigan Press, 1997).
12. Glissant, *Poetics of Relation*, p. 11.
13. Betsy Wing, "Translator's Introduction", *Poetics of Relation*, p. xv.
14. Sergei Eisenstein, *Towards a Theory of Montage, Vol. 2, Writings*, eds., Michael Glenny and Richard Taylor (London: BFI, 1991).
15. Deleuze, *Cinema 1*, p. 180.
16. Sergei Eisenstein, *Nonindifferent Nature*.
17. Deleuze, *Cinema 2*, p.166.
18. Deleuze, *Cinema 2*, p. 167.
19. Deleuze, *Cinema* 2, p. 179-180.
20. Jason Skeet, "Woolf plus Deleuze: Cinema, Literature and Time

Travel" (http://www.rhizomes.net/issue16/skeet.html). *Rhizomes*, Issue 16 (Summer 2008), n.p.

21. The interstice or gap has been much theorised in contemporary discourse and has led to very seductive theories of, for example, the "unhomely" in the writings of Homi Bhabha. I note the importance of Bhabha's deft incorporation of Deleuze, Bakhtin, Lacan and Kristeva in particular in the essay "Dissemination, Time, Narrative and the Margins of the Modern Nation" in *The Location of Culture* (London: Routledge, 1994). Of importance is his idea of the movement of peoples whose lives experienced at the margins generate a flow of memories and cultural traditions that meet and engage with those whom they encounter. The migrant performs both historic encounter and cultural transformation. However, this book will not go into dialogue with Bhabha's work. My concern is with the cinematic and its theorising by Eisenstein and Deleuze. This theorising is used to examine how a writer such as Walcott intuits the filmic and the cinematic as forms through which the idea of void joins with the need to imagine processes of becoming. Moreover, I am concerned with Walcott's concretisation of memory and time to allow the sense of a continuing process of thought and of endless potential that are released within the very gaps left by a history of conflict and movement of peoples.
22. Deleuze, *The Time-Image*, p. 83.
23. Skeet, http://www.rhizomes.net/issue16/skeet.html. See also Deleuze, *Time-Image*, pp. 41-42.
24. Wilson Harris, *Palace of the Peacock* (London: Faber and Faber, 1960).
25. Deleuze, *Cinema 2. The Time-Image*, p. 99.
26. Lisa Åkervall, "Cinema, Affect and Vision", in *Rhizomes Issue 16* (Summer 2008) http://www.rhizomes.net/issue16/akervall.html.
27. Tomlinson and Galeta, translator's introduction, *Cinema 1,* by Gilles Deleuze, p. xvii.
28. Tomlinson and Galeta, p. xvii.
29. Deleuze, "The Brain is the Screen", in Gregory Flaxman, ed., *The Brain is the Screen. Deleuze and the Philosophy of Cinema* (Minneapolis and London: University of Minnesota Press, 2000), pp. 366-367.
30. Gregory Flaxman, ed., *The Brain is the Screen. Deleuze and the Philosophy of Cinema*.
31. Gregg Lambert, "Cinema and the Outside" in *The Brain is the Screen*, p. 253.
32. Gilles Deleuze and Felix Guattari, *A Thousand Plateaus: Capitalism and Schizophrenia*, trans. Brian Massumi (Minneapolis: University of Minnesota Press, 1987).
33. http://deleuze.tausendplateaus.de/wp-content/uploads/2008/01/trent-

final.pdf. This was published initially in *Deleuze and Philosophy*, ed. Constantin Boundas (Edinburgh UP, 2006) pp. 133-159.

34. Wilson Harris, *Palace of the Peacock*.
35. Wilson Harris, *The Mask of the Beggar* (London: Faber and Faber, 2003).
36. Édouard Glissant, *Poetics of Relation*.
37. See the lines "There, in miniature,/ the world was globed like a fruit, since its texture is / both acid and sweet like a golden *pomme-Cythère*, / the apple of Venus…", *Omeros*, p. 275)
38. Derek Walcott, *Another Life* (London: Jonathan Cape, 1973), pp. 58-59.
39. Gordon Rohlehr, "The Problem of the Problem of Form", in *The Shape of that Hurt and Other Essays* (Port of Spain: Longman, 1992), pp. 39.
40. Edward Baugh, *Derek Walcott* (Cambridge: Cambridge University Press, 2006).
41. Derek Walcott, *The Star Apple Kingdom* (London: Jonathan Cape, 1980).
42. Derek Walcott, *The Fortunate Traveller*. See "The Spoiler's Return", pp. 53-60.
43. Deleuze, *The Time-Image*, p. 6.
44. There are a number of versions of *Steel* as film script and as stage play. I use the 2005 version.

CHAPTER 2
THE BODY AS INSTRUMENT. SHOCK AND DISSONANCE AND THE LEAP TO THE NEW

The art of the time-image or the direct image of time engages the artist in the creation of revolutionary structures that affirm the creative power of the imagination and the potential for newness. For Gilles Deleuze, the virtual (the simulacrum) and the cinematic contain the possibility of foregrounding difference and opening up new ways of becoming. This project is at the heart of *Omeros*, which asks at a very deep level, what is the Caribbean? Its answer is "process" that takes as its first principle the differences that are in fact shards of culture, linguistic, performative, spiritual and cosmological. Film, as an art that uses fragments to reconstruct new realities and as an art of illusions and shadows, becomes a seductive mechanism for depicting both the stages of emerging selfhood, and the continuing re-invention that makes the Caribbean a place of boundless possibility.

Film through the combination of fragments generates an explosion into thought, conceived of by Eisenstein as a leap to ex-stasis or from quantity to quality and described in his discussion of *pathos* structure. The most powerful example of ex- stasis leading to new thought processes comes from Eisenstein's description of montage as used in *The General Line*:[1]

> As if by accident and hardly perceptible, shots of intensifying hope gradually brighten, whereas shots of aggravated suspicion – darken.
>
> With the increase in tempo pieces are cut shorter – fragmentation of the change from bright to dark frames occurs more often. The disks spin faster and faster, as if caught up by them, light fragmentation of edited cuts slide into actually revolving "sunbeams", in close-up (done with the help of a technical device – splinters of a mirror pasted on a spinning sphere).
>
> At the appropriate moment, this entire edited sequence is intercut by the muzzle of a separator pipe. For just the right instant it remains empty. For just the necessary length of time at its lower edge, a drop begins to swell.
>
> (Changing faces in close-up.)
>
> For the necessary length of time the swollen drop trembles.
>
> (The disks of the separator mechanism revolve at a frantic speed.)
>
> At any moment the drop will fall.

> (The close-ups flash, intercut with the revolving disks.)
> The drop breaks off.
> It falls!
> And the tiniest spray, starlike scatters, hitting the bottom of the empty pail.[2]

There follows a description of a series of explosions that both signify and mimic the leap to a new consciousness and a new state of existence for the participants of the new communist state.

What this quotation exemplifies is an idea of film montage as containing the potential to change both thought and consciousness and equally to mimic the very processes of this transformation. Walcott interrogates this possibility in various stages. He first explores it thematically, then examines the value of the still shot in opposition to the moving image. He then experiments with the use of conflicting or multiple lines within a frame. This is in keeping with classical montage theory as in Eisenstein's use of images in *The General Line* and his description of their generative explosive power. This use of gradually developing tempo and the calculation of an explosion into the new, arrives at its climax in two of Walcott's works: *Steel* and *Omeros*, both of which use an interplay of several lines or contrapuntal montage to impact on the psyche. This shock leads to a new way of seeing.

Thought through the body

Thought enters the body through cinematic processes that play on the senses. In the stage and film scripts for *Pantomime* one finds an intuition of the differences between an art associated with intellectualisation and cerebral thought and one derived from the body's responses to stimuli and experience. *Pantomime* asks directly how far can the literary contain the diverse sensibilities and experiences of the Antilles and in the film version uses the act of projection and the structures of montage to explore these differences. The calypsonian's skill at improvisation and his adept use of language in a form of verbal stick fight are given prominence and become evidence of the capacity to adapt and reframe, despite adversity. The play, in this use of a language that is seen to refashion the idea of originality and creativity, overtly references Naipaul's *The Mimic Men* and *The Middle Passage* and their insistence that the Caribbean is a place of mimicry and unoriginality:

> How can the history of this West Indian futility be written? [...] The history of the islands can never be satisfactorily told. Brutality is not the only difficulty. History is built around achievement and creation; and nothing was created in the West Indies.[3]

Walcott's play, *Pantomime*, recasts this apparent failure of creativity through the figure of Jackson who declares:

> Jackson: For three hundred years I served you breakfast in my white jacket, on this white verandah, bwana, effendi, baccra, and sahib. I was your shadow, in that sun that never set on your empire, that was my pantomime, and you smiled at me as a child does smile at his shadow helpless obedience, boss, bwana, effendi, baccra, sahib ... But after a while, the child does start dominating the master and, that is why all them West Indian and Pakistani in England have all you vex and frighten. They are your shadow, you cannot get rid of them, boss, bwana, baccra, effendi, sahib.[4]

The mimic man as shadow is thus reinvented as castigator and one who has subverted and usurped hegemonic structures. *Pantomime* reframes mimicry as survival. The shadows or mimics become masters, invoking Lamming's Caliban-Prospero theory, which one finds in particular in *Pleasures of Exile* and *Water with Berries*.[5] Jackson, the waiter, is the master of language in *Pantomime*, in particular through his ex-tempo performance. He "masters" the master, in this way emphasising his relation to the Caliban story. Improvisation, word play and ex-tempo performance emerge as sites of resistance and refashioning.

In its use of calypso, *Pantomime* also grounds both stage drama and film in an aesthetic of the carnivalesque or an idea of performance that is transgressive and disruptive and that undermines hegemonic systems through its use of laughter, the grotesque and the lower regions, in particular the carnal.[6] In the film script, the camera mimics the mocking voice of a calypsonian in its movement and point of view. In aligning this cinematic eye to Jackson (a one time calypsonian and now waiter), the camera eye and movement fulfil the same function as Spoiler in "The Spoiler's Return" of *The Fortunate Traveller*.[7] The calypsonian/camera becomes the note of reality and the acerbic voice that reverberates at different levels in the play for television. It provides the impact of an oral tradition grounded in the reality of a place.

The figure of the goat in the film represents the sensuousness of art and artistic communication. In this it looks towards *Omeros* where the goat is an embodiment of the carnal quality inherent in the origins of great literature. The goat is given a central position in the film version of *Pantomime* and is crucial to the representation of the practical element of creole art. It signifies the will to survive and the rootedness of Caribbean expressions in the soil and specific history of a place. It makes a direct statement about the differences that exist between Antillean art and that of Western civilisation, seen here as tired and removed from such fundamental impulses and instinctual drives.

> *Harry reads his piece of creative writing and Jackson responds*:
>
> Is good, very good. Touching. Very sad. But something missing.
> Harry: What?

Jackson: Goat. You leave out the goats...
The man is not facing reality. He is not a practical man ship wrecked.
Harry: I suppose that's the difference between classical and creole acting.
Jackson: If he is not practical, he is not Robinson Crusoe.

Harry reads from the script again and the goat appears on the window ledge:

Superimposition: The goat on the ledge. Close-up.
It bleats. Soundlessly.
Then Jackson pantomimes the goat and Crusoe in turn.[8]

The goat underlines the dramatic potential of the calypsonian as well as the force of art, as it aligns itself with a people whose sense of self is still located in the earth or the body's attachment to the earth. In *Omeros*, this goat signifies the essential ingredient of oral traditions as emanating from the body: "a girl," says Homer, "smells sweeter than a book" (*Omeros*, p. 284). The goat is also a figure of the origins of Greek drama, so this figure also unites the origins of Greek culture with that of the new beginnings of Caribbean art, which are seen in the film script of *Pantomime* to contain both mockery and mimicry.

A goat on a small buff above his head, studies the performance [of Harry playing Crusoe].
The goat bleats.
Shakes his head.
Harry gives the goat 'the finger'.

The use of the goat in the filmed version of the play gives double emphasis to the idea that Antillean drama of stage and screen are grounded in the historical necessities of life on these isles. In this it looks towards Walcott's development of a vehicle for effective dramatic form, in particular a form that has the body as its primary vehicle of affect. The importance of the body is alluded to in "What the Twilight Says. An Overture".[9] The goat in *Pantomime* and in *Omeros* is a signifier of the sensual needs of the body, echoing the meaning of the Caribbean "you ole goat" and containing echoes of "horning" as part of the element of goatishness or lustfulness. But the goat's resourcefulness and versatility are also commended, since goats can live virtually anywhere and on anything.

The film version of *Pantomime* also foregrounds the use of an audiovisual aesthetic in the creation of an art of resistance. Walcott uses a disjunction of sound and image, as in contrapuntal montage, to demonstrate the sterility of Harry's sensibility. The "crippling" of the imagination (symbolized through Kripalsingh in Naipaul's *The Mimic Men*) is imaged in *Pantomime*, through Harry's fixation on a tape recorder, through which he can capture the artistic expressions of the Caribbean. There are echoes here perhaps of *Krapp's Last Tape* by Samuel Beckett. A Chaplinesque prelude in the film script shows the white proprietor, the pseudo Crusoe, as a man caught between different roles or self-dramatizations.

Harry Trewe, as Crusoe, is "addicted to signs and notices. On his walk towards the hotel and gazebo we pass three others, or more, as the credits roll over" (p. 4). These are filmed in quick alternating shots as in classical montage These signs represent the literary tradition, which seeks to dominate the action. They are shown before Jackson's calypso rendition, which is "played as a voice over as a montage of postcard stills of Tobago, the scene of the action" is projected. These stills represent the island as a kind of paradise. The still shots, as the script dictates, are "beach scenes, of tourists struggling with luggage etc."(p. 14) and provide visual proof of the tourist-dominated ports of the Caribbean where, as Walcott so often reiterated, tourism introduces a form of neo-enslavement and neo-colonialism. The ironic words of Jackson's calypso then act in counterpoint and serve as refutations of the idea of any servile image of both island and islanders.

The calypso has emerged, as has the steel pan, from resistance and powerlessness and the movie camera and the sound track are made the means through which Walcott can explore the vitality contained in a particular local perception and through this exploration can engage in an alternative idea of Caribbean ingenuity. In a particular sense, his use of montage here (that is the opposition of sound and visual image and the use of fragments within a moving line) gives concrete expression to Deleuze's conception of cinema as a brain that mimics the very processes of human thought processing, and its arrangement and realignment of material. This occurs because the oppositional movement forces us to see events in a new light.

The act of montage editing is given pre-eminence through an overt use of the camera, seen as an instrument for projecting images in a manner similar to the ways in which the empire projected an image of the Caribbean onto the minds of those who were its subjects. But the cinematic, through montage editing, subverts this process by showing how creativity works within the actual processes of the mind. The play of opposing lines, in this instance the disjunction between visual or still shot versus the sound of the calypsonian, enables an attack on the very structures of colonialism and neo-colonialism. Walcott places one line in opposition to the other in order to create a leap of consciousness and a new idea. It is not unlike the way advertising often manipulates the viewer to achieve its effect.

The Shock to the Psyche

Pantomime seeks to shock us into new ways of seeing. We are assaulted into thought. Walcott's use of a principle of montage here is not well developed, but opens up the possibilities for further experimentation, which conceives of montage as an aesthetic formal principle through which an idea and an emotion might be conveyed. The notion of projection as a dynamic process becomes initially associated in Walcott's mind with carnival.

The idea evolves first of all through an association or opposition between carnival and revolution. Carnival initially suggests a capacity to remain locked in an illusion and revolution is first perceived only as another chimera. Both are linked, in a somewhat contradictory manner, with the art of photography or the still shot, which is used as a means of examining the calcifying or paralysing effect of an imperial culture on the imagination of the Antilles.

Photography as a motif has long been a recurrent feature of Walcott's work. It is used in *Another Life* to indicate both subjection and unrealised potential and surfaces in many of Walcott's works and most memorably in *Another Life* and in *Star Apple Kingdom* where it represents a fading past, as well as nostalgia for that past. In his discussion of Walcott's treatment of the politics of the charismatic and idealistic Michael Manley in the poem "Star Apple Kingdom,"[10] Baugh notes the use of a faded photo of "the great house inhabitants of bygone days" as representative of "a pastoral dream of his country's past". This dream is now "insidiously active", though diminished.

Walcott explores ideas of cultural petrification through the still image in a film scenario, "Un Voyage a Cythère". This play for television, which was probably written in the sixties, and which has seen many mutations, including its partial emergence into "The Isle is Full of Noises" (a play performed c. 1981, but never published), interrogates the internal conflicts and racism of the French Creole in Trinidad:

> You know that fake painting great-grandfather brought from France, "The Embarkation to Cytherea", I think I understand it now, when you're a child, you grow up around pictures, books, another world, and they are so permanent and ordinary even if they are beautiful. They are going on a journey which they will never take, because there is no such place. It lives in the imagination. The people in that picture are dead, their costumes, their way of life, their beliefs, are dead, that is why they are so beautiful. I thought of that and wanted to join them.[11]

As the character Oswald notes, it represents a point of yearned-for departure, but the figures never leave. This image of a paralysing fictive memory of the past is also associated with Walcott's long-established metaphor of amber, later associated with the half-light of sunset, found in *Another Life*. In this autobiographical poem, art holds the loved one as a calcified memory that neither changes nor is subject to change, and this paradoxical stasis enables the crafting of a beautiful poetic image that partakes of eternity, as will be discussed later.

The French artist, Jean-Antoine Watteau's (1684-1721) creation of a world of ritualistic order (he was the painter of *The Embarkation to Cythera*

(1717), a beauty beyond mortal time, is used in an entire series of Walcott's plays and their revisions, as a metaphor for the embalming light of Empire, equated throughout his oeuvre with the light of sunset. Carnival, in this play, becomes a cultural battlefield in a war between an old perception tied to Europe, and a new revolutionary spirit. The reporter/ art critic appears here to be close in portraiture to Walcott himself. The young Negro, as he is called in the film scenario, even says, "I have no hatred of history either. I accept the past, even though I don't expect much from the future"(p. 6).

"Un Voyage a Cythère" eventually becomes "The Last Carnival", an outline for a film script that precedes the stage version, which was first performed in 1982 and published in 1986. "The Last Carnival", as film, avails of "the concentrated time span of the film"[12] to explore the contradictions of race in Trinidad society. Interestingly the film is conceived as happening over the span of one week, while the stage play traces the historic development and attitudes of a privileged group from the nineteen-fifties, that is prior to independence, up to the time of the seventies and the 1970 Trinidad uprising.

The idea of photographing an assemblage of the remaining members of a white creole family brings into one space the notion of fixity and the idea of carnival as a re-production or re-presentation of the past (film script, p. 7). Carnival resonates with conflicting meanings in the stage version of this work, but it is its audiovisual impact which, aligned with the importance of *movement*, gives it authenticity as an aesthetic. This authenticity is placed in contrast to Watteau's painting, "Embarkation to Cythera", which is seen as a symbol of a dying culture and of a philosophy that locks the artist (in the text) in nostalgia. The use of French as a badly understood language underlines the false pretensions of a group that considers itself superior because of its racial heritage, even though that heritage, in particular the language, is poorly understood. Watteau's painting is further linked to the decadent and static French Creole world:

> He painted his whole civilization as if it were a sunset, because any embarkation is a fantasy. You see those pilgrims in the painting, they can't move; it's like some paralysed moment in a carnival when there's a sudden silence, and it's frightening. This painting says everything about our future here, right here, in Santa Rosa. It's a prophecy. The costumes, the gestures. We cannot move.[13]

The photograph as a still image allows a meditation on role-playing through costumery. The actors or participants of this charade begin to inhabit their costumes and the mores associated with their apparel. The setting of the play in Arima, which is the home of the Carib queen festival called the Santa Rosa festival, situates the play around a particularly vicious relic of the time of French Creole racism, since

Arima was, until the 1960s, the site for what was called by the general populace, "white people carnival", at which coloured people, including spouses of those few French creoles who had married outside their race, were unwelcome.

The irony of the annual carnival celebrations is underlined by Walcott who links it to a creative drive and a desire for harmony, both of which are negated in the play, because the very force which has led to the creation of this unique festival – that is the syncretic merging of African culture and French customs – is denied by all sides, both revolutionaries and white creoles. Carnival thus suggests ambivalence. "Voyage a Cythère" foregrounds the paradoxes of white/black relations in Trinidad and voices the contradictions of carnival's illusions and its pretence at unity.

The Last Carnival, in its overall conception for both film and stage, is a direct response to the 'Black Power" uprising of 1970, which publicly unleashed many of the previously hidden racial attitudes in Trinidad. Moreover, its version of carnival as a projected image of harmony, which is formed through a fusion of sound and spectacle, prepares the way for Walcott's theory of film. The shocks or "breaks," generated by montage splicing, act both as a way of establishing the relationship between different, often disparate parts or phenomena of the real world, and simultaneously create the sensation of a whole.[14] This possibility, through imaginary projection and as a result of the shocks and breaks of history and tradition, provide a philosophical and a formal method for envisioning a new people and a new art in the Antilles.

Walcott's later works experiment even more closely with the oppositions between the still and moving image. He introduces montage structures as a form of dynamism. This movement creates ebbs and flows and literally seeks to "rock" the mind in the intertwining and radiating lines of the narrative of the play or poem. These penetrate the labyrinths of the body to induce what Thomas Docherty has called "the possibility of enchantment",[15] better known as "the postmodern sublime", or a leap beyond representation into an interrogation of psychic reality.

Eisenstein conceived of this penetration as movement induced by vibrations. The continuous flow of fragments reassembled sequentially was complicated by the contrapuntal dance of visual and sound lines that, in their after-effects, were physiologically identical. True montage thinking demanded the ability to apprehend this mutual identity and through this, to create a structured form that would convey emotional and intellectual messages:

> I wrote about the contrapuntal method of combining the visual and the sound image: 'To master this method you have to develop within yourself a new *sense*: *the ability to reduce visual and sound perceptions to a new denominator...*'.

> Whereas *sound* and *visual* perceptions are *not reducible* to a single denominator.
> They are constants in different dimensions.
> But the visual overtone and the sound overtone are constants in a *single dimension*!
> Because, while a shot is a visual *perception* and a tone is a sound perception, *both visual and sound overtones are totally physiological sensations.*
> And, consequently, they are *one and the same kind*, outside the [...] acoustic categories that serve merely as guides, paths to its achievement:
> For the musical overtone (a beat) the term 'I hear' is no longer strictly appropriate.
> Nor 'I see' for the visual.
> For both we introduce a new uniform formula: 'I feel'.[16]

These psychological sensations are generated through the movement of sound and visual working in tandem or through opposition. For Eisenstein and for Deleuze the play of these different lines leads to new thought and the potential for freeing the self from ideological imprisonment.

Coincidentally, one of Eisenstein's most important insights is derived from his knowledge and interest in Japanese cultural forms. It is noteworthy that the Kabuki and Noh theatres also fascinated Walcott during his stay in New York in the fifties.[17] Eisenstein maintained that Japanese art (other than its cinema) was essentially montage. He claimed that in the Kabuki theatre the perceptual apparatus engages in acts of distortion and fusion. The senses are deployed as meditational links in an increasing and unified line of intense projection. This process is constructed (for it is an act of montage construction) through an organization of space and sound wholly subjugated to a particular ideational or emotional purpose. The harmony of the whole is created by the purposeful direction, which infuses the parts, so that lines, sounds, images can become identical with one another because each as an individual element is made to resound with the emotional tone of the whole.

These harmonic relationships can be constructed because, according to Eisenstein, the Japanese have retained in their worldview an essentially undifferentiated perception. The Kabuki artist does not think in terms of perspective, but organizes her world in a manner similar to the Jazz musician, where the essentially democratic arrangement of notes foregrounds all the various musical elements. This notion of flattened space, of arrangements that take cognisance of linear or graphic patterns and volume, rather than of depth is, in essence, a foregrounding based on psychological or emotional imperatives, rather than a rational view of reality; it relates specifically (in *Cinema 2* by Deleuze) to the creation of "sheets of time".[18]

Eisenstein's stress in his discussion of the Kabuki is on what he will later call overtonal vibration. The Kabuki, in the first instance, could be viewed as montage because it fragmented voice from action; the body into its different parts; action into sequential "shots" and the idea into separate particular representations. Each fragment had life in the overall structure only in relation to the general theme or emotion, which was in the process of being transmitted to the audience. The actor reduced spatial and temporal representations to the level of signs aimed at "the sensual organs [and based on] his calculation [of] the final sum of stimulants to the brain, ignoring which path that stimulation takes".[19] Such a method, based on a particular world view or undifferentiated perception, allowed the psyche of the viewer to be assailed by the mutual play of different sensations which had been individually infused with one emotion:

> Instead of *accompaniment* the Kabuki reveals the method of *transference*: the transference of the basic affective intention from one material to another, from one category of 'simulant' to another.
>
> Watching the Kabuki, you involuntarily recall the novel by an American writer about a man whose auditory and optical nerves were transposed so that he perceived light vibrations as sounds and air tremors as colours: that is, he began to *hear* light and *see* sounds. The same thing happens in the Kabuki! We actually 'hear movement' and 'see sound.'[20]

Eisenstein is describing the efficacy of a tendentious line that creates an intense effect on the body of the spectator and leads to the generation of thought. While the kabuki strives for this effect, the cinema as the fulfilment of the promise of all other arts, achieves it. He is also describing the principle of a monistic ensemble in film. The director gauges the effect of a concert of different lines by careful choice of material and for maximum effect. Truth or knowledge is no longer the experience of the intellect, but a felt response of the body. This response is attained because cinema at its outset is forced to imitate natural perception.[21] Through this assemblage, thought is created. Here thought "gushes forth" because the distinctions between mind and body have been unpinned. What emerges is the felt sensation of the body and a visceral reaction that flows from primal sensation.

In Gregg Lambert's words, this allows for "an extremely free and indeterminate range of possible combinations with regards to the elements of expression" and "becomes a physiological imperative, a total provocation of the brain".[22] Lambert is describing the relationship between movement and thought in Deleuze's understanding of Eisensteinian montage, that film is an art of movement and of time, and movement in time generates thought. While in our human act of perception, our eyes move across a page or across space and thus register or elicit the process of thinking by bringing together the fragments of our perception, in film montage this act of movement is already inherent in the projection of images. This encounter between the movement of the mind and the actual movement that maps duration in film gives rise to the "nooshock" of Deleuzian thought.[23]

For Deleuze:

> choreographic or dramatic images remain attached to a moving body. It is only when movement becomes automatic that the artistic essence of the image is realized: *producing a shock to thought, communicating vibrations to the cortex, touching the nervous and cerebral system directly*. Because the cinematographic image itself 'makes' movement, because it makes what the other arts are restricted to demanding (or to saying), it brings together what is essential in the other arts; it inherits it, it is as it were the directions for use of the other images, it converts into potential what was only possibility. *Automatic movement* gives rise to a *spiritual automaton* in us, which reacts in turn on movement.[24]

Deleuze is actually echoing Eisenstein's often repeated ideas here.

The problem of art for Walcott centred on the notion of time and the echoes that an image, in time, accumulated and triggered.[25] These concerns are linked throughout his work with a desire to free the image from its accretions in time and equally to give that image its own force field. Given that both Eisenstein and Deleuze saw cinema as giving rise to a powerful image born of two factors – one fragmentation, the other conflict – then their writings suggest that the Caribbean is already potentially cinematic. What it needs is movement. This is more than a figurative idea. If one looks at Walcott's later poetry in this light, what is apparent is his concerted attempt to theorise the Caribbean as "moving" and to insert movement into his poetry. One of the ways of doing so is by approximating the combustive force of shock as in conflictual montage, so that the images in poetry develop the explosive, vibratory force of filmic images as they are projected on screen. This, in other words, is an attempt to simulate the automatic processes engendered by the cinematic.

For Caribbean artists there is already "shock" that derives from the meeting of different facets of culture and history within one space, and through the combinations that then lead to syncretic arts. For Walcott, film best enables the depiction of this process, which is founded on conflict, so one might say that film is attached to a situation replete with the elements that might generate new ways of thinking. The idea of movement is already implicit in the theme of exile and dispossession, both as past history and present experience. This is so both in terms of successive displacements, and because of the sea and equally because it is constantly changing. The question that immediately arises is whether poetry can ever attain the full impact of a film despite these conditions. What Deleuze saw was that within certain cultures and situations, conditions of shock and dissonance were created that led to a new kind of cinema.

Lambert notes the vast importance to Eisenstein of the need for dissonance or conflict as a means towards the freeing of the shot from its "inertia", and the concomitant need therefore to resist the use of synchronized sound. The problem he addresses is a philosophical one and his focus is on the process through which time is freed from the rigid structures of causality. Lambert, in his reading of Deleuze, also emphasizes the idea of the body as it exists before discourses, or "before words" in his discussion of Eisenstein's discovery of "a new synthesis of the sensible".[26] In this he is referring to the overtone or, as it was described by Eisenstein, to the creation of "a totally physiological sensation" that leads to "I feel" rather than "I see" or "I hear". He is interested in Deleuze's appropriation of this concept.[27] The body feels and is pleasured by memory of sensation as in Molly Bloom's Ulyssean monologue.[28] Feeling exists before thought. This recalls the now famous stipulation by Beckett in his direction of *Not I*,[29] that he wanted this piece to play on the nerves of the audience, not the intellect.

The idea of synthesis and its capacity for generating new ways of seeing is increasingly linked in Walcott's oeuvre to the movement and creativity of carnival and the properties of film. First of all it is their common method of shared production and the ways in which carnival brings together various artists and participants that intrigues. Then carnival, as an illusion, suggests the possibility of transcendence through a leap of the imagination, as does film.

For Walcott, "Carnival bands are managed like film productions."[30] The relationship between film and carnival is made evident at the start of the film script version of *A Branch of the Blue Nile*. This play, which is in many ways a reflection of Walcott's relationship with theatre in Trinidad, is both a tribute to the Theatre Workshop he founded in 1959 and to the players. But it is also gives a sense of the "ole mas" that is Trinidad.

A Branch of the Blue Nile (circa 2007), the film script, opens with a screen that is replete with colour and movement. These visuals are accompanied by the sound of steelband music. The play, which is being rehearsed on stage, is associated initially with carnival as an art that mimics history and concretises memory and which combines, within its production, both sound and visual; and, most important of all, movement. The film version seeks to demonstrate the gap between reality and illusion. The camera focuses on Christopher who plays Antony. He is dancing in a carnival band. These ideas are intensified through the montage cut, which shows a tired Christopher resting by a culvert still in costume. This is overlaid by Sheila's voice, which projects a memory. Carnival then signifies both the production that marshals sound and visual as an intense experience and also its ability to trigger memory through this affective image.

The screen returns the viewer to the mundane present, which is a scene set within the tall structure of a Port of Spain office block. This, as the voice of a news reporter tells us, is a return to normalcy and the business of the city. In one profound sense, history in the Caribbean is performance and this is exemplified in carnival.

A Branch of the Blue Nile is, one might say, a transitional work that seeks to explore the issues of an indigenous stagecraft or poetic that flows from the layering of different traditions. Film becomes a way of providing both the multiple layers and the sense of dream or hallucination that such an imagining might foster. In this, it foreshadows the many strands of both *Steel* and *Omeros*. Many critics and reviewers have commented on the complex narrative structure of *Steel* as a stage play, and most have found it confusing.

In the play, *Steel*, and the film script, movement and carnival are linked to the creativity of a culture forged in violence and loss. This is fused with an idea of art as movement, as in the various lines and dance movements of the play. These are narrative lines as well as lines of temporal movement. There is a direct relation between what Walcott is doing in *Steel* and Laura Marks's interpretation of intercultural cinema. Marks's *The Skin of the Film* examines Deleuze's work as it impacts on our understanding of the visceral effect of the filmic. Her emphasis is on the revolutionary use of the sensuous as a site of remembering and of production in new cinemas, or what used to be called "Third Cinema". For her, Deleuze is most seductive in his advocacy of fabulation, excavation and falsification as part of the process for intercultural cinema makers uncovering lost or hidden histories and memories.[31]

Steel represents very much a process of excavation and also uses fabulation and fiction as ways of arriving at a truth that has been covered by the silt of dominant hegemonic narratives. In the first instance, it invents a story of the birth of the steel pan and uses true events as reference points within a new fiction that seeks a different truth from that of historical accuracy. The dance, the movement of the carnival, the sounds of battle and fête, and the music of *Steel* act with the refrain and songs to create layers of a complex and perhaps perplexing history that is still only in the process of being told. There are a number of changes between the first versions of *Steel* and the script used in the 2005 production in Trinidad. But all share Walcott's desire to produce a complex set of thematic lines that evoke cultural, political, economic and personal histories in Trinidad.

Steel[32] creates a monistic ensemble to attack the nervous system and to "shock" thought into being by harnessing dance, song, movement, illusion, past and present and an array of thematic lines. In attending the rehearsals for *Steel* it became very obvious that Walcott's concern was with affect, that is how the actual acting, dance, song and movement acted on the audience. His attention was focussed to an inordinate extent on the movement of dance as a way of creating spatialised maps of lived historic experience, which he saw as complex and multifaceted.

Steel begins by making a statement about the relationship between creativity and necessity, and creates a parallel with the illusions of film:

> PROLOGUE
>
> (BANDIDOS pan yard. They play. ELI Comes forward with a folded newspaper)
> ELI
> LONG TIME
> BEFORE ITS IMPROVEMENT
> WHEN CRIME
> ~~MEANT~~ THE STEELBAND MOVEMENT
> CARRIED
> THE SAME SOCIAL STIGMA
> YOU'D READ
> IN THE GAZETTE PAPER
> IS BADJOHNS PLAYING LIFE IS CINEMA
> A DOUBLE PROGRAMME AT RIALTO
> WITH BACK TO BATAAN AND THIRTY SECONDS OVER TOKYO
> (mimes a war movie) (p. 1)[33]

The fact that "Despers, Tokyo, all the best ones were named for war-movies and Westerns" is contextualised within the frame of violence and police interventions that come to a climax on carnival day. The cinema is therefore both a form and a narrative to be mimicked and an escape that fuels in some measure the creative newness of an art associated with carnival. It is this phenomenon and this set of conflictual relationships within the history of the steel band that the play seeks to interrogate, through a complex structure that analyses the way history as chaos and time as memory are envisioned.

The confusion and irrationality of violence and the inability of the poor to carve out a living within a structure of economic exploitation as exemplified by Arenkinian and the American presence and developing capitalism, is another thematic strand in the narrative:

> ARENKINIAN
> The steelbands talking about a Union. This is
> Trinidad. It ain't go work. In this island is
> Every man for himself. I don't intend to negotiate
> With no Union with my Record Company and Cosmos travel. (p. 83)

The play is therefore on one level about the forces of capital, and the ways in which the original steel band men resisted these forces.

Steel's complexity derives from a way of thinking about social relationships and the intricate weave of events and inequalities that give rise to what we might call, in terms of a filmic narrative, a moment of high intensity, which leads to the production of something new and transforming. What Walcott does in the staged version is to show the interpenetration of events, both as the past acting on, and resident in, the present and as a series of actions that are in themselves abortive, but yet in combination give rise to something new. Roger is a case in point. He is obsessed with his father and this idea breeds an illusion and a wish for exile. The theme of absent fathers is replicated in the story of Zora whose mother is a prostitute. These absent presences cause the intersections within the film. But because there is no resolution as such, outside of the creative moment of the birth of pan, the play gives the impression of a non-unified and even chaotic work.

Its true impact is to preserve a sense of time as something internal to both characters and events. Time shapes the narrative, both because the play uses the filmic convention of a flashback and because it brings together diverse lines of movement in the many stories. These act against each other and at times intersect with each other, as in the story of Winston's love affair and the story of the steelband and the two accounts of absent fathers.

These multiple narratives also allow the use of varying sensuous images. The first of course is music, in the steel band and in calypso, as well as the repetitions of the chorus. There is also the raga music and the dance of Zora, the sailor dance and the chip chip of the carnival dance. The audience is literally assailed by these many sense-images. But all combine as modes of temporality, in that all have the aura of memory, as events that have somehow remained alive in the present in the very image and idea of the steel pan, which itself has emerged out of myriad traditions. The diversity of theme in *Steel* embraces that of mulatto or mixed-race individuals, since both Zora and Roger have unknown white American fathers, and this leads to the question of a mulatto aesthetic. It also attaches this idea of mixed origins to the lure of elsewhere, as found in both Roger and Zora. It is particularly focussed on the choice between classical art and an indigenous tradition of art.

The character of Lawrence-Bain is conceived as a figure whose idea of culture is definitively European and he plays Chopin "without a music–sheet". In the film-script he is a fine-featured black man, balding with a white moustache" (p. 36). In the stage play he is white. The adversarial action between Lawrence-Bain and Eli should have formed the heart of the matter. It actually does not, which gave rise to severe criticism in 2005 in Trinidad.

In *Steel*, Eli tries to persuade the music teacher Lawrence-Bain to see the pan as a musical instrument, but Lawrence-Bain insists on seeing it as a "dust-bin". In the film version, while Eli Manette demonstrates the high notes and his precision-cutting, and plays "Panis Angelicus", Lawrence-Bain declares:

> It is not music and can never be. A garbage can cover produces garbage. It's fun. It is not music. ("Steel", film-script, p. 36).

Storyboard from "Steel", Zora dancing
The Thomas Fisher Library, The University of Toronto,
Ms coll 136, 1990

The disrespect shown to Eli ultimately leads to Winston's departure.

Within this already intense situation a new one develops, based on land and territory, when Roger declares that he is checking out of Belmont and moving to Woodbrook. This means he can no longer play with Bandidos, since Invaders is Woodbrook. This is part of the issue that Walcott introduces as his version of the history of pan. The violence that erupts when boundaries are broken is both disruptive and a source of breakdown. These perpetually erupting fractures are the breaks that somehow, and perhaps miraculously, lead to creation. The film-script works consistently to produce these shocks.

Steel is an important work, despite the fact that its multiple strands seem to require more careful editing and focus. As a film script it bears a resemblance in many of its sequences to Jamaican Perry Henzell's 1972 film, *The Harder they Come*. One particular scene in the film script version of "Steel" is pertinent; it occurs when Roger, Bones, Centipede and Winston go out to steal a drum to bring to Eli to make into a pan. The guards start shooting and Roger, who turns into a bandit guarding his property, in clear mimicry of a good Western shootout, shoots the guard.

> [But ROGER has climbed into a drum, and both hands around the gun, takes aim, or tries to, on the swaying jitney. He pitches forward as shots ring out from the Security van.]

> WINSTON
> O God, o my God, they shot him. Bones,
> they shot him!

> BONES
> I hope so. I really focking hope so.

> [EXT. The highway, outside Couva. But the jitney's swerve was to avoid the Security van, as it has swung onto a side road, then onto another road, and then through a canefield, the canes rushing past it with the Security van gone down the highway. Silence. CENTIPEDE'S head resting on his shoulders, HEADACHE, head tilted. WINSTON bending over ROGER, BONES gasping against the drums.]

> ROGER
> Since when all you ever hear the starboy could dead?
> ("Steel", film script, pp. 28-29).

This is a direct copy of Ivan from *The Harder They Come* who goes out in a full blaze of gunfire convinced of his invulnerability, because he has become a star boy and a folk hero and thinks himself at one with the iconic figure of a movie star. Both film and film script are commenting on the vulnerability of the Caribbean male to the illusions of the cinema. *Steel* has this as one of its primary themes. What Walcott sought to do in this work for stage and screen was to show how these various facets combine to generate both illusion and imaginative creation – here the creativity of the invention of the pan. So that the chase and near death of the three young men in "Steel", the film script, is followed by ecstatic movement in:

> CUT
>
> [EXT. The same. Night. ROGER, WINSTON, BONES beating on the hollow drums on the bed of the jitney, a wild ecstatic rhythm, with the heels of their palms, the pliers and the chisel.]

The cinematic is an ideal mechanism for suggesting that the Caribbean imagination responds to a set of competing circumstances. Cinema enables Walcott to manipulate time and to produce several strands of narrative as parallel lines, while also giving the dips or caesurae, which suggest loss of history and even culture. The theme of movie as life, and life as illusion is constant in 'Steel", so that even Winston gives the excuse for not doing his "homework" and practising, as his compulsion to attend the double feature at the Globe, saying that the distraction was simply too much to conquer.

The play is also about memory and film as a motif operates as such an image. Film represents desire and the dream of becoming, for those who live in a void of identity. The search for "home" is figured through Reds (Roger) in his move from Belmont to Woodbrook. This quest for a place of belonging leads Reds and Zora to move to America in search of their fathers. This is doubly evoked through filmic leaps in time that mirror the shared Caribbean sense of a history shrouded in shadows and loss. Memory becomes available to appropriation and creation. As Winston sings:

> How long ago did it start, the very first frame
> Of the movie we're still making of our lives? (p. 113)

The "interior camera" that Winston demonstrates through mime in the stage production of 2005, suggests that cinema as a generator of illusions is also available as a mechanism for recreation. But at the same time the Caribbean personality is exceedingly vulnerable to this vehicle of chimeras because of the absence of a past.

But film is also the cure. As a synthesis of the arts, in the sense that as a production it brings together visual, sound and movement, it enables the fashioning of fragments of culture into a whole. The new entity of the steelband exemplifies this.

The work also uses the idea of filmic time, or the capacity of film to condense or stretch time, to show the clash of cultures and events that have led to this creative genesis. Eli comments that steel creates a note that is "perfection", that is "the harmony of spheres", and then reflects that this harmonic music causes him to remember the "night we beat Japan." ("Steel", screenplay, p. 4). This use of time as fluid enables a sense of the interconnections over time and even continents. V.J. night, 1945, is a night that marks history. It marks both a night of musical history and a night of European war history in the harmonics of memory.

This idea is marked very self-consciously by a filmic flashback on stage. The question, "Were you there?" is the point at which Walcott inserts the flashback.

What is particularly interesting in his use of filmic flashback in the stage play *Steel* is its resemblance to the montage forms described by Eisenstein in his discussion of his own films, for example *The General Line*. Here the leap generated by the contrapuntal play of different lines of sound and of visual leads to an explosion like fireworks, that marks a leap to a new dimension, a raising of consciousness or a leap to a new idea.

The analogy is found in Walcott's *Steel* when the moment that peace is declared and the steelband is invented is performed on stage as:

> I WAS SINGING IN A NIGHTCLUB ON WRIGHTSON ROAD, SINGING IN THE BLACKOUT AT CLUB MIRAMAR WHEN PORT OF SPAIN LIKE IT SUDDENLY EXPLODE WITH A CRY LIKE A ROCKET IN THE SPARKS UP YONDER. OVER THE ROOFS AND FROM THE YANKEE BASE DOWN CHAGUARAMAS THE GUNS START TO THUNDER LIKE A BIG BASS DRUM AND THAT WAS THE CASE. (*Steel*, stage play, p. 6)

The combined sound and visual impact is similar to that explosion generated by conflicting lines in movement in montage and is a replica of a classic scene of cinema to which every student of film would be exposed, and already quoted:

> (The close-ups flash, intercut with the revolving disks.)
> The drop breaks off.
> It falls!
> And the tiniest spray, starlike scatters, hitting
> the bottom of the empty pail.[34]

The idea of a leap to ecstasy or *ex stasis* (being beside oneself) is a mimicry of the creative process, where the artist becomes "besides himself" through inspiration. This leap of the material (colour and light) is explained further as a chromatic leap, in other words there are jumps to new levels of perception in the leap to colour, since "montage elevates the level of this shimmer to a new heightened class of intensity – to a shimmer of soaring fire sparks."[35] The various transitions of affective techniques are calculated for maximum impact. They both have a visceral effect and also a philosophical one, since they lead to a change in consciousness, which is in fact the level at which Walcott aims in this complex play. This is reinforced near the close, by ARENKINIAN who in the film script says:

> On the night of the Allied Victory over the forces
> Of Adolf Hitler and Emperor Hirohito, thirty of more
> Years ago in the ecstasy of our jubilation
> The poor in our streets picked up dustbins (sic) covers,
> Angle irons, brake drums, anything they could find to
> Celebrate the end of one struggle, but the end
> Of one struggle was the start of another.
> The struggle to make out of those garbage-can
> covers, rusted and abandoned junk, an
> Instrument that was tempered in fire and
> Determination, the collective determination of
> the underprivileged to make a new music.

This comes immediately after the directions for an interior shot in Queen's Hall:

> [Night. Close-up: A shining silver tenor-pan with a Polaroid picture of ROGER in Marine combat gear holding up a Steel bayonet between two other soldiers and Roger's handwriting: REAL STEEL! Under the portrait. Crossed flags. Trinidad and Tobago, The Stars and Stripes. The pans. The Stage empty. Above the Queen's Hall Stage, a banner STEELBAND FINALISTS: BANDIDOS; CASABLANCA: DESPERADOES.]

Roger's death and remembrance suggest that his sacrifice, despite his own unrealised dreams, in the midst of battles of war, society and economic deprivation, yet enabled the conception and realisation of a new musical instrument – a leap to something new.

> I SITTING DOWN IN A RICE FIELD
> THAT STINKING OF HUMAN MANURE
> I SMOKING AND PLAYING JOHN GARFIELD
> EXCEPT IT IS A REAL WAR
> WHEN I LOOK ACROSS THE HORIZON
> THE RICE LOOKS LIKE CARONI CANE
> WITH CHALKBIRDS AND WATER BISON
> AND I FEEL I AM HOME AGAIN
> HERE IS REAL STEEL ALL AROUND ME
> I THINK OF MY FATHER A LOT
> I'VE FOUND MY PLACE IN THE ARMY
> I GO GIVE IT ALL THAT I GOT
> GLOBE, I'M HERE WHERE YOU FOUND ME
> LET THE MOVIE BEGIN
> AND WRAP OLD GLORY AROUND ME

A HORIZONTAL CITIZEN

BONES+ROGER+WINSTON
LIKE A GANG WAR IN WARNER BROTHERS
LIKE A SHOWDOWN IN R. K. O.
THE NAME OF THE BAND IS BANDIDOS
AND THE SHERIFF IS TEXACO.
YOU MOVIE STARS ABOVE US
TIME FOR OUR DREAMS TO START
WE LIVE THE DREAM OF OTHERS
EDWARD G. CAGNEY, BOGART (*Steel*, stage play, p. 7) [36]

The performance of his death uses close-up, flashbacks and a freeze frame – a technique also used in *Omeros*, both in the poem and in the film script. This pictures life in the Caribbean as a succession of illusions, but in the repeated refrain, also commemorates Roger as a "martyr" for pan and one whose dreams and frustrations led to its birth.

It is his death that is commemorated through film as the steelband men return in triumph to the Queen's Hall stage to celebrate pan at what the script describes as Steelband final between Bandidos, Casablanca and Desperadoes. The audience sees him in Korea, "seated on a knoll, with a view of rice paddies." He is writing a letter. This flashback is staged as a simulation of a movie and occurs during the playing of the steel pan. Film and music combine to project the dual effect of fantasy: one leading to sacrificial death and the other to the creation of the only new instrument of the twentieth century. Both film art and music combine to narrate his death in the rice fields of Korea and to show their relationship and simultaneous co-existence in memory. At this point it is movement that narrates, since the words are rendered almost superfluous.

The quick transition to Growler as calypsonian and articulator transforms the idea of loss and takes it to a new level, as indeed occurs in many of Walcott's works including *Omeros* and *The Prodigal*.

IN A BACKYARD IN BELMONT
IN A YARD BEHIND THE BRIDGE
SOMEWHERE BEHIND EAST DRY RIVER
GROWLER HAD THE PRIVILEGE
OF SEEING HOW PAN WAS BORN.

This is a response to a repeated refrain of Reds.

TIME FOR OUR DREAMS TO START
WE LIVE THE DREAMS OF OTHERS
EDWARD G., CAGNEY, BOGART.

The sense of life as performance is once again reiterated in a dramatic production that includes Indian dance and song and a repeated Shango chorus, as well as the music of steel and calypso. Growler provides the commentary that informs the audience that a Shango meeting is in session and that this is a vestige of Africa with drums from the Congo and drums from Dahomey. This co-exists alongside gospel music and Aunt Jessica's singing. There is an obvious clash of cultures and beliefs but this clash is the energy of the play. Walcott is obviously striving to attack the psyche through all available means.

The hills of Laventille, which are the setting of the action (the stage set for Queen's Hall was designed by Jackie Hinkson and comprised the hills with multiple lights), reflect the history of a place where resistance has bred both creativity and disfranchisement and this contradictory fact fuels both the poem "Laventille",[37] as a meditation on a place in which human suffering and trauma are embedded, and "Steel," which is exuberant in its hope and its illusions.

Carnival becomes aligned to cinema as a production that can bring together these elements and that can act as a screen on which the past can be projected, that is in a manner similar to a carnival band reproducing an event of history. If for Deleuze the time-image is an image of disjuncture that yet gives rise to the creation of the new, then *Steel*, as a film script and as a stage play that uses the cinematic in terms of the movement of images, is seeking actively to make that truth emerge. It does this by eliciting responses through play and through movement and through the careful production of combined effects.

Endnotes

1. Sergei Eisenstein, *The General Line* or *The Old and the New* (1929).
2. Sergei Eisenstein, *Nonindifferent Nature. Film and the Structure of Things*, ed. and trans. Herbert Marshall (Cambridge: Cambridge University Press,1987) pp. 52-53.
3. V.S. Naipaul, *The Middle Passage* (London: Andre Deutsch, 1962), pp. 28-29.
4. Derek Walcott, undated film version of "Pantomime", Box 7, Folder 6, Derek Walcott collection, The Alma Jordan Library, The University of the West Indies, St Augustine, no date. Published stage play, *Remembrance and Pantomime* (New York: Farrar, Straus, and Giroux 1980), p.113.
5. George Lamming, *Pleasures of Exile* (London: Michael Joseph, 1960; MI: Ann Arbor, 1992); *Water with Berries* (London: Longman, 1971; Leeds: Peepal Tree Press, 2016).
6. Mikhail Bakhtin, *The Dialogic Relation. Four Essays*, trans., Caryl Emerson and M. Holquist (Austin: University of Texas Press, 1981).
7. "The Spoiler's Return", *The Fortunate Traveller* (New York Farrar, Straus and Giroux, 1980), pp. 53-60.
8. "Pantomime", teleplay, ts., Box 7. Folder 6, Derek Walcott collection, Alma Jordan Library, The University of the West Indies, St Augustine.
9. *What the Twilight Says. Essays* ([1970] London: Faber and Faber, 1998), pp. 3-35.
10. Edward Baugh, *Derek Walcot*t (Cambridge University Press, 2006), p.115.
11. Derek Walcott, "Un Voyage a Cythère". A play for television, Box 6 Folder 6, Derek Walcott Collection, Alma Jordan Library, The University of the West Indies, St Augustine. c. 1965
12. Derek Walcott, "The Last Carnival", a film outline, four pages, box 6, folder 11, Derek Walcott collection, Alma Jordan Library, The University of the West Indies, St. Augustine, Trinidad, 1978.
13. Walcott, "The Last Carnival", stage play, Walcott's production script, box 6, folder 11, Derek Walcott collection, Alma Jordan Library, The University of the West Indies St. Augustine, Trinidad, University of the West Indies, c.1982.
14. See Sergei Eisenstein, *Nonindifferent Nature. Film and the Structure of Things*. Ed. and trans. Herbert Marshall (Cambridge: Cambridge University Press, 1987).
15. Thomas Docherty, *After Theory* (Edinburgh: Edinburgh University Press, 1996).
16. Sergei Eisenstein, "The Fourth Dimension in Cinema" [1929] *S.*

M. Eisenstein, Selected Works, Vol. 1, ed. Richard Taylor (London: BFI, 1988), pp. 185-186.

17. Laurence Breiner, "The Impact of Japan on Derek Walcott's Early Plays", *Comparative Theater Review*, Vol.13 (English Issue) March 2014. p. 4.
18. Gilles Deleuze, *Cinema 1. The Movement-Image*, trans.,Tomlinson and Habberjam (London: Athlone Press, 1992), p. 3. See also *Cinema 2*.
19. S. M. Eisenstein, "An Unexpected Juncture", *Writings, Vol.1*, published as "The Unexpected" in *Film Form. Essays in Film Theory*, ed. and trans., Jay Leyda (New York and London: Harcourt Brace, 1977), p. 21.
20. Eisenstein, pp 117-118; "The Unexpected", pp. 21-22.
21. "The Unexpected", p. 24.
22. Gregg Lambert, "Cinema and the Outside" in *The Brain is the Screen. Deleuze and the Philosophy of Cinema*, ed. Gregory Flaxman (Minneapolis and London: University of Minnesota Press, 2000), p. 258.
23. Gregg Lambert, p. 258.
24. Gilles Deleuze, *Cinema 2. The Time-Image*, trans., Tomlinson and Galeta (London: Athlone Press, 1989), p. 156.
25. See Walcott's attempt to explain this idea, in his discussion of an image generating echoes at the filmed Bowling Green University symposium, "Imagining the Caribbean, Identity and Aesthetics," in March 1999.
26. Gregg Lambert, "Cinema and the Outside", p. 254.
27. Gregg Lambert, "Cinema and the Outside", p. 254.
28. James Joyce, *Ulysses* (London: Penguin, 2000).
29. Samuel Beckett, *Not I*, in *The Complete Dramatic Works* (London: Faber and Faber, 1990).
30. Derek Walcott, "On the Beat in Trinidad", 5 October 1986, *The New York Times Magazine*, Part 2.
31. Marks, *The Skin of the Film*, p. 27.
32. I am using a personal copy of the stage play used in the World Premiere, September, 2005 production in Queen's Hall, Trinidad.
33. Script for *Steel*, 2005.
34. Eisenstein, *Nonindifferent Nature*, pp. 52-3.
35. Sergei Eisenstein, *Nonindifferent Nature*, p. 53.
36. See also p.16 where the second verse is sung in chorus.
37. "Laventille", *The Castaway and Other Poems* (London: Jonathan Cape, 1965), p. 32.

CHAPTER 3
FILM AND THE TRUE LIGHT OF THE WORLD

Cinema is light moving in time.[1] As a form of communication, light creates images in the brain and does this through the eye. Light, as Eisenstein reiterated, is also a language that operates through vibration and is therefore a harnessing of both the effects of the visual and the impact of sound, since both are channelled by the body to the brain as a series of vibrations. Light is, therefore, one might say a scintillating language of affect. Photography creates an image through light or the effect of light, but photography is still and not moving and therefore does not have the resonating or oscillating effect of the cinematic. This difference is crucial to an understanding of Walcott's works and may be seen to be one of the primary ideas at work in *Tiepolo's Hound* in its move to an audiovisual language of affect.[2]

The vibrations of light exceed the impact or signification of verbal language, and light as a motif and a concept finds its way into works such as *Another Life*, *Arkansas Testament*, *Omeros*, and *Tiepolo's Hound* where it becomes the main theme and in *The Prodigal* and *White Egrets* where it attains a quality through which to mark the passage of time and looks towards death and resurrection.[3] Light in its visual impact also creates shapes that people the imagination. Light emerges as a cluster of ideas that suggests contradiction, or as a motif to examine the sense of double vision imaged in *Another Life* as in, "The sun explodes into irises,/ the shadows are crossing like crows."[4] Walcott suggests that the light of the tropics destroys the stereoscopic capacity of the eye: shots or pictures do not merge as in normal perception when the sun strikes the eye. This stunning physical effect evolves into an image of a psychic split, figured in such works as *Arkansas Testament* as a form of doubling.

Light also has historical emanations through its association with Christianity and the "light of knowledge". This "light", represented as the "true light of the world," by Western knowledge and culture, is that light against which the Caribbean defines itself and sees itself as lacking subtlety, an extension of the physical properties of Caribbean light which moves without gradation between day and night.[5] These ideas which, for Walcott, are at the root of the lack of confidence and self-image of the Caribbean individual and of the Caribbean artist,[6] become pivotal concerns in the poems and essays after the publication of the essay, "What the Twilight Says: an Overture" in 1970.[7]

"The Light of the World" of *Arkansas Testament*, attempts a reversal. It renounces this stereotype, which presumes to suggest that white is equal to goodness and in this poem extends the ideas of heaven and the earthbound to include the suffering of an ordinary simple people. The people of St Lucia become the "true light of the world" because of inherent qualities of beauty and grace. The word "transport" which in the Caribbean means "taxi" accrues a double meaning of sublime transportation. But in examining their words, he also insinuates his own betrayal of their trust in his choice of leaving St Lucia for those very places that have so denigrated them. The patois, "Pas quittez moi à terre", is given the diverse meanings of historic abandonment and his abandonment. But the poem moves to a new idea, which is that the poor of St Lucia need nothing from him, nothing except the act of writing a poem entitled, "The True Light of the World".

Later, in *Omeros* the poet asks, "Where is the light of the world?" (p. 197) and lists as mercenary the art locked up in museums and the "City that can buy and sell us", of benefit only to those who have constructed themselves as having the true light. Walcott extends his use of light as a way of seeing and of being seen into an interrogation of forms for the representation of the complex life of the tropics. Complexity adheres both to the quality of light itself, its changing shapes, and its extension in lightning – which is a source of myth. The search for form evolves into an interrogation of the cinematic as an art of light or light waves. This effect of vibratory activity is achieved in the first instance through the use of conflict, as espoused by Eisenstein, for whom "conflict is at the base of the shot". As previously noted, this use of conflict is most apparent in the oppositions between still and moving image or between photography and the movies.

Cinema, through montage, which is the creation of a moving line or the simulation of movement through the superimposition of still shots, gives Walcott a method to think the new. Through the imposition of movement, as in cinema, memory and art combine to provide a process for moving beyond internalised ideas that "fix" the individual in positions of subservience and inferiority.

Laurence Breiner[8] notes Walcott's fascination with Japanese cinema during his two sojourns in New York (in 1957 and 1958-59). While Walcott did not see a great many Japanese films, the impact of those that he saw was life-long and possible intensified by the fact that he was immersed at the time in the study of stage-craft and film. Breiner notes two films by Akira Kurosowa, *Ugetsu* and *Rashomon*. The influence of Kurosawa, the Japanese film director goes beyond that of theme and representation and has been acknowledged by Walcott on more than one occasion:

> In New York… there was then a very strong popular interest in Japanese cinema – in Kurosawa, and films such as *Ugetsu, Gate of Hell, Rashomon*, etc. I had written one play which was derivative of *Rashomon*, called *Malcauchon* … This was a deliberate imitation, but it was one of those informing imitations that gave me a direction because I could see in the linear shapes, in the geography, in the sort of myth and superstition of the Japanese, correspondences to our own forest and mythology. I also wanted to use the same type of figure found in this material, a type essential to our own mythology. A wood-cutter or charcoal burner.
>
> To me, this figure represented the most isolated, most reduced race-containing symbol. In addition, I have my own associations of our forests, of rain, of mists, plus of course, the inherent violence or despair in a person of that type – the mad woodcutter. […]
>
> I am a kind of split writer: I have one tradition inside me going in one way, and another going another. The mimetic, the narrative, and dance element is strong on one side, and the literary, the classical tradition is strong on the other.[9]

Kurosawa was influenced by Kuleshov, Eisenstein's contemporary in the use of montage in the cinema. According to Russian theorist, V. V. Ivanov, Kuleshov's *The Great Consoler* (1933) is a "direct precursor" of *Rashomon* in the use of two contrasting types of film language, "the montage method, inherited from the silent film, and the theatrically-oriented sound film", for the interrogation of "an identical series of events from two diametrically opposite points of view".[10] *The Great Consoler*, as an exploration of the twin problems of creativity and the artist's "duty to reality",[11] suggests a crucial function for film in Walcott's work and thought.[12]

However, Akira Kurosowa also bequeathed to Walcott an intense experience of light as it can be used in film. Light resonates in Kurosowa's work and the play of light is part of the action and meaning within the thematic and emotional structure. Light and the use of light as a signifying mechanism lead Walcott to think of light as a language linked to silence, which he sees as also resonating or reverberating, both in the mind and in the psyche. Light becomes increasingly significant as a mechanism for exploring hidden trauma or submerged memory as, for example, the silence of the girl in "Cul de Sac Valley" whose language is swallowed like a tongue.[13] Light is also specifically linked to a particular kind of silence which is associated with the woods and waterfalls of the Caribbean, as in the figure of the silent woodsman who "walked without noise, / a shaft of light angling the floor of the forest / without shaking the ferns" (*Omeros*, p. 61).

The poem "The Man Who Loved Islands"[14] (which appropriates the title of D. H. Lawrence's short story)[15] in the collection *The Fortunate Traveller* also plays with the idea of light and examines the ways in which film might be popular and yet address complex issues. The poem is subtitled a "two page outline for a film script". The tentative use of film form in this poem, and the ambivalence to film within the work, has led some critics to see it as a rejection of cinematography. This is far from the truth. Instead, the poem and *The Fortunate Traveller* as a whole should be viewed as a meditation on the importance of conflict in film and on the impact of light and movement.

In this poem, the protagonist who is also a "Shabine", is imaged in a long shot, which foregrounds the concept of a world denuded of its history and its gods; empty of all except memory seen through the motif of the disappearing tanker, "thin ghost of a tanker drawing the horizon/ behind it with the silvery slick of a snail" (p. 37). The figure of the castaway resurfaces here as an image of the West Indian who has been "shipwrecked" on these islands, denuded of his past and forced back on himself and his elemental power in order to survive. "The Figure of Crusoe",[16] delivered as a lecture at the University of the West Indies, St. Augustine, Trinidad, in 1965, explores this idea and is also an early expression of Walcott's attention to the efficacy of film in his comment that the idea of "endurance", which is at the centre of the castaway image, is ideally suited to film, based on a survey of successful films.[17] He is here indirectly referring to Kurosowa's thematic.

The film scenario/poem dramatizes the way in which a scriptwriter and perhaps director might conceive of a film and he discusses the ingredients for a successful "box office" hit. The poem also incorporates the structure of montage, in particular in its use of oppositional lines. This is seen for example in the conflict between stillness and movement, inherent in the figure of the thinker, versus the play of light on water and the implied movement in the idea of chaos.

The "whiteness" which is highlighted in the poem, "The Man Who Loved Islands", allows the theme of colour, that obsession with slight differences of skin colour which is deeply embedded in the psyche of the West Indian, to emerge as a play of visual inflexions (highlights), as in a painting: "whitening hair", "silvery light", "silver chain" are all encircling echoes. Of equal importance is the image of contemplation, which is closely interwoven with this "white" light. By making a connection with the visual arts through the image of the thinker, in the reference to Rodin's sculpture, and the "painterly" texture of the lines in this section, Walcott emphasizes the visual impact of the islands and attempts a very complex series of connections centred on the notion of looking:

> … 'cause there's no kick in contemplation
> of silvery light upon wind-worried water
> between here and the islet of Saint John,
> and how they are linked like any silver chain
> ("The Man Who Loved Islands," p. 37)[18]

The conjunction of thought/contemplation (as an idea and image) with the "chaos of artifice still called the plot", locates the chaos of imperial history in the twin notions of thought/reflection and fiction-making.

History as a fictionalized and selective version of the past, a narrative in which selective shots are mounted together, is later juxtaposed with a "moving" history; a history which includes the emotional and psychic life of the Antilles. This is opposed to a version of the past that views these islands and their peoples through written history or the history of archives and, as such, of wars and events which are extrinsic to the "real" experiences of a people. This is a theme that will later surface with even greater prominence in *Omeros*.

The true history of the islands is contained in movement, juxtaposed to the stasis of contemplative thought, which introduces the notion of tone or rhythm. This tonal quality or rhythmic movement has already, in the earlier sections of *The Fortunate Traveller*, become associated with an oral tradition and a rejection of poetry as a purely literary art. In his 1990 lecture, "The Poet in the Theatre", Walcott described this tonal quality as the expressiveness of voice:

> These first lines springing from memory at random vindicate an argument, which is that an immediacy of tone – the tone of dramatic conversation which can vary in pitch from that of a professor as in Auden, to a middle-class employee as in Larkin, an amateur fisherman as in Bishop, a traveller in Pound; and the others, from Dylan Thomas, e.e. cummings – is dramatic, and by dramatic I mean theatrical, that is they are tonally speakable.[19]

The poem also approximates the cinematic caesura, which is a pause before a leap into a new idea, as perceived by certain montage theorists. "The Man who Loved Islands", in itself, is a pause for contemplation within the collection as a whole, thereby creating another conflict of movement versus stasis, and this dynamic action moves the work in its entirety to a new level. This transition is to an elemental force contained in the fury of the hurricane. This represents the rage of both poet and god at the desecration of a primal setting and the usurping of a native space. This movement in its mimicry of contrapuntal montage here suggests Walcott's familiarity with classical montage structure.

The use of the caesura for both contemplation and action in "The Man who Loved Islands" also means that the contemplating figure in the film/poem has a paradoxical significance. The poem, as a script for a movie, becomes an expression of a dual heritage, one within which conceptualization and psychic immanence are given equal weighting. The second movement of the overall collection flows from the film scenario/poem and is therefore particularly significant. "Hurucan" synthesizes the images and sounds of the Caribbean with the elements (the power of the place) themselves, a strategy again also echoed and more fully realised in *Omeros*. It also moves towards a gathering of the various artistic forces of the Caribbean in the poem that follows, "Jean Rhys".

This poem begins with photographs ("In their faint photographs/ mottled with chemicals") and in this also creates an oppositional movement by locating the still image in a moment of time past. The poem, however, is a decisive re-appropriation of Rhys's work, and situates her 1966 novel, *Wide Sargasso Sea*, within a tapestry of Amerindian myth, perhaps a reference to Harris's essay, "Carnival of Psyche: Jean Rhys's *Wide Sargasso Sea*,"[20] in which such parallels and influences are traced as unconscious assimilations of the myths of a place. In this way she becomes a symbol of the very idea Walcott is trying to formulate. She is the heiress to two quite separate traditions, both of which have been assimilated into her unconscious and transformed through the power of her imagination.

In its realisation, the poem "The Man Who Loved Islands" focuses on the "spectacular" nature of the Caribbean as well as on the subjugation of the islands within a predatory economic landscape. It also makes statements about the interior "meditative" or reflective life of poetry and the need for "action" in cinema, in this way perhaps voicing some of the criticisms that Walcott's film scripts may have generated over the decades. It does succeed in bringing poetry and drama together within a filmic structure nonetheless.

Paula Burnett provides several insights into this collection and focuses on the title poem as exemplifying a response to film. "The Fortunate Traveller" is read as a reworking of Francis Ford Coppola's *Apocalypse Now* (1979), which is in itself also a free-flowing film interpretation of Joseph Conrad's *Heart of Darkness* (1899). Burnett sees this as "a dialectical engagement in which aesthetics are exposed as a political field".[21] She notes the many critics, from Mervyn Morris to Rei Terada and Seamus Heaney, who have commented on Walcott's elaborate use of allusion and echoes in this collection as a whole and she points to the disagreement among such commentators about the possible "deathly" quality of such apparent derivativeness. I agree wholeheartedly with Burnett that *The Fortunate Traveller* is a much under-rated collection and one that is of central significance in Walcott's *oeuvre*.

As a collection that deliberately interrogates the filmic, it points to film's capacity to transform perception, as may be seen in the central value attributed to cinema by the politicians of the former Soviet Union and Soviet filmmakers and political leaders such as Fidel Castro, whose funding of a film school had much to do with his recognition of film's potential as political weapon. Soviet filmmakers saw film montage as a primary mechanism for raising consciousness and achieving the ideals of communism. In this respect, Burnett's statement about the title poem, though she does not identify the power of montage, is quite apt: "The Fortunate Traveller" she says "inverts the dynamic of cultural colonialism, addressing itself, as mission, to the 'soul' of its others, the neo-imperialists, hoping to effect a moral transformation."[22]

Burnett argues that the atmosphere of "The Fortunate Traveller" is suggestive of a "film noir" Europe, meaning that it is associated with a period of film-making prevalent in the post World War Two period and associated with a degree of cynicism. Of course, the use of monochrome here in this poem also suggests early pre-colour cinema, that is cinema prior to World War Two, though the manipulation of colour in cinema existed at a much earlier stage.

It is useful to read this poem through montage theory and its intriguing use of cinematic light. In the first instance, the poem is dedicated to Susan Sontag, whose writings on photography are referenced in the interplay of black and white that is found in the very first poem of the collection ("Black clippers, tarred with whales' blood [...] A white church spire whistles into space", "Old New England") and in the repetition of the idea of stasis in the word "congealed". In "The Fortunate Traveller", there is also a movement from darkness, in the grey and black of overcoats, that echoes Yeats's "The Fisherman".[23] This poem by Yeats is, above all else, about the creation of an image through the reworking of the real by the imagination in the "cold" light of recollection as in, "I will make you an image as cold and passionate as the dawn", which is opposed to the real figure of the fisherman. The grey of Yeats's protagonist, against the greyness of Connemara, is a beginning motif that moves the reader to and through the creative process of poetry-making. Here in Walcott's poem, the greyness merges with the grey tones of the photographic, which Sontag associates with melancholy and death.[24] But for Sontag the photograph also gives the impression of power, as if one owns the experience. Photographs are "experience captured" and beyond this photographs are forms of appropriation so that, for Sontag, to photograph someone is "subliminal murder". Being a photographer also means that one is essentially a voyeur and not capable of interventionist action.[25] It is therefore necessary to consider the relationship between this still "congealed" image and the movement of images that are in this poem defined through light.

The first verse also introduces the idea of "cold ecstasy of an assassin", reinforcing the concept that the protagonist or traitor here is initiating some form of death-like stasis on the country he is betraying. He is the maker of statistics and shadows and he is creating deserts that have fallen victim to the slow, "soft" destruction of the weevil (p. 89).

The poem moves to a "frisson", or movement defined in light, first through the television's "blue storm with soundless snow", that also invokes the idea of ecstasy, in the line "rehearsing ecstasies of starvation" (p. 90), that at the same time anticipates the final verse, in which starvation leads to the ecstasy of Christ's death and resurrection. Starvation is thus marked as a prelude or passage to salvation. The journey to Pity is a simulated one and undertaken in colour. It is "envisaged" in a "flood of light", that is a form of alchemy, which is the transmutation of base matter into gold, linking greed and materialism to what the poet suggests is only a pretence at pity (*caritas*), and that is also seen as an academic exercise. Light also becomes a double motif in that it can also be used to rationalise the selling of one's country and one's people, as in "their rising souls will lighten the world's weight" (p. 93), creating an inner harmonic with Walcott's ironic depiction of light in the collection, *Star Apple Kingdom*,[26] for example. In this 1979 work, light is associated with intellectual knowledge and the "light" of Christianity, and by extension with its use in justifying enslavement.

The play of light in "The Fortunate Traveller" allows the emergence of phantoms and leads to the spectral idea of evil at the centre of Conrad's *Heart of Darkness*. The hollowness at the heart of Kurtz and European civilisation is then explored through a layered image that also uses opposition to create a new insight or idea. The received ideas of the colour white, as equivalent to good, and black to evil, play off against each other and, through word play, create a reversal. Savages become aligned to light, though the matter is made both ambiguous and secret by carefully creating an indistinguishable subject of the action through enjambment ("The heart of darkness is the rubber claw/ selecting a scalpel in antiseptic light" (p. 94)). And equally by creating a montage list that juxtaposes a rubber claw with a scalpel bathed in what is in effect cold light, with mountains of children's shoes, which evokes, in the first instance, Charles Dickens and the poverty and labour of children; and in the use of the sound "tinkling", reminds us of the poem "September 1913" by Yeats where the sound of money in the greasy till reiterates the idea of the greed of "gombeen" men. Here, also, medical instruments usher in the memory of the holocaust and the inhumanity of experiments on incarcerated Jews; these are linked to Christianity, as another experiment in attaining "purity," in the phrase, "white altar".

As in classical montage, through opposition the poem leads the reader/ viewer to a new idea. This transformative leap is already heralded in the summoning of phantoms: "Now I have come to where the phantoms live" and in the figures who move towards the tree of life. This reference signals a relation to the ideas and writings of Wilson Harris, and also marks a mythic transformation. The image of the eternal becomes expressed as a wish that is breathed into the movement of the poem:

> If those who starve
> like these rain-flies who shed glazed wings in light
> grew from sharp shoulder blades their brittle vans
> and soared toward that tree, how it would seethe –
> ah, Justice! But fires
> drench them like vermin,... (p. 95)

As with montage, the truly ecstatic leap is defined through movement that creates energy, in this instance in the movement of the palm trees

(p. 97). Here the use of sibilants in the final verse is scintillating. The climax born of the release of energy is also a moment of apocalyptic vision, as evident in the reference to the third horseman.

still, through thin stalks,
the smoking stubble, stalks
grasshopper: third horseman,
the leather-helmet locust. (*The Fortunate Traveller*, p. 97)

The "frisson" movement, as erupting energy, then leads to apocalyptic transfiguration and in the reference to the locust, connects the "grasshopper" to Christ who ate locusts and wild honey in the desert. It is logical then that the poem, which began as a kind of spy thriller or even detective movie, should end as a movie that directs the reader to an idea of survival and transformation, contained in "The Season of Phantasmal Peace", a poem, quite aptly, twice read at Walcott's funeral.

These two poems from *The Fortunate Traveller* suggest a form of synthesis through light. "The Season of Phantasmal Peace" is both utopic and prophetic. It uses the image of a net, in a way similar to the tapestry woven by Maud in *Omeros*, to construct an idea of potential harmony that will evolve from the babel of language and culture that is "like heaven".[27] The phantasmal light gives material substance to the latent possibilities of Caribbean culture and history and makes shadows move as in film. Its soundlessness is, like light, a resonance that vibrates and echoes through time and memory and into the future.

Both poems place light at centre stage and see its movement as central to the projection of film. Light becomes associated with many meanings, as perception or a way of seeing, as an idea of Christianity and knowledge, and, in *The Fortunate Traveller*, assumes the function of a transcendent reality. It is justifiable then to think of *The Fortunate Traveller* as a precursor for Walcott's more extensive use of film montage in *Omeros*.

In *Omeros*, the poet is stunned by beauty, love and light, and becomes like blind Homer or blind Seven Seas (the black Homer), who can see with his ears and in whom all senses are fused. These bards are his guides. This reversal of sense suggests a primal perception that links the poet to different ways of seeing, The poet is in fact a seer, one who sees beyond the limits of any one sense. On the one hand, light speaks to the poet's imagination, on the other to Walcott's concept of simultaneity and his belief expressed most recently in *Moon-Child* that the "night is full of noises" (p. 19) or that there are presences that people a landscape, an idea evoked as well in *Omeros* as the result of the myth-making imagination, when it is inspired by the movement of half-light or light:

Because in you only, over the wind-wrinkled centuries
of an ageless atlas I catch the antipodal noise
of the troughed lines widening, and see the shambling fleece

of the Cyclone's flock, and praise the bleeding eye
rising over Bois D'Orange, its olive ridges slowly,
whose blinded brightness mistakes a cloud for a ship.

In his light the seeds of almonds guess their tree's shape,
the map-eaten leaf rediscovers the contour of islands,
and a one-eyed lighthouse, seeing the edge of a cape

pauses, a paralysed seraph with wingless hands,...[28]

Light is also the play of light through which the imagination peoples a world. In *The Prodigal*,[29] and *Arkansas Testament* among others, and in *Tiepolo's Hound*, and the stage play, *O Starry Starry Night*, with its elision of the boundaries between the artistic world of Paris, Europe and the Caribbean, light becomes an extension of the desire to see equivalences and to suggest that the Caribbean represents a new way of seeing and the potential and the possibility to create a new art form, as in the art of Pissarro. Walcott suggests in *Tiepolo* that this artist from St Thomas inspired Cezanne and the post-impressionists. Light is therefore a complex metaphor and also a philosophical statement attached to an idea of structure. It is useful to look briefly at the way light evolves as a cinematic principle throughout Walcott's work.

In *Another Life* the poet declares, punningly, "Gregorias, listen, lit,/ we were the light of the world!"[30] This is at one with the stated ideal not only of giving things their names but also of beginning a new Renaissance in St Lucia. Light is also expressed in terms of artistic complexity in the much quoted line, "a crystal of ambiguities", through which Walcott sought to differentiate the steadfast "plain" seeing of St Omer, who painted things as he saw them, with a "virginal" force, allowing the unpainted world to exist as it were in itself, and his own more tortured approach to that world. Walcott's poetry, in his own eyes, expresses the contradictions of both race and class and imposes a cerebral layer onto the world he sought to render truthfully.

The play of light on landscape evokes and maps particular mythologies. Land, sea and light are the shaping factors of our perception of the world and this idea is also explored in the little film script "The Loupgarou" (1972). Here the vagaries of Caribbean light literally breed presences in the movement of light on the earth's surface and in the half-light before the close of day. These shapes give rise to the belief, fed by the unscrupulous, that there are presences and evil powers and in particular shape-changing beings. "The Loupgarou"[31] anticipates the tale of Manoir from *Another Life* and foreshadows the poem "White Magic" from *Arkansas Testament* where the poet declares that, " Our myths are ignorance, theirs are literature (AT, p. 39). But "The Loupgarou" also leads to *Omeros* and its unpinning and reweaving of the syncretic relations that define the true "is" of the Caribbean through that combination of light and imaginative re-creation.

The essay, "What the Twilight Says: An Overture", foregrounds the notion that twilight or semi-light represents both a brief moment before the end of the day or its opening and is also a time that generates hallucinations. "What the Twilight Says" begins with twilight (the dying sun of empire), and focuses attention on the relations between language and art and the perception of the artist as this complicates the process of achieving what is true to both memory and art.

"What the Twilight Says" and *Another Life* are works written in tandem with each other. "What the Twilight Says" begins with twilight (the dying sun of empire), and as Edward Baugh has pointed out, both are about the act of remembering and about seeking to actualize the reality of a new people and a new art and culture. The act of naming becomes a vital part of this process. While Walcott remembers and envisions, he is also reserving the right to name.[32] Home is "both subject and object" of "an imaginative quest." But this quest, while it begins in nostalgia, does not leave us there according to Baugh, but becomes focussed on the impact of the past on the present and the informing shape of the past on both present and future. This is the true subject of *Another Life*.

But the object of the work is also the St Lucia of Walcott's youth, as this becomes both objectified as an image of his memory and as an object of his art – the thing locked in amber and made something other than what it is. This is a lesson well learnt from modernists of perception such as Virginia Woolf and W. B. Yeats. Both are concerned with the fixity of the past when the past moment is transfixed by an event that makes it for some reason memorable. Yeats in "Among School Children" explores that image which appears, seemingly out of nowhere, because, on the one hand, the children before him conjure, through similarity, a past-remembered image of Maud Gonne, and on the other hand, the emotion of that past moment makes the image powerfully present as in, "And thereupon my heart is driven wild:/ She stands before me as a living child".[33]

Light as a way of seeing

Memory is crucial. The past, or memory, is in *Omeros*, as it was in *Another Life*, the silence which is the world resounding in the poet's mind. This silence is inserted as a pebble that sends ever widening eddies on the poem's surface in the "race-containing symbol" of the woodsman; it is a silence that reverberates and is linked to ancestral traces in land and language:

> Through stumps of brown teeth he pointed out the hillcrest
> with gaping, precipitous valleys, where smoke rose
> from a charcoal pit, and under the smoke, the lines

of a white, amnesiac Atlantic, then with a bow,
and a patois blessing with old African signs,
as soundless as light on the road they watched him go. (*Omeros*, p. 61)

The silence of the woodsman of *Omeros* is conceived in terms of light and as an energy that derives from shared relationships of place and memory. The woodman's silence reverberates through the "energy, which is light" and, by extension, suggests the silence of those who have been repressed or rendered silent. Light gradually emerges as a language that goes beyond sight and beyond sound. Instead it creates echoes that resound in the body.

This reverberation through the body is repeated as a recurring unifying chime throughout *Omeros* and resounds in several keys. Philoctete, for example, feels an ant crawling across his brow and he "felt the village through his back" (pp. 21-22).

Silence suggests submerged memory and repressed pain. The silence of the woodsman who walks in light is a silence which is the vestige or the trace of memory and of myth, and combines with these "loud-mouthed forests on their illiterate heights"(*Omeros*, p. 61) to generate the force of history, and of vestigial traces on the communal psyche. The poet as bard gives voice to that energy contained in memory and the latent beliefs that reside in the transplanted seed buried in the soil of the new place.

Silence as vibration is associated with a movement into the psyche and with the process through which an image emits reverberating associations that connect to a past buried in memory. Light waves are also physically vibrations that are pure energy, and suggest Wilson Harris's use of the word "quantum" to describe the force of an image in its opening up of new ways of seeing and being.[34] Light also allows Eisenstein to think of sound and visual image as identical in terms of affect.[35] Walcott extends the force of both sound and image. The silence that resonates in between these two signifying mechanisms becomes pure reverberation and acts on memory to allow pure time to flow.

The theme of *Omeros* may be said to be that of light, that is, the light of dawn. The opening movement of *Omeros* introduces the idea of sunrise. This as an image of a new beginning, and is formulated as an "O", a reverberating space which is synonymous with the primal innocence of a child, in which the realities of two worlds can be made to cohere because there is still wonder and a capacity to dream. It is this sense of an Adamic world, with spectres always somewhere present, which allows Walcott to engage "in a deeply significant act: that of claiming and signing a purposive relationship with [the] world…[In doing so the] New World comes to hold, in Walcott's view, the possibility of a revitalization of a human purpose.[36] This is linked to an ethical project that becomes most evident as *Omeros* progresses and brings into its movement the death of the Aruacs and the first peoples of the Americas as a whole, as well as the transportation of enslaved peoples from Africa.

Interestingly, the stage production of *Omeros* at the London Globe in 2014 used candlelight to light the stage and light became the focal point of the performance.[37] Light in the film script is also used to carve or sculpt out figures, as with Helen who is described as having a "face of carved beauty", which the camera overtly seeks out. For those familiar with the work of Wilson Harris, the chiselling effect of light here also gives contour and a sculptural appearance, akin to the use of the mask in Harris's *Mask of the Beggar*,[38] for example, or Brathwaite's "Ogun".[39] Light as a shaping mechanism creates portals between time past and present and serves as entry points into memory, as in the portals created by the eyes of the beggar and the mask carved by the artist in Harris's 2003 work. The effect of sculpturing also suggests ways in which time "carves one out", psychologically speaking, and gives to light the potent capacity to reveal psychic layers of meaning or memory.[40]

This idea is used in *Tiepolo's Hound* to create an audiovisual aesthetic that leads to an idea of Caribbean light and perception as powerful creative forces that can cross cultures, epochs and races. *Tiepolo's Hound* is, as Paola Loreto suggests, about light and the metaphoric significance of light.[41] But light in *Tiepolo's Hound* is embedded in the theme of memory, which the book pursues in its narrator's search for the source of that "stroke of light that catches a hound's thigh" (p. 58). Memory is located in the body's memory or sense perception, or as a flash of an image leading to recollection. Light in *Tiepolo's Hound* also allows a meditation on time, in its temporal passage and as something that can be "petrified" through paint (p. 43) and also as seasonal change (p. 106).

Most specifically light is linked to language (p. 10) and in Walcott's descriptive phrase: "he painted in dialect", is made equivalent to a way of seeing and perceiving that has a specific relation to place. So the painter Pissarro remembers the markets and "the straw-hatted vendors and his palette's/ explosion of primal colours, the African sounds/ of their shouts and bargains in Charlotte Amalie (p. 54). He therefore painted the ordinary in a new light. Place and memory dictated his mimetic gift.

The act of painting and the painting of light, inseparable from colour and its application on canvas, relates to a way of remembering light and its visual impact. This act of remembering creates a particular language of art that Pissarro, we are told, transferred to Paris, thereby influencing a new aesthetic language through the vibrant palettes of painters such as Cezanne and Gauguin.

Pissarro, as Walcott puts it, carries the light of the tropics within him to Paris and remakes modernism, because he brings a new and exuberant use of colour. His sensibility, despite his "treachery" in not painting the ordinary folk of St Thomas, is important to Walcott and the Caribbean because it is a realisation of the potential of that light and the transcultural nature of language and art.

Light becomes a figure and an associated leap of transcendence in *The Prodigal*, after the sorrows of many deaths, including that of his brother Roderick. The leap to light at the end of this poem is magical and heals the passage of time and the pain of death. Light is also a "veil", "Through which phantoms move", thus connecting the idea of light with the fragile or gauze-like borders between life and death, so that ghosts are always close to hand:

> ...you could feel it shift
> in the shadow of the almond on the open terrace,
> in the sweet stink of the shallows by the sea-wall,
> in the rough dark sand of the beach, the frowsty umbrellas
> that echo a beach on the other side of the world,
> drizzling Pescara, the light became a veil
> through which phantoms moved, pirates and beggars
> behind the high walls that hid Márquez's house. (*The Prodigal*, p. 47).

That line of light signifies movement and separation from an elsewhere, that is both actual and spiritual. So Walcott closes with, "that line of light that shines from the other shore" (*The Prodigal*, p. 105), which, to quote Edward Baugh, "is the eventual radiance which Walcott's work has always sought".[42]

Endnotes

1. See William C. Wees, *Light Moving in Time. Studies in the Visual Aesthetics of Avant-Garde Film* (Berkeley, Los Angeles and Oxford: University of California Press,1992). Wees looks at the ways in which light is processed by the eye and brain.
2. Derek Walcott, *Tiepolo's Hound* (New York: Farrar, Straus and Giroux, 2000).
3. See Patrick A. B. Anthony and his essay on the after death, "'Wherever it is loved friends go': Death and After-death in the Poetry of Derek Walcott" in *Interlocking Basins*, ed. Jean Antoine-Dunne (Leeds: Peepal Tree Press, 2013), pp. 244-258.
4. Derek Walcott, *Another Life* (London: Cape, 1973), p. 57.
5. See J. Michael Dash, *The Other America: Caribbean Literature in a New World Context* (Charlottesville: UP of Virginia, 1998) for a clear discussion of this phenomenon and its historical underpinnings.
6. See J. Michel Dash in *The Other America*.
7. Derek Walcott, introduction to *Dream on Monkey Mountain and Other Plays* (New York: Farrar, Straus and Giroux, 1970), pp. 3-40.
8. Laurence Breiner, "The Impact of Japan on Derek Walcott's Early Plays", *Comparative Theater Review,* Vol.13 (English Issue) March 2014: 3.
9. Derek Walcott, "Meanings", *Savacou*, (1970), p. 48.
10. V.V. Ivanov, "Functions and Categories of Film Language," trans. Stephen Rudy, *Film Theory and General Semiotics*, ed. L.M. O'Toole and Ann Shukman (Oxford: RPT Publications, 1981), p. 7.
11. Ivanov is here quoting from N. Zorkaya.
12. Edward Baugh comments in his book, *Derek Walcott* (Cambridge: Cambridge University Press, 2006, p. 73), that Walcott adapts something of "both situation and style" from Akira Kurosowa's 1950 film, *Rashomon*. I argue that it is really the figure of the woodsman and Kurosowa's use of light and silence that influence Walcott.
13. Derek Walcott, "Cul de Sac Valley", *The Arkansas Testament* (London: Faber and Faber, 1987), p. 9.
14. Derek Walcott, "The Man who Loved Islands", *The Fortunate Traveller* (London: Faber and Faber, 1982), p. 37.
15. D. H. Lawrence, "The Man Who Loved Islands", *Love Among the Haystacks and Other Stories* (Harmondsworth: Penguin, 1960), pp. 97-123.
16. Derek Walcott, "The Figure of Crusoe" in *Critical Perspectives on Derek Walcott*, ed. Robert Hamner (Washington: Three Continents Press, 1993), pp. 33-40.
17. See, "I once read somewhere that a survey conducted on the most successful films proved that they were ones which dealt with endurance

and survival, much more so than those whose themes were sex, or romance", in "The Figure of Crusoe," p. 37.

18. The image of the silver chain is reinforced in the unpublished play "The Isle Is Full of Noises" (c. 1986). The use of echoes of previous works is an important constituent of the overall tapestry of images which later, in *Omeros*, becomes the process of interweaving crucial to the use of audiovisual counterpoint in the novel/epic-poem.
19. Derek Walcott, "The Poet in the Theatre", *Poetry Review* 80.4 (1990-91): 25.
20. Wilson Harris, *Explorations* (Denmark: Dangaroo Press, 1981), pp. 125-153. This essay explores, in Jungian terms, the importance of the mythic unconscious in the construction and naming of a Caribbean aesthetic.
21. Paula Burnett, *Derek Walcott. Politics and Poetics*, p. 180.
22. Burnett, p. 177.
23. William Butler Yeats, "The Fisherman", http://banteerns.ie/wbyeats/the-fisherman. Accessed 17 May 2017.
24. Susan Sontag, *On Photography* (New York: Farrar, Straus and Giroux, 1977).
25. Sontag, *On Photography*.
26. Derek Walcott, *The Star Apple Kingdom* (New York: Farrar, Straus and Giroux, 1979).
27. Derek Walcott, *The Antilles: Fragments of Epic Memory* (London: Faber, New York: Farrar, Straus and Giroux, 1993).
28. Derek Walcott, "Omeros" draft, Box 25, Folder 10, Derek Walcott Collection, Alma Jordan Library, The University of the West Indies, St Augustine. (1986), p. 6.
29. Walcott, *The Prodigal* (New York: Farrar, Straus and Giroux, 2004); *The Arkansas Testament* (London: Faber and Faber, 1987); *O Starry Starry Night* (New York: Farrar, Straus and Giroux, 2014).
30. Derek Walcott, *Another Life*, fully annotated by Edward Baugh and Colbert Nepaulsingh, ([1973] London and Boulder: Lynne Rieiner Publishers, 2004), p. 152.
31. Derek Walcott, "The Loupgarou", Box 6, Folder 8, Derek Walcott Collection, Alma Jordan Library, The University of the West Indies, St Augustine.
32. Baugh, *Memory as Vision*, pp. 2-3.
33. William Butler Yeats, http://web-books.com/Classics/Poetry/Anthology/Yeats/Among.htm. Accessed 17 May 2017.
34. See in particular Harris's description of quantum in *Mask of the Beggar*.
35. See Sergei Eisenstein, "The Fourth Dimension of Cinema" [1929] S.M. Eisenstein, Selected Works, Vol. 1, ed. Richard Taylor (London: BFI, 1988).

36. Pat Ismond, “Naming and Homecoming”, *ACLALS Bulletin 7th series. 2* (1985), p. 27. See also *Abandoning Dead Metaphors* (Mona: UWI Press, 2000).
37. *Omeros*, as stage play, first performed in 2014 at the Globe, London.
38. Wilson Harris, *The Mask of the Beggar* (London: Faber and Faber, 2003); and Edward Kamau Brathwaite, “Ogun” in *Islands* (London: Oxford University Press, 1969), pp. 85-86.
39. See Harris, *History Fable and Myth in the Caribbean and Guianas.*
40. Andre Tarkovsky, *Sculpting in Time. Reflections on the Cinema*, trans., Kitty Hunter- Blair (Texas: University of Texas Press, 1987).
41. Paola Loreto, *The Crowning of a Poet's Quest. Derek Walcott's Tiepolo's Hound* (Amsterdam: Rodopi, 2009).
42. Baugh, *Derek Walcott*, p. 229.

CHAPTER 4
CREATING AT THE INTERSTICES

For Walcott, meaning and affect occur at the space of the in-between of the many lines of narrative, voice, colour and time as these are shaped in movement in the poems *Omeros* and *The Prodigal*, in particular. The interstitial space is at the heart of Deleuze's argument and the difference between Eisenstein's aestheticisation of what he called "overtonal resonance" and what Deleuze called "the interval and interstice" constitutes the most important relationship between the two. This idea of a gap as a way of generating an image of thought appears in Deleuze's discussion of the movement-image. First of all, for him, Henri Bergson is startlingly ahead of his time because he intuits "the universe as cinema in itself, a metacinema."[1] Secondly he saw in Sergei Eisenstein a filmmaker whose theorising of the organic spiral and whose conception of the film attraction had caused the interval to take on a new meaning.[2]

For Eisenstein this "filmic" phenomenon, shaped by and through movement, emerged as an effect of light and sound waves in themselves. For him, the vibrations of light and sound were reducible to a single sensation and further could generate ever-deepening perceptions and could act as a means of forging a trajectory into the psyche.

Walcott's lesson from classical montage, then, was that film, through montage, could provide a form which would allow him to go beyond verbal language or the word, and also to go beyond speech into the sphere of reverberating silence, in particular those echoes that resound after speech, and those that are given shape in gesture and intonation. Film, therefore, provided a model for a new language of art.

The unifying rhythm of the musical composition is analogous to the rhythmic movement which fuses the montage construction as a whole. In effect, this rhythm is the "generalizing image" of the work. It is the materialized form or contour of the director's purpose and idea. The dynamism generated by the conflict of these newly assembled parts, which is also a process of intensification, creates the psychological impact or "overtones" of the work that lead to a form of "spatialised time". The "overtone" is a name given by Eisenstein to the vibration in the psyche which results from this juxtaposition of shots in their movement in time, as he explained in a note included in the draft version of his essay on "Laocoön":

> I have defined the 'overtone' as the summation, or rather the *general* emotional 'resonance' that derives from the sequence. It is general in that it arises from both content and structure; from the style of playing (by the actor) and the play of linear elements; from the emotional associations of form and the interplay of the forms themselves, etc. etc.
>
> I established the feasibility of the montage editing of sequences on the basis of individual component factors (e.g. movement, light, etc.). This interpretation of 'overtone' also fits in with the examples that are analysed here: it is an *emotional generalization* about all the elements in a sequence (a definition which differs from the concept of 'overtone' in musical terminology).
>
> When it is simultaneously an idea which has not yet assumed any other form of expression, the overtone begins to sound like an overall image of the sequence. One further step – and we read it as the 'meaning' of the sequence. We should not forget this – but it is more dangerous to remember *only* this![3]

The distinction made here between the overtone as understood by its use in music and overtone as a generalization that creates a vibration or resonance in the mind and psyche of the viewer/auditor is important. The overtone or overtonal resonance is the sum of the monistic ensemble of the work. It is evoked through the careful calculation of the effect on all sensory perceptions and the careful infusion of a general idea into all facets of the work. The overtone is the full "affect" generated by this combined ensemble. Eisenstein saw montage activity as a way of jolting the mind into new ways of seeing, or as Taussig puts it:

> [T]he juxtaposition of dissimilars such that old habits of mind can be jolted into new perceptions of the obvious. In fact we have been surreptitiously practising montage all along in our historical and anthropological practices, but so deeply immersed have we been in tying one link in a chain to the next, creating as with rosary beads a religion of cause and effect bound to a narrative ordering of reality, that we never saw what we were doing, so spellbound were we by our narrativizing – and thus we repressed one of the very weapons which could resist, if not destroy, intellectual colonisation and violence.[4]

Kamau Brathwaite's use of the filmic is perhaps of greatest significance here, in particular since he calls his technique montage. His development in the eighties of what he called Sycorax Video Text format is linked to the desire to bring together sound and writing and to make the graphic resonate with the impact of the oral. In 1984 Kamau Brathwaite published his *History of the Voice*[5] through which he sought to provide a theoretical framework for the use of black music and the voice of the Afro Caribbean individual as formal principles in the writing of poetry. *The Arrivants*, his first major work and the first two parts of his second trilogy, *Mother Poem* and *Sun Poem* apply these principles,[6] but it is not until *X/Self* and the recreation of these three poems into *Ancestors* that Brathwaite arrives at a system through which to make sound concrete. Brathwaite's work, perhaps more than that of any other writer in the Caribbean, has exerted a continuing fascination for Walcott, whose earliest reviews of Brathwaite's poetry are an odd admixture of admiration and condemnation.[7] Walcott's work, it may be argued, has moved increasingly close to Brathwaite's in the past three decades.[8]

Brathwaite's theory of the voice is concerned with the historic significance of music and sound, as in the guttural tone and rhythmic beat of the voice of the Black in the Caribbean and in the vocal qualities and rhythms of Black music in the Americas. He advocates the use of metric patterns more aligned to the sound-systems of the Black whose music and speech, as he maintains, contain the historic residue of a people and the influence of the land and elements: "The hurricane," he says, "does not roar in pentameters".[9] Brathwaite has chosen to use the term "Nation Language," in the first instance to remove the sense of inferiority attached to dialect and "people speech" as well as to reinforce the idea that Nation Language is more than dialect:

> First of all it is from ... an oral tradition. The poetry, the culture itself, exists not in a dictionary but in the tradition of the spoken word. It is based as much on sound as it is on song. That is to say, the noise that it makes is part of the meaning, and if you ignore the noise (or what you *think* of as noise, shall I say) then you lose part of the meaning. When it is written, you lose the sound or the noise, and therefore you lose part of the meaning.[10]

The breaks and discontinuities of this "music" contain the *immanence* of a people, that is "the power within themselves" on which they depended "in conditions of poverty ('unhouselled', with its intimations of religious sacrament) because they come from a historical experience where they had to rely on their very *breath* rather than on paraphernalia like books and museums and machines."[11]

The other point relevant to "Nation Language", and Brathwaite's recrafting through Sycorax, is that it needs an audience for completion. It is based on *performance*. Performance includes what both Walcott and Brathwaite have designated as *total expression*. As a poet, Brathwaite has been concerned to get at the "noise" and the idea of the very reliance on "breath" that has shaped the rhythms and tone of Caribbean expressive products. It is this that drives his concern with shape and the breaks as well as discontinuities within a poem, and that give rise to the use of font variation and a concern with graphics that one can see and sense. These techniques deriving from concepts of montage, approximate the fragments of a film that are then edited together to create immediate impact and resonance. The essence of a film is its direct signification.

As a dramatist, and the founder of the Trinidad Theatre Company with Beryl McBurnie's Little Carib Folk group, which was primarily dance oriented, Walcott was concerned with the relationship between the various artistic forms of the Caribbean in their use of body language and the entire range of folk expressions of the oral tradition. Part of the dilemma he faced as a writer was that of reconciling within theatre the two traditions he inherited. In a 1977 interview with Sharon Ciccarelli, he commented on the importance of a theatrical structure that could retrieve a sense of community through a combination of voice and other modes of primal expression, and elaborated on the problem, as he saw it, of drama and its place in society:

> The modern reader is an individual. The whole custom of reading to the family ... has been replaced by television and the cinema. Today, the visual narrative entails an individual spectator who is not *read to*. No one is told a story by a living voice.
>
> The narrator as a performer does not exist any more except in primal societies. And by primal society I mean any tight, familial, tribal society in which the reader or poet has a function. This society could be the society of Homer or the society of a Swahili tribesman.
>
> Literature developed from the ear first, then the eye. That is, from an oral to a written tradition. So the society that existed before printing was invented, e.g., Homer's society, and the one that still exists without printed literature become the same in terms of oral narrative. West Indian society is within an oral tradition [...]
>
> Story-telling, singing and other forms of tribal entertainment continue with such phenomena as the calypso tents. That tradition is also African...
>
> If one begins to develop a theatre in which the drum provides the basic sound, other things will develop around it, such as the use of choral responses and dance. If we add to this the fact that the storyteller dominates all of these, then one is getting nearer to the origins of possibly oral theatre, but certainly African theatre. Oral theatre may be Greek, or Japanese, or West Indian, depending upon the shape the percussion takes.[12]

The shape of the percussion provides another point of similarity between Brathwaite and Walcott in their desire to give concrete expression to the Caribbean, its oral traditions, its memories and its rhythms. For Walcott it became a problem to be resolved through a synthetic merging of the dramatic potentials of the stage, the deep reflective capacity of poetry and the inflections of voice and body. Walcott, in seeking such a synthesis, arrived at the potent possibilities of the filmic. I am therefore looking at the creation of this spatialised movement as a phenomenon in itself.

Page 8 from the storyboard for "Omeros": Build up to the battle of the saints.
The Thomas Fisher Library, The University of Toronto
Ms. Coll. 136, Box 65, November 198?5 or 1986

The space between two lines

The power of the in-between is also to be found in what Paula Burnett has identified as Walcott's adept use of doubling in language.[13] This is demonstrated in the capacity to make words double their meaning and also to create a succession of meanings through a carnivalesque appropriation, where meaning is transferred through repetition of sounds or the repetition of words which then accrue double meanings. This double talk is best exemplified in robber talk, picong[14] and calypso. Language here appropriates the power of rhetoric as it has been assumed in Caribbean carnivals and also demonstrates the iconoclasm of the carnivalesque as defined by Bakhtin. For Bakhtin medieval carnivals and their celebrations privilege the lower body, the genitals and excrement and use laughter and parody. Laughter brings the object up close as a way of ridiculing those with power. The privileging of the lower body returns language to the primal or instinctual drives and opposes the symbolic or law-giving status of the word. Power is reclaimed through linguistic exuberance, and a release of animal functions that disrupt the order of what is considered rational and civilised. As Burnett points out in reference to "The Spoiler's Return", for example, this may entail ironic "mis"-appropriation, as in Walcott's translation of Shelley's, "Hell is a city much like London". Through this manoeuvre a series of parallels is set up between the idea of civil and civility, and what constitutes "civilization". It involves the positioning of two meanings that emerge as the interplay of power and the breaking of hierarchical positions as in Helen's response to Maud: "I dere," which is interpreted in two ways: its meaning as creole, "I am here and I am ok", but also in the subversive, "I dare", which Maud interprets it to mean.[15] Helen's daring sets up the first explosive movement to change in the poem where she "dares" to take off all her clothes "'cause she dint take no shit/ from white people and some of them tourist" (*Omeros*, p. 33).

In *Omeros*, the space between two lines is perceived as originating, in the first instance, in a pause such as, "Time halts the arc of a javelin" (p. 33), suggesting that certain acts have universal and reverberating significance, so that Helen's words resonate through the ages and enter into play with the events of the Homeric. This space is also imaged through the two oars that are placed side by side in the boat ("like man and wife", p. 9) and also in the space between the wings of the swift. The wings of the swift, which open and close like the "lace troughs" (p. 130), have a mesmeric quality that induces a trance-like state. Its flight is then imaged as a projector or a machine that tows the fishing boat, after Achille sees his father's ghost. This boat, "its shearing motion/ whirred by the swift's flywheel into open ocean" (p. 131), takes Achille back to Africa. Time emerges within the space

Storyboard images of Hector hurling his javelin. The Thomas Fisher Library, The University of Toronto, Ms. Coll. 136, Box 65, November 198?5 or 1986

shaped by the oscillating movement of the swift and the poem as both move back and forth through several layers of time.

The use of a multidimensional and multifaceted form in *Omeros* is, from one perspective, due to the dialogue it sets up between the artists of Walcott's generation. One of the strands in this complex poem is that of a conversation between Rhys, Naipaul, Brathwaite, Harris, Glissant, Chamoiseau, and among others, Conrad, Yeats, Joyce and Ellison and of course, himself. The poem therefore introduces the key discourses with which each may be identified over the past several decades. These include the idea of mimicry associated with Naipaul; dream time located in the work of Wilson Harris; orality, the process of creolisation as a language of poetry and the importance of Africa in the work of Kamau Brathwaite; and cross-cultural dynamics and questions of the rhizomatic nature of Caribbean language and identity found in Édouard Glissant's *Poetics of Relation* and *Caribbean Discourse*. It is also in conversation with Walcott's entire body of work, which we hear resonating throughout the text. In this it achieves a multi-layered texture through repetition of words and images and sometimes lines, that "chime" throughout the poem.

As Anne Reckin has noted, Brathwaite's poetry is in itself a blending of Glissant's ideas of return and detour, and more importantly that Brathwaite "reaches back to Africa", but does so "without losing sight of the Caribbean situation". She notes further that his essay "Timehri" emphasizes "the primordial nature of [African and Amerindian] cultures and the potent spiritual and artistic connections between them". But what is ultimately at stake is the point of entanglement.[16] Walcott engages in similar processes of entanglement and seeks equally to enter into dialogue with the primal. He does this through the many voices and lines of narrative the poem *Omeros* composes and through a dialogue with those like Brathwaite and Glissant and Harris who have sought to create an art of multi-vocal intensity and cross-cultural complexity.

The vertical and horizontal lines of the poem emerge as historical necessities as it seeks to construct an image of the Antilles and the New World as a whole. The horizontal takes the reader across space through America, its plains and its cities and to London and St Lucia. Its vertical lines enter into the past as these descend into the sea of the Middle Passage and into the soul and memory of the past, whether these are the forgotten Aruacs, who rise like smoke, or the burning of Castries. The ascent of the smoke that constantly filters into the poem suggests the presences that hover in air and memory as near forgotten ephemeral presences, and are recovered in sound. These lines graph the essential disparateness, the fragmentation of New World history and experience and, moreover, allow the construction of a system through which harmony can be envisaged.

These several narratives of history and myth also imply that the bards of past and present, of two hemispheres, are being placed in parallel cultural positions and given equal classical stature, imagined in the novel-poem as the two oars placed in parallel positions in the skiff. The importance of echoes already identified in my discussion also reinforces the notion of audio-visual counterpoint through the various thematic lines, which resonate with an identical idea-image. This merging process enables the movement to an idea of a new beginning or way of seeing.

Film, as Walcott concludes, provides the means to a graphic depiction of the psychic landscape of a people and their cultural and geographic location, and leads to a mapping of a journey where presences or ghosts clamour for recognition. The movement seems to be between what Walcott has been "taught to see" and his quest for individual knowledge, truth and a way of seeing that refuses to conform to outside influences. Walcott returns to this theme again in *Moonchild* when he makes Ti Jean, another saviour, refuse communal wisdom and choose instead reliance on himself – what Walcott calls the difference between a Methodist and a Catholic doctrine of salvation.[17]

His work, as an example of a "minor" literature in the Deleuzian sense of a literature that comes from the margins and achieves a distinctive and perhaps revolutionary change, is associated with the cinematic in its use of lines that act as catalysts to moments of shock that force the protagonists into sudden changes or to leap beyond the confines of their accustomed actions.

The poem *The Prodigal* exemplifies this process. *The Prodigal* begins with the creation of two moving lines that evoke a tunnel. The movement of the journey on a train is both actual in its movement through space and as a journey through time and memory and as a meditation on the shaping of the poet's imagination. Time is made to issue forth from these moving lines through the conflict generated by past and present and the disjunction between an accustomed view of perceived reality and a new way of looking at what the poet has been taught to see.

The poem therefore exists in its entirety within the space of two moving lines. The first figural representation of that space is the tunnel through which the train passes and which, as an enclosed or constricting space, forces the reader to hear the echoes of racist ideologies and sounds.

The movement of space and time is therefore concomitant with the tracing of a circuit of memory and time within the poet's consciousness, which is both his individual consciousness and that of his race. The poem has been creating tunnels through a system of parallel lines from its inception. These create echoes in memory, that are memories of old racial hurts as in the "tunnel's skin" (p. 4), which suggests how the black is seen in America and the prejudice he endures. There are metaphoric connotations in the editing or construction of the images, as in the "gripped" face which suggests the travelling black as well as the tensions marking the lines of the face of one who is always ill at ease and unwelcome. These metaphors are built, as in film, through their movement in time, as in the movement that directs the gaze to the mapping or retracing of Columbus's journey and that builds a scaffold of myths to reinforce the layering of belief systems that have gone into the making of the Americas and the creation of lines of refugees or the movement of peoples.

The journey introduces the myth of the prodigal as a biblical reference that acts as a continuing line of development and unifies the whole. As part of the theme of journeying it embraces ideas of loyalty and betrayal, love and family and forgiveness, as well as the waste of time and inheritance. This mythic fabric allows Walcott to superimpose several ideas that derive from Christianity; the first being the received notion that a white God or a religion derived from a Western tradition is somehow the same as an idea of civilisation and salvation. As such, the poem moves to a new level where the personal becomes the communal and then the universal.

The theme of whiteness surfaces as a series of inflections or lines of colour first associated with another kind of myth, that of the legend of the white Ice Maiden, whose beauty hides her evil. The line of whiteness progresses throughout the poetic narrative and incorporates the lust for white women, the hypocrisy hidden under a whited sepulchre and the horns or treachery of whiteness that lead to war, savagery and ultimately to genocide. This line of whiteness or colour moves in parallel motion with the developing line of sound that is first a faint echo issuing from the tunnel, and then becomes a roar of pain and suffering, changing frequency in the pitch of sound emerging from the historic resonances of ghostly presences (pp. 26-33) that include Joseph Brodsky.

As with *Omeros*, *The Prodigal* sets several moving lines in motion, beginning with an idea of travel in the movement of a train. It also operates through a system of echoes that deepens in meaning and significance as the poem progresses. *The Prodigal* as a poem creates "blocks of stanzas" (p. 3), that set up the idea that a book is an imaginative journey that brings together frames of time in a montage construction. In its determined progression to a history of atrocity hidden under images of so-called civilisation, the poem traces a journey towards the discovery of what is hidden between lines of sight and of myth, and leads to a climactic sequence that engenders the awareness of the ways in which surface beauty hides bigotry. It does this through the use of a metric system that often cunningly persuades and lulls with its lyricism. The musical line that leads ingenuously to the beautiful woman from Serbia, for example, leads the reader unawares to the hardened emphasis of the final words:

> whose name, she told me, was a mountain flower's
> but one that was quite common in her country,

> spoke softly as the drizzle on Pescara's shore-front
> of Serbia and its sorrow, of the horrors she had seen
> on the sidewalks of Kosovo, and how it was, all war,
> the fault of the Jews. Yet she said it with calm eyes. (*The Prodigal,* p.19)

The continuous flow of these lines brings the beauty of landscape into sharp focus and links it to an idealised image of Western beauty, completely at odds (like the Alps) with the reality of racism. The photogenic quality of these descriptions, set as it were to music, suggest that Walcott is thinking not visually, but audiovisually as he has done, for example, in setting his poem, "Forty Acres" (written for Barack Obama) of *White Egrets* to music.[18]

The contradiction of evil hidden beneath "sublime" beauty opens the movement of the text to "The tidal motion of refugees, not the flight of wild geese", in this way bringing together historic acts of ethnic cleansing throughout the world, and including Ireland in the flight of the "wild geese" who were the princes of Ireland who, after the battle of Kinsale in the seventeenth century, at which they were defeated by the English forces, left the country of Ireland for the continent of Europe. The flight across borders is a moving image with several close-ups of "huge bundles", "axles creaking", "joints and bones" that are audible, and shapes that become "dissolving" frontiers. These fragmented images reinforce the sense that Walcott, as imaginary film editor and director, has carefully chosen each shot for maximum emotive affect, and has built a line that dissolves the boundaries of place and time. Time is circular since the "shot" of "the wagon without horses" merges with both the European refugees and the movement of wagons in the plains. This makes identical the effects of the holocaust that destroyed the first peoples and the holocaust that murdered Jews (*The Prodigal*, p. 20), and becomes a universalising image.

By part two, these echoes and lines of white have moved the reader to an emotional intensity that shares the poet's grief in the combined atrocity of the death of the young female soldier in South America, and that acts to create that orchestration of grief that emerges at the point of the caesura, marked by the taut lines of a telegram announcing the death of his twin brother, Roddy. The progressive and accumulative texture of the poem operates through a series of shocks that then creates a transition to new levels of intensity, until the final moment where the poem leaps to a point of transcendence.

But before this occurs, these intensities are built or, one might say, "compressed" through lines shaped as conflicting movements. The second such movement is in language. The poet who queries whether he may have been "halved by language/ as definitively as the meridian/ of Greenwich or by Pope Alexander's line" (p. 62), which introduces the carving up of the New World by the imperial powers, then attempts to work through the contradictory nature of Caribbean language, its debt to Europe and the poisonous taint of this inheritance, in terms of Europe's evil and treachery, which is also a legacy, and their enforced structures on a people whose languages are now termed, as in "The Season of Phantasmal Peace"[19] and *The Antilles*, "a Babel" (*The Prodigal*, p. 62).

The poem sets up further parallels that are spatially similar to the shaping of the tunnel through which echoes emanate. In the instance of the parallels between the right-hand margin of the page, and the left-hand margin, he deliberately courts these echoes as residues of antiquity. So that the ancient wood is "veined" and goes "far back in time and deep in roots". The echoes suggest the long traditions of old England and these are reinforced when Walcott insinuates the relationship between Britain and Homer as two ancient or long established traditions through the rhyming set up between "comber's centuries" and "Homer's centuries". This rhyming also suggests that the English literary tradition and the Homeric derive from oral forms. The "tunnel" shaped by the movement of the poem is now linked to sound and a sense of hearing. At this point Walcott also reverts to the sounds of old England in:

> ...This ocean, English and this forest weald,
> this clattering natterer "burn," this distance, mist,
> kept its high columns marching as my pen moves (pp. 62-63)

Language here, as a carrier of history, assumes the rhythm of a marching band and the woods now suggest an army at war or set on conquest, linking Britain's deep roots to those roots that, as Glissant suggests, see themselves as singular and therefore create hierarchies of tradition that lead to subjugation. A war of words ensues between a tradition shaped through writing and dominance versus "the bright salt arc of a bare unprinted beach". The war for dominance extended to language means that the poet Walcott is also suggesting that he has been conquered by print, and the "delight" derived from being thus vanquished is connected to a form of magic, since its logic cannot otherwise be accounted for. He includes here, by association (since these are part of the accumulative fabric of the poem), the magic of Hans Christian Andersen and magical tales that enthralled the poet as a boy. This is seen, for example, in: "... all these leaves and lines that/ still rasp with delight with rhyme and incantation/ pages of shade turning into translation" (p. 63). This deep enthralment leaves no possibility of rejection since this spell is set in memory and imbibed in the body.

The system of accumulative meanings via the route of repeated words and images becomes richly layered with several meanings. The reference to ancient runes also has introduced another kind of magic that serves perhaps, to further enforce the idea of the magic of the white Ice Maiden.

Here the ancient wisdom of the druids endows England with the power and authority of antiquity, derived from knowledge. But Walcott opposes this line with that of a column on the left hand margin that is "not their opposite or their enemy", suggesting that between these two lines something new will emerge. The language here is fresh and of nature, and is seen "drawing its thumb to mark the dog-eared wave" (p. 63). This is a different kind of writing and one that engages in a musical language that reflects the art and vitality of history carried in an oral tradition. Interestingly, the repeated use of the word "still" reinforces the sense of a resonance that emerges from silence, and that is more effective than the language of words. This is language felt in the skin as in the "tunnel's" skin, (p. 4), where one feels with one's flesh and nerves. The poem moves here to a new intensity that brings language into line with that of the echoes of memory and felt pain and the healing power of faith in, "except for the wireless harp of the frangipani/ that still makes its music out of extreme stillness".

But the moments of intensity that now emerge, through the oppositions of two woods that enable a space between two lines, are increasingly spiritual and come from the depths of soul and being. The word "palate" recalls the tongue that receives the gift of holy communion, and the words "pain and *pain*" act as superimposed images that combine in language to suggest that suffering and trauma lead to spaces where something new and transcendent occurs, a miracle perhaps of healing and salvation

The movement here is from suffering to the holy communion of Christianity and the exaltation and resurrection already hinted at on page sixty-two. The religious density of the following sequences mimics Christ's suffering in the desert in:

> The dialect of the scrub in the dry season
> withers the flow of English. Things burn for days
> without translation,... (p. 65)

The desolation is contradictory, for the wilderness, as language which is "dialect", is perceived, on the one hand, as something that "overruns" but also moves towards a blessing through the rain and the rainbow that follows from this. The blessing is in creole: "*arc-en-ciel*". Emotion and several layers of meaning once more penetrate language. The compression of different lines through highly evocative images and conflicting movement evokes a leap of transcendence in the sighting of a rainbow. This rainbow, as a symbol of colour, is also an image of the intensity of light through its prismatic quality.

There follows a new caesura that marks a transition to a higher level, which is the proof of the creative imagination of the creole. This is given as evidence of the transforming nature of suffering or repression, again conceived in language and through the malleability of language. The evidence is to be found in the construction of a folk tale out of old fragments of mythologies: "The sun fought with the rain in the leaves and won". This new myth also poses the question, how are myths formed? It also references Kamau Brathwaite's use of folklore and Nation Language and brings the St Lucian Sesenne's singing into the developing line of a new creole aesthetic:

> The earth grew music and the tubers sprouted
> to Sesenne's singing, rain-water, fresh patois
> in a clay carafe, a clear spring in the ferns,
> and pure things took root like the sweet-potato vine. (p. 70)

Music is here intrinsically related to natural history, but also introduces a further dilemma for the poet, since he now asks whether "his whole life [is] a language awaiting translation? (p. 70) There is no doubt a note of regret here in the suggestion that his poems are not in that "clear" "fresh patois", which further reinforces the continuing validation of Brathwaite's *History of the Voice,* begun in *Omeros.* Is this a regret for writing in Standard English?

The descriptions become ideogrammatic and in this sense deeply filmic, or one might say that, as in the language of hieroglyphs in *The Fortunate Traveller* and Walcott's constant use of the figure of the egret for pen and writing, the images here act as signposts to their meaning. The descriptions are close to hieroglyphs or symbols. They are also magical in their evocation of the flamboyant and the egret as inscriptions that herald a spiritual passage (p. 75).

The question that still remains, since he has been "gored by language" and the culture of Europe, is whether it has "come to this, to have to choose?" (p. 77). As a way of resolving the issue, the poem becomes strictly audio-visual. "Do not diminish in my memory" summons images of visual memory that he hopes will, like the photograph, fix these memories of "villages of absolutely no importance" (p. 78) in his mind. The images called up to the mind are moving images that combine the sound and vibration of a "rattling bridge", and a river that is enshrined in light through the aid of the internalised idea of Yeats's "stone is the midst of all" taken from "Easter 1916", which forms a rippling movement in the words, "stone-bright river".

The combination of words and images also operates through antithesis. There is the conflict inherent in the opposition of images of "un-ornate churches", as distinct from the baroque splendour of Europe or, again, chapels that are very opposite in their sunlit placement in the tropics from those that are situated in "light-exhausted Europe". The movement to audiovisuality, again a play of two lines – in this instance the written and the oral – is sustained in the dialogue that follows, which contains in sustained counterpoint the idea of seeing and sounding:

> The sound of Paris in the rustling trees
> when the leaves talk traffic and the withered pods
> of the acacias are dried spices in the cafés
> that season reputation; "You don't know Paris?"
> "No. Never been there." "You've got to go."
> "Why?"
> More repulsion: "Why?"
> "Yeah. Why?"
> "Because it's Paris, that's why."
> "I see."
> "No, you don't see, you're being stubborn."
> "Maybe when I get there I'll see."
> "It will change your life."
> "I like my life."
> "You think here is enough?"
> "For me it is."
> "Fine."
> "Anyway I can see Martinique from here."
> (*The Prodigal*, p. 78)

I have quoted this at length because its form is equally part of the meaning in the play of opposites. The structuring on the page sets up a visual contrast between the two people arguing, and there is yet a peculiar balance achieved as the positions are articulated. As a strategy, this continues the series of oppositions through which various new leaps, or one might say epiphanies, occur. The idea is also shaped by the opposition between what is seen and what is heard, since it is the "rustling" of the trees that carries the idea of "withered pods and traffic" (congestion and noise) and also insinuates the idea of an old, perhaps dried-up world. The combination of sound and sight leads to an idea that appears to carry truth and knowledge: "You don't know Paris?" It is not however an unqualified or absolute given, since each assertion is met with a refuting statement. In the first instance the answer displaces the meaning of the word "see" and turns it to its opposite, "I don't see". This moves to a questioning of what is the meaning of a transforming moment. Or, what indeed does give meaning, since Martinique is both here in the Caribbean and is also "little Paris", and a department of France. In a circular movement "here" becomes "there" and resolves the issue of sameness, by making that place which is different have the meaning and significance of a culture which has taken upon itself the privilege to assert or define the ideal and to dominate the other.

This established, the poem as a whole then moves to embrace a version of the magical real and in its final movement leaps to new spiritual heights or images of transformation, fully articulated as an arch that is like "the way thoughts rise from memory" (p. 104). It is exactly the description of film as passage to thought given by both Eisenstein in *Film Sense*[20] and by Deleuze.

The various moving lines of the poems *Omeros* and *The Prodigal*, and the stage and screen plays for *Steel*, suggest that Walcott sought a form of image -making that issued from the forced emergence of echoes or resonances that are in the first instance perceived by the body and that through leaps or moments of intense experience lead to new insights or beginnings. These filmic movements enable thought to be constituted not through a cerebral apprehension, but through visceral effect. The use of oppositional lines also generates a concerted ethical response to trauma and atrocity throughout the ages and across the globe.

Endnotes

1. Gilles Deleuze, *Cinema 1, The Movement-Image*, trans., Tomlinson and Habberjam (London: Athlone Press, 1992), p. 61.
2. Gilles Deleuze, *Cinema 1*, p. 38.
3. Sergei Eisenstein, *Towards a Theory of Montage*, p. 402, n. 9.
4. Michael Taussig, *The Nervous System* (New York and London: Routledge, 1992), p. 45.
5. Edward Kamau Brathwaite, *History of the Voice* (London: New Beacon, 1984).
6. Edward Kamau Brathwaite, *The Arrivants*, published initially as *Rights of Passage* (London: Oxford University Press, 1967); *Masks* (London: Oxford University Press, 1968) and *Islands* (London: Oxford University Press, 1969); *Mother Poem* (Oxford and New York: Oxford University Press, 1977); *Sun Poem* (London: Oxford University Press, 1981); *Ancestors. A Reinvention of Mother Poem, Sun Poem and X/Self* (New York: New Directions, 2001).
7. See, for example, Walcott's review of *Rights of Passage*, "Tribal Flutes", *Trinidad Guardian* Sunday 19 March 1967: 2-3. These newspapers reviews and articles are edited by Gordon Collier, *Derek Walcott, The Journeyman Years. Occasional Prose 1957-1974* (Amsterdam: Rodopi, 2013).
8. See Rhonda Cobham-Sander, "'An Enemy So Was a Compliment': Walcott, Brathwaite and the Formal Possibilities of Creole", in *Interlocking Basins of a Globe*, ed. Jean Antoine-Dunne (Leeds: Peepal Tree Press, 2013): 100-122. Also her monograph, *I and I. Epitaphs for the Self in the Work of V.S. Naipaul, Kamau Brathwaite and Derek Walcott*, (Mona: UWI Press, 2016).
9. Brathwaite, *History of the Voice*, p. 10.
10. Brathwaite, *History of the Voice*, p. 17.
11. Brathwaite, History of the Voice, p. 19.
12. Sharon Ciccarelli, "Reflections Before and After Carnival: An interview with Derek Walcott", *Chant of Saints*, ed., Michael Harper and Robert Stepto (Chicago: University of Illinois Press, 1979) 296-97. Reproduced in *Conversations with Derek Walcott*, ed. William Baer (Jackson: University Press of Mississippi, 1996), p. 35.
13. Paula Burnett, "The Smell of Our Own Speech: The Tool of Language", *Derek Walcott. Politics and Poetics* (Gainesville: University Press of Florida, 2000), pp.125-158.
14. Picong has been described by Gordon Rohlehr as stick-fighting in words. It is making fun through language that uses various techniques, including irony, double-talk and jibes.
15. Burnett, p. 150.

16. Anne Reckin, "Tidalectic Lecture. Kamau Brathwaite's Prose / Poetry as Sound Space", http://scholarlyrepository.miami.edu/cgi/viewcontent.cgi?article=1048&context=anthurium.
17. Jean Antoine in conversation with Derek Walcott, filmed in St Lucia on 24 October 2015.
18. Derek Walcott, *White Egrets* (London: Faber and Faber, 2010).
19. Derek Walcott, "The Season of Phantasmal Peace", *The Fortunate Traveller* (New York: Farrar, Straus and Giroux, 1981), pp. 98-99.
20. Sergei Eisenstein in *Film Sense* discusses cinema's affective impact by showing that film montage uses the same structure in principle as does the mind in its apprehension of images in memory.

Designs for "Marie Laveau": Overseer
The Thomas Fisher Library, University of Toronto
Ms. Coll. 136, Box 62, denim notebook, December 1981

Designs for "Marie Laveau": Sam and Marie
The Thomas Fisher Library, University of Toronto
Ms. Coll. 136, Box 62, denim notebook, December 1981

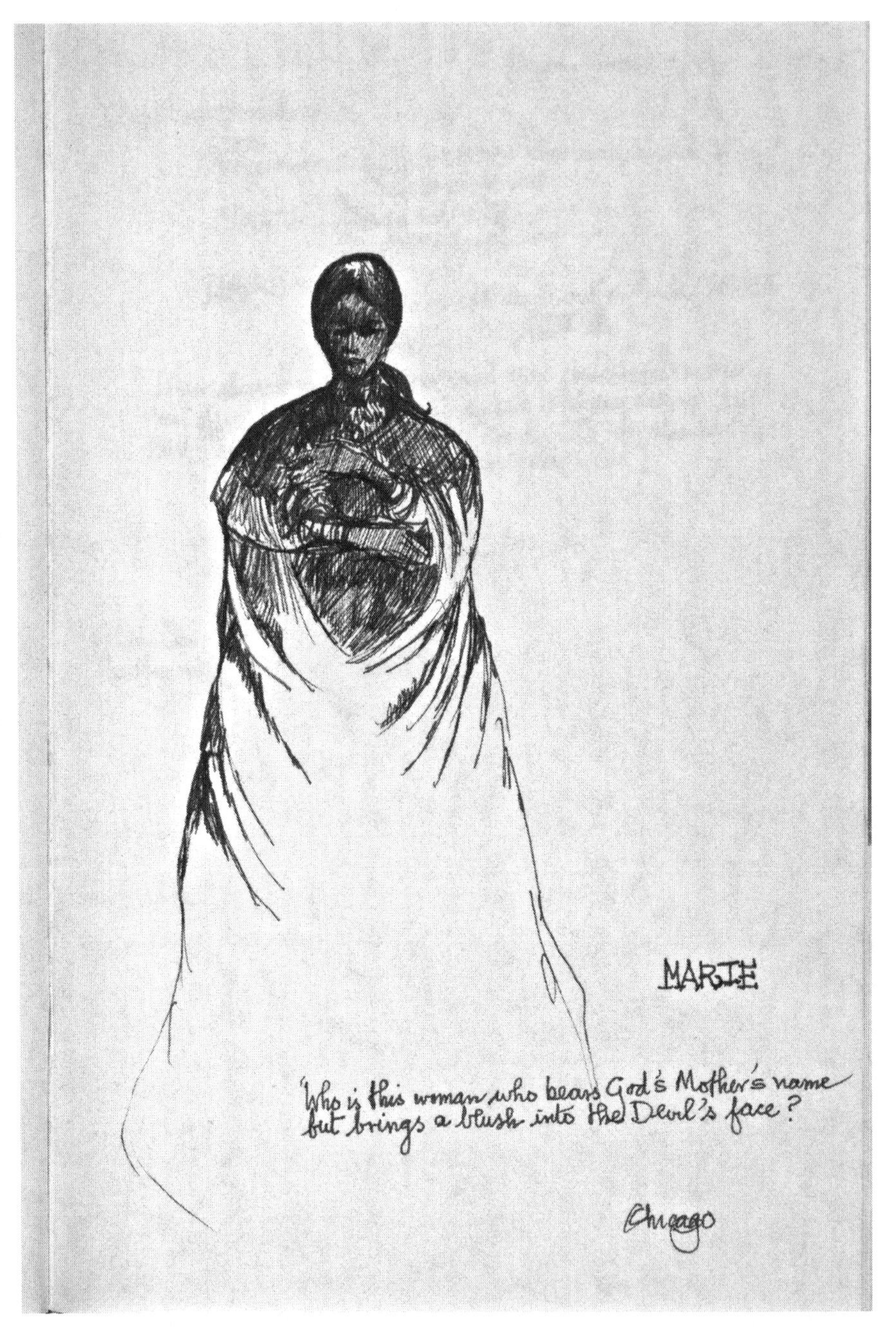

Designs for "Marie Laveau": Marie
The Thomas Fisher Library, University of Toronto
Ms. Coll. 136, Box 62, denim notebook, December 1981

Designs from "Remembrance"
Courtesy of the private collection of Michael Gilkes

CHAPTER 5
LINES OF SIGHT AND SOUND AND A LEAP TO THE SUBLIME

The play of sound and sight and the use of dissonance become increasingly important in Walcott's later work and is a distinctive feature of the poem *Omeros*. In this poem, historic ideas are shaped through a system of sound and visual lines moving together, and infused with one specific idea: that of the constant return of enslavement and pain and the possibility of transcendence. The very sights and sounds of the market hold this cycle of atrocity. Its noise is more than a memory of the roar of pain of the previously enslaved and is in fact a residual memory of enslavement, which acts as the unifying element of the following sequence:

> Where did it start? The iron roar of the market,
> with its crescent moons of Mohammedan melons,
> with hands of bananas from a Pharaoh's casket,
>
> lemons gold as the balls of Etruscan lions,
> the dead moon of a glaring mackerel; it increases
> its pain down the stalls, the curled heads of cabbages
>
> crammed on a tray to please implacable Caesars,
> slaves head-down on a hook, the gutted carcasses
> of crucified rebels, from orange-tiled villas,
>
> from laurels of watercress, and now it passes
> the small hearts of peppers, nippled sapodillas
> of virgins proffered to the Conquistadores.
> (*Omeros*, p. 37)

This travelling shot along a Caribbean market signifies the trans-generational trauma of enslavement and its continuing effect in the present of the Caribbean. Here in this sequence, the stalls retain, as Brathwaite notes in *Contradictory Omens*, the very look of an African market. Submerged memory surfaces as an active agent in the present, and not simply as a moment of recollection: "the physical resemblance of present-day Afro-West Indian peasants, for instance and present-day Ashanti and Yoruba, say, is remarkable [...] and the organization of the markets [...] are almost exact copies of markets in Lagos, Accra, Abomey, Ibadan". Brathwaite suggests further that the only way to give a sense of this uncanny sameness or resemblance is through "photographic and cinematic/tape recordings to illustrate that the rhythms and sound patterns of West Indian and West African markets are also similar".[1] The idea is that the market, through its images, retains a deep connection with an African past that the ruptures of time and the Middle Passage have not dissolved. The camera's lens in Walcott's *Omeros*, quoted above, both interprets and establishes the image of the market as a moving image and as a memory jolted by the semblance of a "look". Further it reinforces the idea that the trauma of this rupture is still an open wound.[2]

These superimposed memories emerge through resemblance and create an illusion in a manner similar to that shaped by editing processes, where one image can be co-joined or placed on top of another to create a distinctly new idea. This editing imposes several layers of history and leads to the idea that the past remains constantly present in the lived experiences and daily lives of Caribbean peoples. The sound or, as Brathwaite suggests, the rhythm, is also a unifying factor and here the "roar" of the market facilitates the emergence of a resemblance between Africa and the New World.

Since each fruit and product creates an image/idea derived from the memory of several histories of enslavement, it also gives the effect of layers of parallel narratives. The structure in this section of *Omeros* is derived strictly from montage. This formal manoeuvre is also found in Kamau Brathwaite's use of Sycorax video text format or his use of montage. Paul Naylor notes in his analysis of "Julia" of *X/Self* that:

> In the "magical montage" of this poem, Brathwaite juxtaposes at least three historical periods in which an empire is in a moment of crisis: Rome, as it begins to decline, America, as it is confronted by the demands of African-Americans, in the late 1960s, and America at the time the poem is being composed, the mid 1980s when the culture industry "produced" the simulated presidency of Reagan/ Headrest. The figure of Julia cuts across all three frames". [...] this montage of images "arrests" the narrative of progress in a number of ways. First it suggests that the role of women as window dressing has changed very little. [...] secondly it suggests that people of mixed race are simultaneously marginalized and exploited [...] third that "the products of contemporary consumer culture are merely "pacifiers" and fourth [...] that mainstream poetry may also participate in the commodification of culture.[3]

"Julia" also incorporates Brathwaite's awareness of the culture of dependence both on heroin and fame and material objects, so Julia is "hooked on all these" in her rise to stardom. The poem, "Letter from Roma", is even more condemning of the cycle of "the products of contemporary consumer culture", figuring the emperor as an individual both nursed by women who feed his need and his addiction for luxury. They also simultaneously feminise him by simply emasculating him.[4] Power is a need and an addiction that resurfaces in every age and is there as long as there are sycophants and greedy merchants who can manipulate the easy victims. The re-writing of many of his poems with only slight variations, but increasing pessimism, suggests that time is a closed circle for Brathwaite, but that artistic process is of increasing importance to the precise conveyance of historic and personal pain.[5] As filmic projection, Brathwaite seeks to give that sense of recurrence by making both word and poem exist as a montage of successive images that all lead to the same idea of a closed or enclosing circle of time.[6]

In *Omeros*, the density of time is the density of myth or poetic vision. It is a sensibility that has accrued layers of experiences, like scales, and has become, like the shell or the coral, (an image derived from Brathwaite's *Mother Poem*)[7] impervious to the ravages of history. Coincidentally Earl Lovelace uses an identical image to figure the resilient history that is stitched into the costume of the dragon in *The Dragon Can't Dance*.[8] Walcott projects an idea of time as an intersection of the cyclical and linear through the metaphors of the coral, the conch and the crab. The movement of the spiral, in which the inter-penetrating or interlocking lines of time form the origin of the circle as a tentacle, or outward thrust to change, replaces his earlier conception of cyclical time. The image most conducive to this idea is that of the conch shell and *Omeros* traces this pattern both in terms of its movement inward into the ear and in its privileging of the shell as an image of sound that penetrates the ear and enters the body. The process of the poem as a sound-visual system is also one of interiorisation or penetration into layers of being. The shape through which that spiral is enacted is that of contrapuntal montage, through a formal arrangement of several lines of narrative that intersect and the many voices and wounds that layer the work. *Omeros* is a poem of many voices in counterpoint.

The migratory birds that carry the seed of the cure and transplant it in the new soil also image the transplantation of many language systems. The seed of language is carried in the sounds and rhythms the African has brought with her and him and in the names of flora and fauna. Ma Kilman's trek through the forest following the ants, signifiers of black women, is therefore a journey through memory and self acknowledgement:

> She saw the course
> they had kept behind her, following her from church,
> signalling a language she could not recognize. (p. 238)

Her journey to self-recognition is extended to include a recognition of the African gods and their power:

> so the deities swarmed in the thicket
>
> of the grove, waiting to be known by name; but she
> had never learnt them, though their sounds were within her,
> subdued in the rivers of her blood. (p. 242)

The poet becomes, like Maud Plunkett, a gardener involved in enabling or participating in an organic process of growth and transformation. This is linked implicitly with coral architecture and perceived as a universal, as well as a New World potential. The word becomes a means of "spreading the Japanese peace" (p. 266) of *Les Nympheas* (a reference to Monet's series of paintings), because of its ability to act as a harmonizing and transforming agent. What is important here is that the very sound of the language, including its rhythms (caused by the impact of various tongues) is an integral part of the process of spiritual and cultural identification. This process spreads like the ripples caused by a stone cast in a pool. Once again the idea of something potentially transformative as well as rhizomatic is noted. Art creates ripples like light and these are always changing, as in reflections in water.

Language becomes the frame within which various experiences and sensibilities interact and transform through time. The refusal of any of these responses or affects creates a wound, or a split in language. The climax of the poem becomes an achievement in sound and synchronization, which is the result of the interaction of the historic relics of the past and the retained sounds of that past. This is marked by the X of the crossroads and the swift and the cross ("the swift whose wings is the sign of my crucifixion", p.134). This X is the mark of intertwining forces and the cross of past and present in their intersection. This idea of harmony burgeoning out of multiplicity is facilitated because the intersection of lines constructs the shape of a spiral, which is the graph of growth and new beginnings.

The accumulated images of this section bring together the many enabling movements of the poem. The container for the "bush bath" is a relic of the colonial past now given new purpose and made a vessel of change. It is "one of those cauldrons from the old sugar mill". It has, now, accrued the silt of time. The pyre, too, is a ritual re-enactment of Aruac loss (already perceived as a loss of language), and also the potential for rage and rebellion. It is the ultimate symbol of the harmonic power of the poetic imagination. Here as the burning of the detritus of the past it emerges as the culmination of the many "fires" and "rages" of the epic. Philoctete's cure is a closing "of a mouth around its own name" (p. 248). The acceptance of self, the closing of the wound, is also the return to the stasis of home:

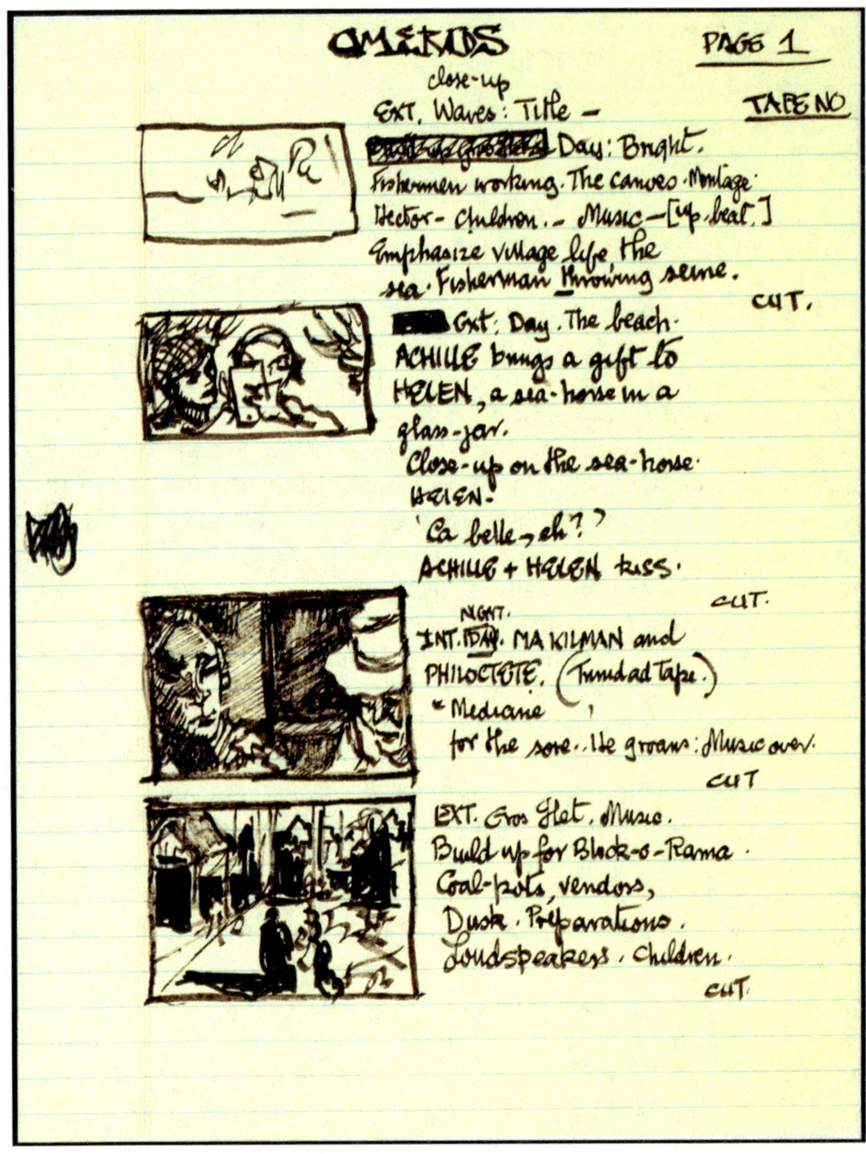
OMEROS PAGE 1

TAPE NO

EXT. Waves: Title – [Close-up]

Day: Bright.

Fishermen working. The canoes. Montage.

Hector – Children. – Music – [up-beat.]

Emphasize village life the sea. Fisherman throwing seine.

CUT.

Ext: Day. The beach.

ACHILLE brings a gift to HELEN, a sea-horse in a glass-jar.

Close-up on the sea-horse.

HELEN:

'Ca belle, eh?'

ACHILLE + HELEN kiss.

CUT.

INT. NIGHT. MA KILMAN and PHILOCTETE. (Trinidad Tape.)

"Medicine for the sore." He groans: Music over.

CUT

EXT. Gros Ilet. Music.

Build-up for Block-o-Rama.

Coal-pots, vendors,

Dusk. Preparations.

Loudspeakers. Children.

CUT.

Storyboard for "Omeros", page 1.
The Thomas Fisher Library, University of Toronto
Ms. Coll. 136, Box 65, November 198?5 or 1986

> ... the right journey
> is motionless; as the sea moves round an island
>
> that appears to be moving, love moves round the heart –
> with encircling salt, and the slowly travelling hand
> knows it returns to the port from which it must start.
> (*Omeros*, p. 291)

In the synchronous projection on the screen of the mind and page – the past made co-existent with the present – Walcott reformulates the idea of history. He gives authority, through his craft, to the subjective Caribbean imagination to rephrase its past according to its own priorities. It also allows him as a "new historian", who is inscribing, through the narrating of a previously unwritten history, to write that new version of history. In rearranging the past as a new story through its filmic projection, Walcott is giving a privileged reading or viewing to this particular version. The histories of the first peoples of the Caribbean and the Greeks, contained within the one frame, make them equivalent as stories, myths, fictions, or histories. By implication, the legends and the lives of the original peoples are legitimized.

This legitimization, as a reconstruction of the past, as in the assembling of montage, is a means of re-evaluating the events which have happened in time but also, and of greater significance, a process towards a cure, a leap beyond the confines of that past. In this telling of a tale, through which the events of the past are re-constructed in ever-changing configurations, the associational logic of retold events engenders a new conception of the truth – of personal and historic reality. Fiction or narrative as a reconstruction of facts and events (rather than the piling up of fact and fact), leads to new knowledge of self and of the events of the past through constant retelling.[10] As such, it is a leap beyond the confines of history to the new. In the poem *Omeros*, the figure of the goat becomes aligned to the poet, Homer, as an originator of classical poetry that has its basis in an oral tradition. The two, Homer and the goat, parallel the mocking role of the calypsonian. This is Walcott's attempt to show how a particular kind of language and art born of a people who suffer and endure, can give rise to classical myth and poetry, both in Greece and in the Caribbean.

"The Aegean's chimera is a camera" (*Omeros*, pp. 282-283) encapsulates this resourcefulness and also the twin attributes of Antillean art in the dual meaning of the word "chimera". Here, in this word, which connects goat and flight of fancy, Walcott affirms the role of both imagination and the earthiness, the "gravel" of true art. On page 290 the difference between the camera as a producer of fixed images and the chimera as a creator of imaginative creations is emphasised in the lines, "Just as the nightingales had forgotten his lines, / cameras not chimeras, saw his purple sea / as a postcard archipelago with gnarled pines…" Homer skips down the goat track, (along which Ma Kilman has already travelled on her way to the cure), like an "old goat". His "goatishness" links him to the "eros", which in the first draft is formed from Hom/eros. Homer asks the poet "Did you, you know, do it often?" (p. 284), in reference to the girl who gave his name.

The camera as a vehicle of illusions is linked to the power of the imagination and equally with self-delusion. But its primary function here is as a projector of images that enthral. Cinematography is potentially a form and a language for true dialogue and transformation. Against a history of colonialism and imposed, negative valuations, film form can allow the restoration of a true self-image by those whose material circumstance had led to incarcerating images constructed by the myopic eye of other perceptions. Montage provides an artistic structure for the emergence of the psyche whose instinct for survival has led to submergence or "the self in maroonage", the African resistant self that has retained its memory of Africa and of its difference. In Eisensteinian terms, the individual then, as a cell of society, can be viewed as carrying the incipient seed of social transformation.

The use of audiovisual contrapuntal montage allows for an articulation of the inherent contradictions of human kind but also enables a process of communication, or a new mechanism for transmitting those differences hitherto rendered silent and invisible. Eisenstein's notion of the shot as a montage cell, or of montage as leading to burgeoning movement and leaps of consciousness, allows for a perception of culture as constant process. Through montage form the Caribbean poet can structure a poem that replicates the processes of conflict and recreation that have led to the making of Antillean art and culture.

The poem *Omeros* as film process arrives at a particular peak moment when Omeros or Homer says, "forget the gods", and then, "read the rest" (p. 283). The poet has admitted that he has not read the Homeric text all the way through. But at this stage Walcott has done several sleights of hand, one of which is a trick of language. At this point in the narrative the poem becomes as close to a movie as a poem can. There is an edited version of the Medusa legend, whose association with history the reader remembers since this poem in many ways refers us back to "The Muse of History", where history is seen as a medusa. The figure becomes reversed in *Omeros* where she is seen as a symbol of the retrieval of self from the "eye-vision" of modern consciousness.

The poet's admission to Homer that he has never read the book "all the way through" is a statement that refutes the idea of the dominance of a written classical tradition, in *Pantomime* associated with Trewe, and with Lawrence-Bain in *Steel*, and locates the author's love of Western art in a different idea.

> The lift of the
>
> arching eyebrows paralyzed me like Medusa's
> shield, and I turned cold the moment I had said it.
> "Those gods with hyphens, like Hollywood producers,"
>
> I heard my mouth babbling as ice glazed over my chest.
> "The gods and the demi-gods aren't much use to us."
> "Forget the gods," Omeros growled, "and read the rest."
> (*Omeros*, p. 283)

The word "babbling" links the poet to "the talkative brooks" that carry the tale of Philoctete's cure, and recalls the silence that "is sawn in half by a dragonfly". So we are warned that the silence that encases the poet as he turns to ice and is submerged in the sea, will be "sawn in half" when he undertakes the journey with Homer across the sea. But that journey is now connected to a kind of production, like film. But it is also the poet's recognition of his self-reliance in, "Forget the gods". The final movement before home is therefore perceived as submergence into the depths of one's own self, a self that has been previously strangled. The poet's project is here to release those voices from their silence and to give those lives and feet the visibility that they have hitherto lacked.

> Why waste lines on Achille, a shade on the sea-floor?
> Because strong as self-healing coral, a quiet culture
> is branching from the white ribs of each ancestor,
>
> deeper than it seems on the surface; slowly but sure,
> it will change us with the fluent sculpture of Time,
> it will grip like the polyp, soldered by the slime
>
> of the sea-slug. Below him, a parodic architecture
> re-erected the earth's crusted columns, its porous
> temples, stoas through which whipping eels slide, (*Omeros*, p. 296)

These verses point to an idea of a simple race and a people seasoned in the life and trials of the tropics and its histories. The past has been outfaced as these ghosts rise as images of terror while the will to survive has brought triumph. Like the coral, a new architecture, which is art, is built slowly but surely and steadfastly from these multiple deaths and ancestral pasts. From the many traumas, lacerations and fissures, a new people and a new aesthetic have emerged in crystal form.

The verses refer to the idea of a rhizome in the figuration of a branch and its emphasis on fluency. It emphasises the necessity of living with and through difference, while returning to the theme of mimicry in the word "parodic" and in this way recognises that culture and so called identity will always be a process of sameness and difference, of repetition and change. Moreover the verses in their emphasis on the importance of change and in the oppositions of grip and slime, summarise the elements that give unending potential to Caribbean culture in its clash of opposites, its movement of peoples and its perpetual confronting of the need to build and rebuild, no matter what time and circumstance present.

This process is encapsulated in the figure of Ma Kilman who is both seer and the mountain La Sorcière, which has the shape of a woman, and she thus combines the human, the land and historic vestiges. She is led by the ants, down a goat track to the seed buried in the soil of the place. Ma Kilman, as surrogate poetic self, unpeels the layers and accretions of time and history so that she can truly see. Her journey follows the path of instinct in the slow recovery of sense perception and memory, as well as another sense, which is a sixth sense. This entails the gradual recall of "a language she could not recognise". Seeing becomes more than sight in *Omeros*. It emerges as the acceptance of difference and different ways of seeing and evaluating reality. The language which the ants speak is beyond the logic of rational comprehension or a so-called "civilised" way of life. As an interrogative language it delves into the "unconscious variables"[11] of the human soul. It also suggests the jouissance, which for Julia Kristeva energises the semiotic.

In *Desire in Language* and in *Revolution in Poetic Language*, Kristeva describes the ways in which the poetic in writing, not simply poetry, unsettles the thetic and the symbolic in language.[12] Through the instinctual drives and the activity of the chora from which rhythm emanates, the poetic transgresses the ordering principle of the symbolic in language or the law of the father and acts through the carnivalesque to shatter the surface of the text and to wage ideological battle. This space of transgression is polyphonic and often achieves its force through breaks in punctuation and syntax or "play". Through such disruptive writing, the subject positions herself in an "historical space" to "refashion time".[13] The poem *Omeros* situates itself within that space of transgression. Walcott writes:

> Besides I have always thought in two margins. It has been the rigid benediction of my life, and to think in two margins, one on the right, and one on the left, obviously, is to serve a life-long sentence. [...] I mean both the sweet and chafing prison which the soul chooses and which it calls, since apparently everything must have its noun, poetry, but it is also to see poems as simply parentheses, asides of that life-long sentence, as now a phrase of Dylan Thomas's springs to mind: '*that poetry is statements made on the way to the grave.*'[14]

These two margins, which among other things signify the dichotomy between prose and poetry, also indicate the difference between conceptual thought and instinctual imaging or perception through sense and emotion and psychic experience. Walcott continues:

Storyboard for “Omeros”, page 10. Ma Kilman comes out of the church
The Thomas Fisher Library, University of Toronto
Ms. Coll. 136, Box 65, November 198?5 or 1986

> I have a horror ... of the intellectual veneration of rot ... no amount of masturbation can induce the Muse. What do I mean by masturbation. Well, you take your hand and you write from the left-hand margin and stop when you have achieved some spasm of self-recognition that may not breed but will appear to conceive, and that is known as literary philosophy...
>
> I cannot think because I refuse to, unlike Descartes. I have always put Descartes behind the horse, and the horse is Pegasus ... the one with wings.[15]

For Walcott, in this essay, conceptual thinking is equated with a language that has become an end in itself and the vehicle of a culture nearing sterility and impotence. As such, his fascination with the language of Lowell's poetry,[16] which is crucial to much of *Omeros*, is with a language, which allows the crude impact of life on the nervous system and the senses to resound. Such language opens itself to areas of experience, which are not subject to reason, definition or proof:

> The years that brought this difference, this reconciliation with ambition, lie in the prose word "ticking". It is the sound of cracking ice, of a bomb, of wheels, of a clock, of the floe, fated to melt as it gets near the ocean, and every word around it is ordinary. That is, it is ordinary at first, then it is wonderful.[17]

The "wound of a language I'd no wish to remove" (*Omeros*, p. 270) is, therefore, emblematic of the reconciliation within the psyche of the differences, the disparateness of every individual history; and the refusal to reduce this fragmented past to a blandness or forgetfulness. The cure to the wound of history is the new capacity to see the thing as it is without the embellishments of received ideas, to think its difference. He returns to this theme in *The Prodigal* (pp. 62-64).

This shock of the banal which in 1964 Walcott identified as, "one of the prerequisites of American art", derives from "a manic strenuousness of self-examination that no longer takes comfort from European tradition, that has produced the shrill fury of a novelist like Mailer or Burroughs, this teetering, dangerous balance of a poet like Lowell, the visceral explosions of abstract expressionists, action painters, hard-edge painters and their self-destructive drives."[18] In locating this impact in a newly emerging American artistic tradition, Walcott is also suggesting that the New World aesthetic is founded on the drive for renewal, the remaking of the old, and the potential this manic drive has in a situation where old and new come into collision with each other.

This need for self-renewal is voiced by Wilson Harris as an ideal of harmony and healing which, as a Guyanese writer who was in his youth accustomed to open spaces and the expanse of the unexplored interior, is weighted by that sense of unbounded possibility of both time and space:

> To put it in other words – the impact of the human mind and body on the hard world, in constructing something and destroying something, has a unity or combination that is both secret and plain, immaterial and material, showing forth the power of passion, the limits and order of being. What is truly particular is not isolated or static but is an association of numerous factors. Value or spirit is the illumination of dark energies. The new architecture of the world must be a profound understanding and revelation of all factors that combine into the phenomenon of effort and achievement not for one race of men but for all mankind together. Not simply for a glorious name or tradition in the historical sense but for an identity that is purposive and vital in a universal and manifestly human sense.[19]

What he means by "vital" in a universal and manifestly human sense is that art must take cognisance of the marginalised. In order to do this he fashions a cross-cultural aesthetic.

This cross-cultural dynamic creates an arc of communication through which the old and new worlds are made to dialogue with each other. Harris's subterranean explorations of the mythic unconscious map new passageways. As such, he is also (he was, in fact, in reality) a surveyor and analogous to the iguana who, in *Omeros*, represents an ancient right of possession that infuriates Plunkett in his effort to record history:

> "Every spear of grass on this ground
> is yours. Read the bloody pamphlet. Did they name it
> Iounalo for you?"
>
> The lizard spun around
>
> to the inane Caribbean. Plunkett also. (p. 92)

This latter, through its name and shape, becomes a symbol for Walcott of the remapping of the Antilles. Walcott's desire for concrete expression and imagistic impact evokes Harris's theory of the need to fashion a new architecture of the word, through which the artist can create a concrete aesthetic image of reality and a portal to enter into the layers of the unconscious, the subconscious and of time.

Myth and The Flight of the Imagination

"Vangelo Nero", "The Loupgarou" and the film, *The Haytian Earth*, are myth creations and therefore privilege the idea of an imaginative flight or a leap beyond the real.[20] The concern with myth and landscape is also to be found in the pivotal essay, "The Muse of History". Walcott advocates a mythic tapestry as opposed to a fixation on history. For him the New World in its relative openness and emptiness enables exultation, awe and potential and in particular, elation. According to Walcott, writers of the Antilles and the Americas share these qualities:

> Even in Borges, where the genius seems secretive, immured from change, it celebrates elation, which is vulgar and abrupt, the life of the plains given an instant archaism by the hieratic style. Violence is felt with the simultaneity of history. So the death of a gaucho does not merely repeat, but is, the death of Caesar. Fact evaporates into myth. This is not the jaded cynicism, which sees nothing new under the sun; it is an elation, which sees everything as renewed. Like Borges too, the poet St.-John Perse conducts us from the mythology of the past to the present without a tremor of adjustment. This is the revolutionary spirit at its deepest; it recalls the spirit to arms.[21]

Here the landscape and its associations or living presences provide a weave of timelessness shared by these New World writers. They have gone beyond the confrontation of history (p. 38) and share an essential idea of the sameness of human cruelty. But the New World's complexities of history and its myriad cultures, as well as its loss of memory, enable that sense of boundless potential that Walcott celebrates here and elsewhere. The word "potential" for Deleuze summons an idea of openness and unending becoming, akin to Harris's "unfinished genesis of the imagination" and foregrounds the necessity for the New World writer to participate in a discourse between the inside of his own experience and the outside of an unknown past and future, and to imagine. The jubilation or elation of such boundlessness gives the imagination its particular power.

This power is associated with a return to an originary consciousness. Those who "burrow" in the dark or the blackness seek a return to an essential image of the human that Deleuze, in his re-reading of Henri Bergson, calls "a machine assemblage" that exists on a "plane of immanence". This "bloc of space-time" or "material universe [...] is the machine assemblage of movement images [...] it is the universe as cinema in itself, a meta cinema".[22] Film as a replica of this universal image through its automatic movement enables a language of a self without borders. This is read as an image of the self before categorisation or division of consciousness. Film as an art of abstract space enables a leap beyond the actuality of lived experience, but as an art of time enables the development of a relationship between self and other that goes beyond thought into psychological and emotional spheres of existence.

The filmed and televised version of *The Haytian Earth* and the stage play produced for the Government of St Lucia in 1984 evolved from a much revised film script about Haiti.[23] The raconteur who is speaking to the boys as the film opens tells them that, "these buildings have more history than

Design for "The Haytian Earth"
The Derek Walcott Collection, The Alma Jordan Library, UWI, St Augustine. Box 33, folder 8.

Design for "The Haytian Earth"
The Derek Walcott Collection, The Alma Jordan Library, UWI, St Augustine. Box 33, folder 8.

sugar have ants" and promises to take them on a journey of discovery if they are good. This quest is one in which the spirit is summoned through ritual. The speaker has already suggested that the boys in front of her bear the traces of spirits of the past, since one resembles Dessalines another Toussaint and the other Christophe. Spirit then is transmitted from one generation to the next. Film assumes the goal of giving this transference an embodied presence. There is also, here, an echo of George Lamming's novel, *Of Age and Innocence* (1958), where the boys of different ethnicities assemble to listen to Ma Shepherd's tale of the tribeboys and the warrior ants, but they also engage in their own "work" with this story, to go beyond Ma Shepherd's inherent conservatism.

The Haytian Earth as a film does not make use in any significant way of filmic technique, other than the use of the close-up and the two-shot. The first enables Walcott to focus on the implements of war, and on small, significant details and to paint the face in light. One primary example is the face and skin of a black woman who appears before the group comprising the student, the Matron and Calixte-Breda. The two-shot and the use of a close-up provide him in this sense with something close to a canvas on which he can depict a face or a portrait in what is often a new light, and there are a number of such shots. In a 1990 interview he notes of this scene where Calixte-Breda is speaking to the matron shortly before the torture and execution of Ogé that:

> I was making a video film of a play I had done in the Caribbean and I was beginning to do some shots just to see what some of the actors would look like. Now St Lucia has some very black, very fine featured, very beautiful women, and the blackness is very much part of their beauty, because of the texture of the skin, it's beautiful. Now there was this girl, in ordinary life she was very beautiful to look at, but the cameraman set up a shot, taking a picture of her in a madras head tie. And then he called me and said, come and take a look at this. And I looked through the lens and I just stepped back, because he, a professional photographer, had brought the girl into close focus, and she was just staggering. Something had happened between the beauty of the woman in ordinary daylight, and what the camera had done to her. The same thing happened to two or three other women.[24]

The use of the close-up became a dominant feature of all of Walcott's attempts at film-making and filtered into his poetry. It became a new way of perceiving the world and of conceiving Caribbean beauty.

The first evidence of *The Haytian Earth* as film is to be found in a manuscript dated Nov. 12 in the Walcott Collection. Alma Jordan Library, The University of the West Indies, St. Augustine. The script was presumably also written in 1972, the same year as "Vangelo Nero". The alternate title, The Black Emperor, also appears and it is conceived as a

T.V. Epic produced by Crysalite Productions and as A Television Mini Series in Nine Episodes.

The idea of revolution and resistance demanded for Walcott a large canvas that would allow time and space to be fluid. Film gave him the freedom to cut from one place to another and to suggest the revolutions of time within national and cultural consciousness. But the theme of resistance is also important. This traverses all his film attempts from *Ti-Jean* right through to the most recent works for either television or cinema.

The undated typescript, "The Loupgarou" and the film script/scenario, "Vangelo Nero" dated 1972,[25] are both also myth creations. They engage in an act of linking myth to landscape. In a literal sense the "earth emanated influences."[26] "The Loupgarou" is based on the legend of the *jã gajè* already incorporated into *Another Life* and *Ti Jean* and *The Arkansas Testament*.[27] It tells the story of Manoir the Merchant (who also appears in the "cinematic transition from chapter four to chapter five"[28] in *Another Life*), who sells his soul to the devil to gain financial and business success. It is a fairly common story in the West Indies. It suggests that the stories that abound in the Caribbean are the result of quite specific atmospheric conditions, in particular in semi-light and these create both illusions of other worldly presences and feed into mythology.

"Vangelo Nero" seeks to build on the scaffolding of the Christian myth. It narrates the story of a black Christ and is within that tradition of naming through the appropriation of biblical myths that critics such as Pat Ismond have described. Both film scripts ("Vangelo Nero" and "The Loupgarou") attempt an audiovisual synthesis as part of their myth enactment. "Vangelo Nero" begins with a "long drawn" celebratory sweep over the African landscape of which we are reminded in Walcott's 1992 Nobel Acceptance speech:

> The sigh of History rises over ruins, not over landscapes, and in the Antilles there are few ruins to sigh over apart from the ruins of sugar-estates and abandoned forts. Looking around slowly, as a camera would, taking in the low blue hills over Port of Spain, the village road and houses, the warrior-arches, the god-actors and their handlers, and music already on the sound track, I wanted to make a film that would be a long-drawn sigh over Felicity. I was filtering the afternoon with evocations of a lost India, but why 'evocations'? Why not 'celebrations of a real presence'?[29]

The work, "Vangelo Nero", is significant not only as an early example of Walcott's writing for cinema, but also because it is a template in several respects for *Omeros*. For example, the beat of the shot in "Vangelo" re emerges in the accentuation of lines at the beginning of *Omeros*. This movement maps a continuous flow that is itself part of the strategy of a naming process. "Vangelo Nero" uses camera movement and the editing of shots to introduce a rhythm that approximates to the idea

Design for "Vangelo Nero": Drawing of several figures.
The Derek Walcott Collection, The Alma Jordan Library, UWI, St Augustine. Flat box 1, dated 30 May, 1972

and the experiences of a rebirth of consciousness, figured in the boy Christ. The setting is Africa, however, and not the Antilles.

This film script also links the opening or birth of new consciousness in the figure of the boy-child Christ to dawn and an idea of a revolutionary consciousness. What is significant in this is that Walcott is making a direct connection between a primal consciousness and a particular kind of editing technique as conceived in a shooting script. He is here, as well as in the opening sequences of *Omeros*, approximating the directions for a shooting script as outlined by Sergei Eisenstein who claimed that the shooting script uses a form of primal language in its breakdown of a concept into a chain of concrete single actions, seen in "Vangelo Nero" as:

> A river, at morning. Africa
> Dawn, a long shot, our eyes travel the river bank.
> Our gaze does not disturb the herons, the rushes in the light
> wind of morning.
> A sky pale, hard and blue, without a cloud.
> It is like the beginning of the world, the stillness waking.
> Far down the shallows of this river, through whose murmurous
> glaze the pebbles show clearly as a mosaic,
> within its centre, a man, in robes stands up to his calves,
> and in front of him, a half-naked boy.
> Still, in long shot, but approaching carefully as if the camera
> did not wish to disturb the rite
> we come nearer to the two,
> to the wizened, bearded, wild-visaged gaze of the robed man. (p. 1)

The fragmentation of the action first provides a visual map of an original world, and through the movement of the camera we are also directed to an image that is also an idea of a world in which human and nature are at one. In emphasising this return to an originary unity, the poet suggests a reawakening of mythic potential, a time of naming or identifying, and the creation of a narrative structure through which this understanding of the world can be given a scaffold for future belief. The film scenario thus combines two ideas: the ineluctable unity of man and nature and the possibility of making new. The directorial movement leads to the simulation of a form of primal consciousness where it is "like the beginning of the world". The word "like" is important because throughout this script Walcott reinforces the fact that this is not the Jesus Christ of Jerusalem, but rather a simulation or a return.

The idea of return or indeed repetition enables a discourse on the possible futility of all revolutionary idealism. In this sense "Vangelo Nero" is another layer in Walcott's long standing depiction and quarrying of figures who have become legends and whose motivation appears to be in one sense or another questionable. "Vangelo Nero" places the human qualities

Design for "Vangelo Nero": Drawing of Vangelo Nero.
The Derek Walcott Collection, The Alma Jordan Library, UWI, St Augustine. Box 6, folder 5.

of the black Christ above all else. He is susceptible to pain and hunger and thirst and comes close to being a fallen figure like Lucifer when he is tempted by the mirage, which is his double, suggesting a duality within men of legend. Christophe, Dessalines and Toussaint are shown to have fallen prey to hubris and in the case of Christophe, to the temptations of the flesh. Legends or mythical figures become the objects of his scrutiny through a form of cyclical return.

These figures are viewed as heroic as much for the qualities or actions that make them immortal, as for their frail humanity. It is possible that Walcott saw himself thus divided, and used mythical figures in a manner similar to Yeats, who used the Ulster hero warrior Cuchulain to explore his own persona.

It would have been exceedingly difficult for "Vangelo Nero" to have been made into a successful movie, not only because, as Bruce King suggests, its action is interior, but because the language of expression is a form of poetry that does not give the immediacy of impact, nor the emotional and psychological effect of a good film. I have noted Albert Laveau's comment in 1992 that as Walcott became immersed in film and writing for film, his language in drama became less poetic and more plain. "Vangelo Nero" and *The Haytian Earth* demonstrate where he had to move from, in terms of writing for film.

"Vangelo Nero" also gave Walcott an insight into the possible tonal variations available through film. Landscape, and its evocation, become a prelude to the boy's burgeoning consciousness and emerging authority. The visual representations: dawn, the herons in paradisal freedom, the gently moving rushes, the cloudless sky, the clear water in quiet movement are rendered as tonal equivalents to the "murmurous glaze" and the baptismal scene. All the figures are in accord, sounding an identical note through which the idea of genesis is conveyed as in "the stillness waking". The rhythmic unity and tendentious movement provide a form of "montage on the dominant", where one concept sounds throughout, but in different notes.

Walcott achieves a particular tonal quality through this combination of sound and sight and this method is taken up in the poem *Omeros*. For example, the rhythm of the moving line which carries Philoctete's tale through mountains, birds and brooks all the way to the sea (*Omeros*, p.4) is forged through a similar use of continuous flow whereby fragments of shots (images) move to a particular beat and the sweeping movement of a simulated pan, that unifies human, land, and bird life, waterfall, rivers and sea. As in *The Fortunate Traveller*, and in his later works, the egret signifies by its look and movement, the act of writing. The rhythmic movement, forged by a chain of single actions, unites man and nature in a "secret" bond that solidifies the unique force of a particular people and the way of life that is shared and that is not available to outsiders. This marking of difference, which is discussed by Glissant in his theorising of the importance of opacity as a way of safeguarding difference, is mediated through synaesthesia and facilitated and shaped by movement.[30]

This method equates to the process of myth-making. *Omeros* is in itself a fiction of the poet's imagination, not simply as a work of art, but because at its heart the poem seeks to demonstrate that all history is fiction and made up of fragments of memory that are transformed into an appearance of a unified whole. As poet he asserts that he can create a myth or a story that is equally as valid as any other and manipulates imagery to create a series of illusions. For this simple reason then, film is the ideal form. It allows the accretion of time through simultaneous layers of history and gives free reign to the flight of the imagination.

The poem *Omeros* is also a myth and partakes of dream reality or a reality that borders or sometimes slides into dream, and in one of the most overt of these dream sequences in Book 5, it references Kamau Brathwaite and his inventive use of the filmic as a way of forcing the emergence of the "self in maroonage". This process begins with an image already loaded with significance from earlier works.

I am referring here to the image of the cyclone, or the cyclops, which feeds into the impact of the hurricane as a force for change. The Cyclops image is subsumed into *Omeros* as a signifier of that process to change. The eye of the Cyclops (the eye of the hurricane) already carries the double burden of imperialist eye and the eye of the poet, in its echo of its earlier use as in the lines from *Sea Grapes*, which locate the Cyclops as a giant eye:

> Or, as I
> paddle this air, breathe this new sea, am I
> still swimming through one gigantic eye? ("Natural History", "The Walking Fish", p. 38).[31]

Here the poet sees himself possibly as a perpetrator of the incarcerating power or "one channelled way of seeing" which language and education have inbred in him. The Caribbean is also still caught in received images and subject to mimicry. This idea of a return of forms of colonialism and domination is reinforced by the camera eye of the opening sequence of *Omeros* and in the "caught cries" of the boys who, imaged as monkeys "doing tricks" (p.73), represent a form of mimicry and an acknowledgement of V. S. Naipaul, in suggesting an enthralment to a new colonial power, that of tourism.[32]

Omeros transforms what Walcott calls a one-channelled way of seeing, into a folk tale, in this way connecting the energy of "Hurucan", which is a tribute to Caribbean writing as noted previously, and the new assertiveness of Philoctete, who refuses to tell his story to the tourist.[33] So the writer and the art of imaginative reconstruction are aligned to the imagination of the Caribbean, which has created folk tales through a process of syncretism that privileges the elements and weather systems of the Caribbean but combines these with received narratives:

> The Cyclone, howling because one of the lances
> of a flinging palm has narrowly grazed his one eye,
> wades knee-deep in troughs.
> (*Omeros*, p. 51)

The audiovisual impact of the new "musical" which the poet includes in his epic, has already been prefigured in the "yesterday" section ("All my yesterdays") of Helen's hallucination or, more appropriately, the film sequence that flows from her moment of hallucination, in that here too one finds a merging of mythologies: of Greek myth and the myth of cowboys and Indians generated by cinema.[34]

The co-mingled images of the folk tale of Ma Rain have their origins in a story recited by children in the Caribbean (thunder and lightning equals the devil and his wife fighting). In Walcott's new version these trans-cultural figures dance to a West Indian beat, and allow Walcott to suggest that sound and rhythm are the unifying connections between two traditions, the West and Africa. And further, that as echoes of the past these myths have a new life in their transformation into a West Indian folk tale. Their existence as living elements is ensured because they are firmly embedded in the newly created "sound systems" of New World sensibility.

Not only is there a synthesis of myths (Zeus, Shango, Neptune, "Zando-li-lizard") but their story is narrated by the voice of a Caribbean storyteller. It has the beat and the dramatic sweep and tension, the tonal expressiveness of the Antillean folk tale. It must be spoken to ensure its full affective impact.

> ...the abrupt Shango drums
>
> made Neptune rock in the caves. Fête start! Erzulie
> rattling her ra-ra; Ogun, the blacksmith, feeling
> No Pain; Damballa winding like a zandoli
>
> lizard, ...(*Omeros*, p. 52)

The story insinuates the history of endured pain of the New World Black, in an echo of Ma Kilman's "no Pain café" in which Philoctete seeks to forget his own pain, remembered as a wound from a rusted anchor. Philoctete's howling in the yams and his sojourn in Ma Kilman's rumshop are reflected in Ogun who feels "No Pain" and in the howling of the cyclone. In this way, the gods of two cultures, historically in conflict, unite in the suffering of the New World. The merging of myths suggests that the New World psyche is, in the first instance, hospitable to influences, but also deeply creative in its reconstruction of these multiple inheritances. In the restaging of these myths, Walcott is also giving the "old gods" equal parts in the enactment of the process of transformation.

The memories of history and myth are merged through the dynamic of sound and vision and through rhythm and the elements specific to the Caribbean space. The rage of the Cyclops becomes the rage of the tropical hurricane. Walcott, despite his use of Standard English, as a Caribbean poet privileges a West Indian rhythm, and embraces Edward Kamau Brathwaite's theory that "the hurricane does not roar in pentameters".[35] *Omeros* suggests that the poetic structure of Caribbean poetry and its rhythms must accord with the rhythms of life lived with hurricanes and historic trauma.

By Book 3, the reader has already associated change with the force field of Caribbean monsoons. So that, as this section of the poem opens, the transition between the cyclone and the movie-making or generating mirage is smooth. It evokes the ghosts of the past and those yet to come.

Imagination is then a projection of the mythic unconscious; it derives its power to construct images from the traces and marks left by those who have peopled the place. Walcott returns to an idea of a primal perception based on the need for self-preservation and renewal. He places against received ideas of self, imagination and thought, a view of history and artistic creation that, while admitting the necessity of a language system through which complex ideas can be conveyed, seeks to free language from its now corrupted myths and ideas and to valorise the systems derived from the transplantation in new soil. In Deleuzian terms he states that thought (ideas of reality and one's relation to reality) changes according to the needs of the time and circumstance, as the circuits of the brain transform themselves and make new associations to accommodate new eras.[36] As Deleuze writes:

> Thought is molecular. Molecular speeds make up the slow beings that we are. [...] The circuits and linkages of the brain don't pre-exist the stimuli, corpuscles, and particles [*grains*] that trace them. Cinema isn't theatre; rather it makes bodies out of grains. The linkages are often paradoxical and on all sides overflow simple associations of images. Cinema, precisely because it puts the image in motion, or rather endows the image with self-motion, [*auto movement*], never stops tracing the circuits of the brain.[37]

Endnotes

1. Edward Kamau Brathwaite, *Contradictory Omens. Cultural Diversity and Integration in the Caribbean*, 1974. See pp. 17 & 42 in particular.
2. See Dominick La Capra, *Representing the Holocaust: History, Theory, Trauma* (New York: Cornell University Press, 1996); *Contemporary Approaches in Literary Trauma Theory*, ed. Michelle Balaev (London: Palgrave Macmillan 2014) and Paula Morgan, *The Terror and the Time* (Jamaica: University of the West Indies Press, 2015).
3. Paul Naylor, *Poetic Investigations. Singing in the Holes of History* (Evanston: North Western University Press, 1999), p. 170.
4. Ibid.
5. Kamau Brathwaite, *Ancestors. A Reinvention of Mother Poem, Sun Poem and X/Self* (New York: New Directions, 2001), p. 383.
6. See Kamau Brathwaite, *Born to Slow Horses* (Middletown: Wesleyan University Press, 2005).
7. See Melanie Otto, *A Creole Experiment. Utopian Space in Kamau Brathwaite's "video-style" Works* (Trenton, New Jersey, Africa World Press, 2009).
8. See Rhonda Cobham, "'An Enemy so was a compliment'", in *Interlocking Basins*, pp. 100-123.
9. Earl Lovelace, *The Dragon Can't Dance* ([1979] London: Faber and Faber, 2003).
10. I am indebted to Pat Colgan and a lifelong friend, Fr. Miceal O'Regan (deceased), for this insight.
11. For Wilson Harris's "unconscious variables", see *History, Fable and Myth in the Caribbean and Guianas*, (Calaloux Publications, 1995).
12. Julia Kristeva, *Desire in Language. A Semiotic Approach to literature and Art*, ed. Leon S. Roudiez, trans. Thomas Gora , Alice Jardine, and Leon S. Roudiez (New York: Columbia University Press, 1980).
13. Julia Kristeva, *Desire in Language*, pp. 159-209.
14. Derek Walcott, "Caligula's Horse", in *After Europe*, ed. Stephen Slemon and Helen Tiffin (Mundelstrup: Dangaroo Press, 1989), p. 138.
15. Walcott, "Caligula's Horse", p.140.
16. Derek Walcott, "On Robert Lowell", *What the Twilight Says. Essays* (London: Faber and Faber, 1998), p. 91.
17. Derek Walcott, "On Robert Lowell".
18. Derek Walcott, "American anguish, Canadian calm", *Trinidad Guardian* 22 July 1964: 5. See George Collier, ed., *Derek Walcott. The Journeyman Years Occasional Prose 1957- 1974. Vols. 1 &2*, Cross/Cultures 171 &172 (Amsterdam: Rodopi, 2013).
19. Wilson Harris, *Tradition, the Writer and Society* (London: New Beacon, 1967), p. 9.

20. Derek Walcott, "Vangelo Nero", Film script, Box 6, Folder 5 & Box 6, Folder 9, 1972; *The Haytian Earth*, TV series, Box 5, Folder 4, St Lucia, Warwick Productions, 1978 and 1984, Derek Walcott collection, Alma Jordan Library, The University of the West Indies, St. Augustine.
21. Derek Walcott, "The Muse of History", *What the Twilight Says. Essays* (London: Faber and Faber, 1998), pp. 37-38.
22. Gilles Deleuze, *Cinema 1*, p. 6. See also, "But through relations, the whole is transformed or changes qualitatively", p. 10.
23. Bruce King, *Derek Walcott, A Caribbean Life* (Oxford: Oxford University Press, 2000), p. 434.
24. Derek Walcott in Conversation with Jean Antoine, *Poetry Ireland Review 34*. Spring 1992. 2015, pp.75-76. See also the documentary, *Walcott as Poet and Seer.*
25. "The Loupgarou", Box 6, Folder 8, Derek Walcott Collection, The Alma Jordan Library, The University of the West Indies, St Augustine.
26. Walcott, "Meanings", *Savacou 2*, 1970, p. 50.
27. A *jã gajè* is an evil being who has sold his soul to the devil in exchange for material gain. This pact allows him to assume animal shape. If anyone wounds him in this shape, however, he becomes 'degajè', or freed of the spirit, and also retains the inflicted wound.
28. Edward Baugh, *Memory as Vision: Another Life*, p. 30.
29. Derek Walcott, *The Antilles: Fragments of Epic Memory* (London: Faber; New York: Farrar, Straus and Giroux, 1993), p. 8.
30. Édouard Glissant. *The Poetics of Relation.*
31. Derek Walcott, *Sea Grapes* (London: Cape, 1976), p. 38.
32. V.S. Naipaul, *The Mimic Men* (London: Andre Deutsch, 1967).
33. See Glissant for whom "a generalizing universal is always ethnocentric"... "so that opacity becomes a site of difference and therefore subversive and necessary to ensure the defeat of the monolingual which has sought through arrogance an essential transparency (*Poetics of Relation*, pp.110 -20).
34. Derek Walcott, *Omeros*, pp. 34-37.
35. Kamau Brathwaite, *History of the Voice* (London: New Beacon, 1984), p.10.
36. Gilles Deleuze, "After Image", "The Brain is the Screen, an Interview with Deleuze", *The Brain is the Screen. Deleuze and the Philosophy of Cinema*, ed. Gregory Flaxman (Minneapolis: Minnesota Press 2000), pp.365-373..
37. Deleuze, "After Image", p. 366.

CHAPTER 6
REVOLUTION AND RETURN

Many of Walcott's film scripts are concerned with revolution and, as we have seen, *The Last Carnival* invokes the resemblance between revolution and carnival. Carnival enables not simply a concretisation of an illusion but also a way of making past and present simultaneous. "To Die for Grenada",[1] while returning to other well known themes of exile and belonging, and the care (or carelessness) of creativity in Trinidad, focuses on political hubris, the futility of idealism and the triumph of deceit and lies. Its main project is the depiction of the idea of revolution and how revolutionaries may be viewed and represented. In this light, the film very overtly invokes Eisenstein's theory of film as both a vehicle of revolution and as a way of representing revolution. It also uses several of Eisenstein's techniques for making the viewer see events in their true horror and with full emotional impact

This script, which is located at the Fisher Rare Book Library at the University of Toronto, focuses on the growing isolation of Maurice Bishop and is prophetic in forecasting the return of tragic events. In retrospect, it anticipates the attempted Muslimeen coup in Trinidad of 1990 (which occurred after the conception of the film) which seemed an echo of the Grenada event. Walcott creates a series of parallel events in Port of Spain and in St Georges, Grenada, and while he was probably still thinking of the 1970 attempted Trinidad revolution, in retrospect events that occurred in Port of Spain only seven years after the Grenada invasion and two years after writing the script, take on the uncanny feel of a return.

Walcott's film script is accompanied by an essay or monologue that begins by conceiving the Caribbean as a place constructed through media images and without value in themselves:

> The islands were colonies, then, their opinion was not required. On these beaches I thought of the desolation of the Pacific islands. Dead soldiers in the surf, rusted landing craft that we saw in Life Magazine, Colliers, The Saturday Evening Post. It was a radio and magazine war then. And, of course, the movies (p. 2).

He adds: "This small tropical war, on TV, reduced everything to a uniform drabness. [...] It looked like Vietnam (p. 3). He is thinking of Coppola's

Image from "To Die for Grenada" or "Monos".
The Thomas Fisher Library, University of Toronto
Ms. Coll. 136, Box 67, November 1985.

Image from "To Die for Grenada" or "Monos".
The Thomas Fisher Library, University of Toronto
Ms. Coll. 136, Box 67, November 1985.

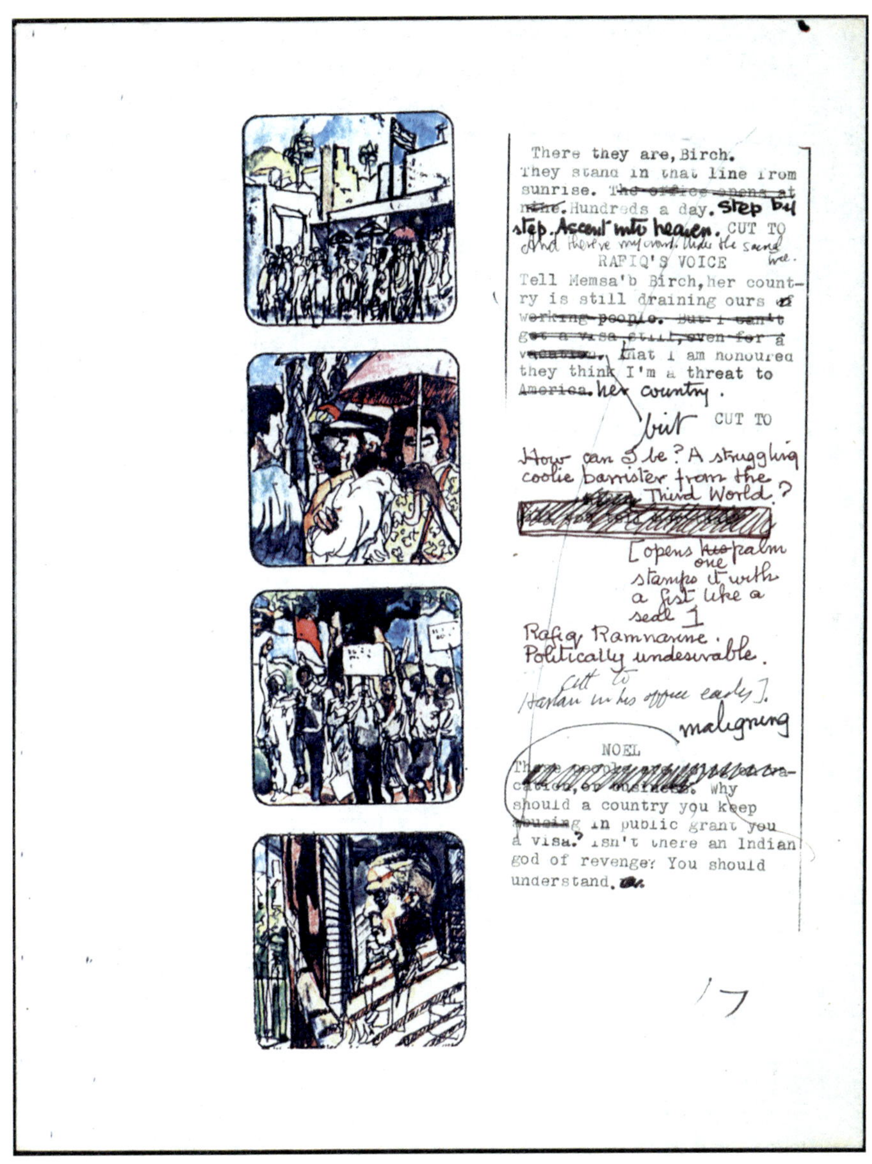

Storyboard from "To Die for Grenada" or "Monos".
The Thomas Fisher Library, University of Toronto
Ms. Coll. 136, Box 67, November 1985.

Apocalypse Now, which according to one of the comments included with the draft, Walcott saw as a film that aestheticizes war. His script is then conceived as a film that uses memory, but that also explores the idea of film as a form of false remembering, as in Jean Baudrillard's theorising of film as a "demonic image".[2] Everything that happens in Grenada is "insulted" and "reduced" by its appearance on television (p. 4). He is suggesting that televisual images both trivialise and create false ideas.

But the film script is also about colour and privilege:

> The short ladder of West Indian privilege is still complexion, in which the lowest rung is black. That was a moral fable of my mother's, in which a black man boasted of his achievement by crowing, 'I have reached Olympus and kicked down the ladder.' So that those who wanted to climb, his own people at the bottom, had nothing to hold [...] In this part of the world, revolution cannot be separated from race (p. 5).

The revolution has, for Walcott, changed nothing since "there was always the matter of complexion [...] and even after the revolution, the Self-contempt of racial distinctions remains the real challenge, more than economics".

The message of this monologue or preamble (it is unclear) is that history returns, because the Caribbean mind has been indoctrinated, so that those who have left the islands and then return to them, see through hallucinations. So that:

> what is important in these ex-colonies, those immediate successors of slavery, is where does this corruption blind itself again, so that again, it does not see properly in the darkness, but only senses figures and numbers like phantoms, and begins that distance that talks no differently from the imperial voice, about 'the people'. 'The people' and 'the natives'. Same thing, but different (p. 13).

The script is here talking about the value of revolution and the sense that since nothing changes, Bishop's idealism must also be seen as suspect, and even deeply cynical. Bishop, despite his idealism, is another corrupt being. For Walcott, at this point, slavery "is in our blood, our bones" (p. 19).

Film as an art form is then both a curse and a form of resistance. It has power, exemplified for Walcott by Coppola's *Apocalypse Now*, which "is saying that there is no difference between the fouled ecstasy of those American helicopters scything destruction after them like the Valkyries, and the Nazi ecstasy of Aryan wrath." What Walcott sees in this iconic sequence from the 1979 film is the power of sound and visual, in opposition, to generate, on the one hand, a sense of the horror of the Vietnam war as the soldiers bomb a village, but also simultaneously to give the experience of the joyous evil that permeates the film and that we share. He says, "'Apocalypse Now' celebrates what it condemns; it tempts itself closer and closer into the magnetic thrill of the horror. We do not look away" (n.p.). It achieves this enthralment through its audiovisual aesthetics.

The crux lies in what the artist now represents. For Walcott, here the artist has lost his conscience and his idea of truth. In this, the artist is at one with the politician. Therein lies the evil and the power of the cinematic. In the film script "To Die for Grenada", Walcott meditates throughout on the power of film, whether as cinema or as television. Film makes us feel without allowing us to think for ourselves. This, then, may be the point of the opening shot which is a close-up of sheep moving across the frame. That one version of the opening of "To Die for Grenada" is set in Greece in 1982 is one way of demonstrating in 1988, two years before the publication of *Omeros*, that history returns and that there are deep interconnections between Greece and the Caribbean. Here the action in Greece – unlike its use in *Omeros* – is in the recent past and aids in enabling the viewer to see the events of Grenada in a different light. The Grenada invasion is viewed as no isolated or laudable action, but rather the nation is seen to be caught in a web of events calculated and plotted by external forces. The reference to Greece also underlines the importance of myth-making and the function of the artist in this enterprise as a true revolutionary. For "revolutions cannot be imported, no matter how much one terrain resembles another" (p. 24).Walcott describes the similarity of the images of Grenada revolution to another film, Roger Spottiswoode's *Under Fire* (1983). This was a political thriller set in the last days of the Nicaraguan dictator, General Somoza. It was criticised in some quarters for using a real bloody war as the backdrop for an entertainment feature about American newsmen. The sense of war as television is doubly reiterated: what Walcott sees in Grenada are mirror images of films he has seen before.

Despite the obscurity of the argument and the theme, this work provides an interesting glimpse at Walcott's film sources and techniques. He uses techniques such as parallelism and superimposition, both of which he transfers into *Omeros*. But the most important sequence for my argument is in the almost direct transposition of tone of one of the most famous scenes in cinema, the Odessa steps sequence from *The Battleship Potemkin* (1925). The use of this sequence signifies the revolutionary techniques of montage, but these are also techniques for generating intense revulsion through oppositional movement and the emotional play on the body and mind of the viewer. Eisenstein's analysis of *Potemkin* in *Nonindifferent Nature* is of movement and the calculation of rhythm that leads to intense *pathos*:

> Let us do this in terms of *movement*.
>
> First, there are the *close-ups* of the figures rushing chaotically, then the *long-shots* of the figures rushing chaotically.

> Then the chaotic movement passes over into the stamping of soldiers' feet rhythmically descending the steps.
>
> The tempo quickens. The rhythm grows.
>
> And now the increasing rush of movement *downward* is suddenly reversed upward, the *dizzy* movement of the masses downward passes into the *slow, solemn* movement upward of the solitary figure of the mother with her dead child.
>
> The masses. Dizziness. Downward.
>
> And suddenly:
>
> A solitary figure. In triumphant slowness. Upward.
>
> But only for a moment. And again a reverse leap to the movement downward.
>
> The rhythm grows. The tempo quickens.
>
> And suddenly the tempo of the *flight of the crowd jumps* into the next stage of fast movement – to the *rolling* baby carriage. It rushes with the idea of rolling down into the next dimension – *from rolling understood "figuratively" to actually physically rolling.* This is not only a different state of *tempo*. This is also a leap in the *method of illustration* from the figurative to the physical, which occurs within a presentation of rolling movement.
>
> Close-ups leap to *long-shots*.
>
> Chaotic movement (of the masses) to *rhythmic movement* (of the soldiers).
>
> One aspect of the speed of movement (people rushing) – to the next stage of that same theme of fast movement (the rolling baby carriage).
>
> Movement *downward* – to movement *upward*.
>
> *Many* volleys of *many* guns – to one shot from one muzzle of the battleship.
>
> Step by step – a leap from dimension to dimension. A leap from quality to quality. So that in the last analysis it is no longer a single episode (the carriage) but *the entire method of the exposition* of a whole event also completes its leap. The narrative of exposition as well as the *roaring (jumping) lions* is hurled into a figurative method of construction. Visual rhythmic prose seems to jump over into visual poetic speech.[3]

This may be compared to *Die for Grenada* (p. 94) where Walcott directs:

> Ext: Grenada – Day
> THE TV SCREEN – CLOSE UP, PULL BACK, THEN WIDEN:
>
> Soundlessly, at first, then loudly, then with modulated volume, scores of screaming, terrified GRENADIANS are running downhill from the walls of a fort. SCHOOL-CHILDREN, in uniform, with their TEACHERS, including TWO NUNS in white, trying to organise them in the panic. SOME OF THE SCHOOLCHILDREN stumble, fall. OTHERS are heading in the wrong direction, that is towards:
>
> CUT TO:
>
> 153.
>
> EXT: SAME – DAY
>
> An armoured carrier with its swivelling cannon. The cannon fires above the heads of the CROWD. A LARGE BLACK WOMAN, carrying a banner marked RELEASE MAURICE, suddenly stops, gasps, leisurely

examines a wound in her stomach, then wobbles slowly, amazed, to the ground. She picks up her eyeglasses, holds them up.

CUT TO

154.

CLOSE UP – SANDRA's FACE
No sound

Noel (VO)

The sound ("To Die for Grenada", p. 94)

This mimics the sequence from *Potemkin* which follows the slow development of emotion-filled terror where the woman with the child moves upward towards the mounting feet of the soldiers and in reverse montage and tempo, we see the mass of people running. The build-up of tempo here is perhaps the most quoted in cinema and is the image which encapsulates through the close-up that intensification of experience, and that has been used by painters since its production. This use includes several iconic paintings by Francis Bacon who used the image of the woman with pince-nez. Here Walcott chooses this particular image of the schoolteacher used by Bacon and the smashed eyeglass, and emulates the beat of the montage sequence to elicit a response that is meant to be dramatic and heartrending.

He tentatively uses the oppositional play of sound versus silence, as in the close-up with no sound, versus the voice-over with sound. Sandra's face in close-up in *To Die for Grenada* mirrors the horror transmitted in *Potemkin*. The concentrated shot of the eyeglass held up by a black woman as she dies in slow motion provides the visceral effect of movement that fills both the viewer on television (Sandra) and the audience who might view Walcott's work. The two-shot also provides the mechanism for a new leap of dramatic emotion. The film within the film acts as a doubling that both distils and deepens the significance of what is happening on screen. This is war as a simulation of a simulation, emphasised in the direction, "TV SCREEN – DRAW IN, THEN WIDEN". Its unreality shows the ludicrous waste and the senselessness of the American invasion as a war played out in the media.

This scene is transferred to *Omeros* at the moment of Hector's death. The close-up as fragment becomes an important element for this purpose and is used to make the viewer/audience connect at a deep level with the action. The close-up has several functions here. It simulates the photograph and serves to rivet the gaze of the viewer. The object distils the force of the idea through synecdoche and as a partial and disoriented image forces a distillation of the experience. Inner emotion and outer reality are made to merge, adding several dimensions to the viewed object.

The close-up can be used as a space of conflict in terms of juxtaposition between, say, fluid movement and the fixed frame itself. Its particularisation gives psychological intensity to one fragment and can oppose this particular to the more general idea or surface. The close-up forces the image/idea onto the body-sensation of the audience, so crowding the space of seeing that there is room for nothing else, and acts here as a kind of "deformation" that attempts a similar impact to that of the montage films of the classical masters. The malleability of the object (its plasticity), enables an injection of tonality and emotional resonance that is in excess of the still shot, and as a result, the object (image) becomes both fixed and fluid since the still shot or fragment is made to participate in a moving line of the film.

The close-up

Colin Gardner makes a most pointed statement about the applicability of Eisenstein's theories to Deleuze in his 2012 work, *Beckett, Deleuze and The Televisual Event. Peephole Art*:

> If we reread *Cinema 1*'s movement-image in light of *Cinema 2*'s time-image, we find the latter always already immanent in the former (we might re-read Eisenstein, for example, less in terms of the dialectical shock *across* images and their intervals, and more in terms of the immanence of the unrepresentable that lies hidden *between* them, in their interstices). This is the time of the Deleuzian event itself, for like future and past time, events don't exist in physical form but are attributed to incorporeals as happenings or becomings which exist in the time of Aion – a time not yet here and time only just past – the 'split' moment that evades the fixed present.[4]

One way of reading this comment is to say that the event is that moment when the enthralling present leaps over into a state of becoming, through a mechanically achieved process. This process, for example, occurs through the use of superimposition, in that one image is placed on top of the other, giving a sense of simultaneous happening. The two images in their combination become more than past or present since they now exist in a shared time that is fluid or "unfixed". This is the time of the in-between and is that time that Walcott attributes to art. Art, in this case poetry or drama and film, through the use of a lesson learnt from montage theory, engages in the process of becoming more than past or present. It creates an event that is frequently conceived of as a moment of high intensity.

In the poem *Omeros*, the close-up is used at the climactic sequence of Hector's death:

> Cut to a leopard galloping on a dry plain
> across Serengeti, Cut to the spraying fans
> drummed by a riderless stallion, its wild mane

> scaring the Scamander. Cut to a woman's hands
> clenched towards her mouth with no sound. Cut to the wheel
> of a chariot's spiked hubcap. Cut to the face
>
> of his muscling jaw, then flashback to Achille
> hurling a red tin and a cutlass. Next, a vase
> with a girl's hoarse whisper echoing "Omeros,"
>
> as in a conch-shell. Cut to a shield of silver
> rolling like a hubcap. (*Omeros*, p. 230)

Each "cut" here denotes a close-up. Each is a moment of intensification, recalling other such moments, as in the close-up of "Cut to a woman's hands/ clenched towards her mouth with no sound", which references Edvard Munch's expressionist painting, *The Scream* (1893). The montage sequence also points to significant moments of colonial and neocolonial history and the effects of such history. Its existence as a simulation of a film sequence allows the simultaneous existence of key evidence of the plunder of the land by the destructive forces of capitalism, materialistic greed and neo-colonialism through tourism, perceived as a kind of death. Serengeti is a famous national park in Tanzania and an international tourist resort as is the Scamander in Tasmania and their inclusion here points to the repetition of events that reinforce the lines "rewind in slow motion" (p. 230) and the exploitation of the natural world. This further suggests the death of civilisations, as in Troy and Africa. Serengeti is also a spectacle, and something to be viewed in the same way that one views a film, for entertainment. The sequence also references the controversial removal of the resident Maasai people and their relocation to the Ngorongoro Conservation Area in 1959, ostensibly to preserve wildlife. Scamander is a holiday resort situated in Tasmania between St Helen's and St Mary's, so that it references St Lucia and also suggests the removal of indigenous peoples when virtually the entire native Tasmanian population was exterminated by white settler troops in the genocidal "Black War" of 1828-1830, a bloody echo of the slaughter of the Trojan wars.

The various shots generate a silent scream, again signifying that the conflict of shots of different times and places has led to a system of reverberations that are now seen to flow through time, uniting past and present. Death, whether imagined or real, becomes a bridge between the real and the unreal and between the visible and the unknowable. The poet's own imagined death now subsumes all other deaths he has created into a theory of the poetic; death becomes a loss of self, submergence into the void, the dark reaches of the human unconscious. Death confronts and causes terror and it is this fear that, as a tremor in the psyche, cracks the surface of the visible world and allows the imagination through sustained effort to glimpse for a moment a truth beyond words. Poetry becomes a leap beyond "death" that can now see the interior depths of a people and the shaping effect of their past and present histories.

Hector's burial scene parallels the submergence into the sea of the poet's own memory before the act of poetry can be completed. Hector's death and burial and Maud's death and burial leave their partners with a deepened understanding of the rituals and life of the island. In the same way, the poetic journey, which has been a submergence into the sea of Antillean history, has left the poet with a new humility, and a stillness and acceptance. It is a loss of self and ego before the transfiguring flame of poetry and pain (signified in the name of Hector's Comet). The submergence of the self into the opening fissures of time leads to a new birth and baptism.

Baptism and rebirth evolve from an acceptance of difference and disparateness. The harmonic unity which the poem seeks is evoked in the carnival ritual, which is preluded by an extended image of Helen's pregnant stomach, which seemed to Achille:

> to bear not only the curved child sailing in her
> but Hector's mound, and her hoarse, labouring rhythm
>
> was a delivering wave. There, in miniature,
> the world was globed like a fruit, since its texture is
> both acid and sweet like a golden *pomme-Cythère*,
>
> the apple of Venus, and the *Ville de Paris*
> that he had dived for once, in search of a treasure
> that was kneeling right there, that had always been his. (*Omeros,* p. 275)

The curved stomach becomes simultaneously the mound of the grave and the womb that protects new life. Despite the paternalistic overtones of this image and the poet's representation of Helen, she nonetheless appears as the powerful image of contradiction that *Omeros* has sought to introduce. Helen carries within her the essential contradictory nature of human existence: its pain and its joy. The deliverance of mankind is to be found in the simple truth of this contradiction: that the human body carries within itself the seed of its continued existence and its death. This "simple" fact leads to an acceptance of the truth of human power, that home is always somehow within us and that our many journeys in search of that home and that becoming lead to an acceptance of the "bitter-sweet" reality of the self.

The carnival dance extends the impact of the other synthesizing movements of Book Six. The frenzy of the dance mirrors the apocalyptic force of the hurricane. The hurricane as both destruction and benediction merges Christian and Pagan mythologies and their shared belief in the organic necessity of death as a passageway to new life. This Christian/Pagan syncretism is enacted in the possession rite of the Pocomania cult, which is woven into the carnival dance. The apocalyptic force of this ritual, perceived by Brathwaite as emitting from the residual spaces, such as the "rusty holes of our shacks", which exist at the cross roads of culture and through which the god enters and possesses the soul of the dancer,[5] extends the ideas of death and resurrection which the whole of Book Six of *Omeros* repeats insistently.

The darkness of the land after the hurricane is equated with the darkness of the netherworld into which the soul descends. This submerging movement opens the way for the rain from which a fresh land and a fresh people, or a freshness of spirit, can surface. Time as cycle is merged with a return to primordial perception in which the senses are synthesized and which acknowledges the "Janus face" of both poet and culture:

> Ah, twin-headed January, seeing either tense:
> a past, they assured us, born in degradation,
> and a present that lifted us up with the wind's
>
> noise in the breadfruit leaves with such an elation
> that it contradicts what is past! The cannonballs
> of rotting breadfruit from the Battle of the Saints,
>
> the asterisks of bulletholes in the brick walls
> of the redoubt. I lived there with every sense.
> I smelt with my eyes, I could see with my nostrils.
> (*Omeros*, pp. 223-224)

Walcott here seeks to create an impact on all the senses; an impact equivalent to that caused by film and by Trinidad carnival.

The carnivalesque enables a use of the burlesque and reminds us that Bakhtin and Eisenstein both noted a relationship between laughter, the circus and the close-up of film. The circus led Eisenstein to his theorisation of what he called "the attraction".[6] The attraction was "*any aggressive moment in theatre, i.e. any element of it that subjects the audience to emotional or psychological influence, verified by experience and mathematically calculated to produce specific emotional shocks in the spectator in their correct order within the whole* [the italics belong to Eisenstein]."[7] This calculated impact, as it became increasingly nuanced and located in film montage, also increasingly became aligned to the close-up.

For Bakhtin, the circus was a direct descendant of the carnival.[8] Both lead to descriptions of qualities to be found in the carnivalesque. According to Bakhtin, the carnivalesque enables the destruction of "hierarchical" distancing through laughter:

> Laughter has the remarkable power of making an object come up close, of drawing it into a zone of crude contact where one can finger it familiarly on all sides, turn it upside down, inside out, peer at it from above and

> below, break open its external shell, look into its center, doubt it, take it apart, dismember it, lay it bare and expose it, examine it freely and experiment with it.[9]

It does the work of the film close-up. In other words, the close-up has a potential for affect that is already seen within laughter and the grotesque and in their use in the oral traditions of Europe and the Caribbean. Film-makers such as Eisenstein deduced that film brings the traditions of orality and performance to a new power. The manipulation of a fragment can have an impact similar to and beyond that of the traditions that Walcott notes in his remembrance of Sidon, his story-telling aunt, for example.[10]

The carnival ritual used in *Omeros* is a less elaborate version of the Trinidadian festival and more apt in this context because the event is held at Christmas time. The concept of renewal is therefore implicit in the synchronous act of the masquerade, which allows the past to co-exist in the present and through this, to engage in a process of renewal.

The light of the dawn that begins the movement to synthesis quickens the senses so that each distinct smell, each colour and sound can be savoured (pp. 221-223). It is that rejuvenating freshness when the earth renews itself and as a "fresh people" Antilleans participate in this renewal. The carnival incorporates within itself, in its sensuous impact, all the various sense-lines of the poem. Achille, having washed himself in preparation for the masquerade, smells "like a flower", in antithesis to the flower which stank on Philoctete's heel. He is garbed in bright colours which have, in the previous chapters, in their variegated hues, become associated with conflicting ideas: the contradictions of life and history. These colours together have built up a tonal or colour line that is part of the unifying, transforming pattern of the whole. The red for example, which has accumulated the meaning of red Indian, flame, leaves of autumn, rage and Hector's "Comet", and therefore death, is changed into the flashing lights of the mirrors which adorn the dress Achille wears. Changed too is the yellow of the butterfly wings which has now accrued the meaning of the golden *pomme-Cythère* and the dream of gold. The predominant tones/notes of white and black frame the poem as in a photograph and become linked to the theme of a black/white racial dichotomy. By the end of the poem, the white has become associated with the white whale and the white snow, which is also the white obliteration or death administered by white settlers. It has become attuned to the white light, which is affirmative and akin to the white foam of the sea. Through the apparatus of sense, the various contradictions appear as reversals. They become part of that movement through which the synthesis, which is also that leap to change, can occur.

Endnotes

1. Derek Walcott, "To Die for Grenada", Ms COLL 136, Boxes 38-42 & 67,Thomas Fisher Rare Book Library Ms. "To Die for Grenada", Ms. dated 1987.
2. Jean Baudrillard, *The Evil Demon of Images* (Sydney: Power Institute Publications, 1987).
3. Sergei Eisenstein, *Nonindifferent Nature. Film and the Structure of Things*, ed. and trans. Herbert Marshall (Cambridge: Cambridge University Press, 21987), p. 31.
4. Colin Gardner, *Beckett, Deleuze and the Televisual Event. Peephole Art* (London: Palgrave Macmillan, 2012), pp. 30-31.
5. Edward Kamau Brathwaite, *Islands* (London: Oxford University Press, 1969), p. 32. Thereafter in *The Arrivants* (London: Oxford University Press, 1981).
6. Sergei Eisenstein's "The Montage of Attractions" was first published in the magazine *Lef*, no. 3 (June-July) in 1923, on pages 70-71, 74-75.
7. Sergei Eisenstein, "The Montage of Attractions", *S.M. Eisenstein, Writings*, p. 34.
8. Mikhail Bakhtin, *Problems of Dostoevsky's Poetics*, ed. and trans. Caryl Emerson (Minneapolis: University of Minnesota, 1984), p. 31.
9. Mikhail Bakhtin, *The Dialogic Imagination*, p. 23.
10. Derek Walcott, "Animals, Elemental Tales and the Theatre", MS Coll 136, Box 1, Folder 1,Thomas Fisher Rare Book Library.

CHAPTER 7

THE RIG AND OMEROS AS FILM

The Rig was filmed and produced by Banyan for Gayelle and televised in 1984. It was originally conceived as a television series, but became a single film. Despite its flaws, it introduces a key concern in Walcott's work, and that is the building of a rhythmic line. This may seem rather obvious for a poet, but his concern in this film is with the construction of a filmic rhythm through which a specific and often single idea is projected through multiple means and for maximum impact. This entails the building of a tendentious line and the careful calculation of the beat of each shot, as well as the pauses and transitions. How long can one shot endure? How effective would the placing of one image immediately after another be in shaping an immediate idea? Given the fact that film time appears in the viewing of a film to be far longer than ordinary time, what should be left out? The question of editing is paramount. I have referred to the creation of a monistic ensemble, which is evident in *Omeros* the poem and in *Steel*. *The Rig* demonstrates the evolution of the idea of feet providing the beat, which is such an important consideration in *Omeros*.

Building a Rhythmic Line

The Rig uses steelband music to create a sense of the Caribbean and in particular Trinidad. It also uses dance, both as a recurring unifying motif and as a symbol of indigenous culture. The dance is initially intercut with the movement of the car as the film opens, and here Walcott engages in a careful construction of sound and image in movement, using the camera as a directorial device. The film therefore opens with a successful sequence of shots achieving a rhythm that keeps the camera in orchestrated union with the sound and the movement of objects, as the movement rhymes with the beat of the shot as the camera cuts in and out of the action. The dancers are therefore dancing both to the beat of the steel pan and to the beat of the camera. The intercutting movement of dance with the movement of the car sets up an immediate

Photograph on the set of *The Rig*
Photograph by and courtesy of Bruce Paddington

dichotomy between the fears that Laurie has of losing her dancers to the interests of money, and the developing narrative, which is about the encroachment of big capitalist interests.

The Rig is a complicated film, which has a primary story line of the threat to indigenous culture by growing money interests that are fuelled by the oil economy and the increasing wealth in Trinidad. It has many other plot lines, however, including the desire to make reparation by a white creole descendant, Phillipe, who attempts to write a thesis on the profits of the slave trade, which he abandons. Phillipe, we discover towards the end, is an undercover agent for the oil company and protects their interests, in particular as there is a fear of a plot to destroy an oil rig. He becomes involved with the passionate folk dancer, Laurie. The film is also about leaving Trinidad. *The Rig* was filmed in Mayaro and this allows for beautiful shots of sea and landscape.

The film makes constant use of intercutting, often using quick cutting montage which serves to create a series of opposing movements and furthers the main plots. The destruction of an idea of culture by materialist interests, for example, is found in the shot of the hovel or small house and the quick cut to the palatial mansion. Money is talking in Trinidad. The beauty of the landscape is frequently paralleled to the seascape, but the natural environment is shown as opposite to the tubular steel fabrications of South City, in a truly effective travelling shot. The film also uses circus techniques to win the attention of the audience as in Phillipe's monkey play when he is wooing Laurie, which is copied in the boys diving like monkeys in *Omeros*. The bele dance is given some prominence and is opposed to the sensual dancing, signifying the prostitution of culture, of those who have been wooed and won by Steve, Laurie's former boyfriend.

These are effective techniques and later Walcott introduces this kind of intercutting and syncopation into *Omeros* and *Steel* and in a more sophisticated manner into *The Prodigal* and *White Egrets*. The action is intensified and is, in this sense, effective. The same is not true of many other scenes including the final scenes, where the action slows and the film becomes uninteresting.

Despite the various successful film techniques, which also include Caribbean symbolism as in the use of the corbeaux (by now a hackneyed image of the predator), who circle and are filmed in a long shot, indicating that the vultures are out and circling, the film does not hold the viewer's interest to the end. The diminution of tension is seen most particularly in the scene where the actors congregate to view the body of "the fella with the big boat", who is found dead on the beach. The body is never shown and there is little psychological build up. Everyone looks. Nothing happens. This represents the core of the problem, since what *The Rig* lacks is *sustained* dramatic tension. The pauses are often too long. The speech is at times too measured. The director too often tries for poetic, rather than filmic resolutions.

One particular sequence, which includes the love scene, seems to suggest that Walcott and his crew were aware of the need to build up the line of high tension. But the beat is wrong. We have what is in effect a caesura where idyllic scenes are privileged, and a romantic setting created by the camera. The couple, Phillipe and Laurie, swim, play on the beach, and there is a cut to the shack, and a close up of the jeep. And then the words, "I love you", which is the moment to which the line has been building. But the tempo is wrong. Then the rhythm quickens, with an increase in the pitch and volume of the music in an oppositional movement, which suggests that the moment of quiet has gone, perhaps forever. The idea here is that peace and romance have been destroyed by Phillipe's involvement in an undercover operation relating to the oil rig. The scene cuts to Phillipe in a crowd and the music becomes jarring and discordant. This works in conveying the idea, but as the action becomes more static, interest wavers. *The Rig* then presents the problems of construction where some things work and others do not. There is an obvious knowledge basis, but little experience, in terms of implementing consistency and timing.

There are also technical problems, such as poor sound and colour correction. Sometimes the cinematography is not as good as it should be. But what works, in terms of film technique, Walcott takes into his poetry and drama. In particular, he uses syncopated sound and image, as well as the use of quick-cutting montage and the collision of land and sea, as well as the potency of the movement of the body. *Omeros* and *White Egrets* demonstrate that after *The Rig*, he thought through and researched the matter carefully.

There are multiple themes in *The Rig*, which we also find in both *Steel* and *Omeros*. In *The Rig* these include the battle of local culture for financial support and survival in the face of selfish interests, symbolised by the lawyer and in particular Laurie's former boyfriend, Steve, who represents corruption. There is also the theme of exile or impending departure, again through Laurie, who is thinking of emigrating to the big city, and Phillipe who has been abroad and has just returned after failing his thesis, which he ceremoniously tears and scatters in the sea, in a move echoed by Laurie at the end when she tears up her visa. There is the theme of paralysis, evident in the line, "We born blight". There is also the theme of betrayal and entrapment introduced by Sancho, who owes Steve Fisher "plenty money", and who says, "He trap me, Mr Phillipe. He trap me". There is the theme of physical movement figured through dance. As with so many of Walcott's stage plays and other scripts, including, in particular, the dynamism and energy of *The Joker of Seville*, the movement of the female body helps to carry the action. The dancers are a repeated motif throughout the film and this becomes one of the most effective devices throughout.

In the 1995 version of the film script for *Omeros*, which is one of several versions, Walcott experiments with several of the structural processes that we see in *The Rig* and that he sought to introduce through simulation of effects in the epic poem. The moment of intense experience is often marked by the use of a close-up. In this 1995 film script[1] Walcott rewrites the epic poem and concentrates much of the action into parallel narratives: the narrator's writing of a poem and Plunkett's writing of a history of St Lucia; the battle between Hector and Achille, which is superimposed on to Achille's return to Africa and slaying of a slaver; the story of Helen's self assertiveness and pregnancy; and Ma Kilman's trek into the forest and curing of Philoctete.

Initially Walcott in his writing of this film version began by focusing on the fishermen and village life. The story boards begin with a montage of key characters, Achille and Helen, then Philoctete with his wound and Ma Kilman (see illustration on page 105). The storyboards are dated 1985?-86 by the Thomas Fisher Rare Book Library. This suggests that the film conceptualisation predated the poem, *Omeros*. The first two pages of what seems to be the final version of the film script, dated 1995, create intense soundscapes and pan over the land in an establishing shot that takes in the pitons, the alleys and the mountains, all of which assume figurative and spiritual dimensions. The initial setting is the wharf and the date is given as 1938. A reverse shot of the town gives the point of view of the coaling ship and a montage cut separates this tourist's view from a close-up of black women's feet, crusted with dust, accompanied by the syncopated beat of a drummer and the sound of a chant as they ascend the gangway. The chant at this point "sometimes breaks off from exhaustion." The film within its first minutes has condensed the history of the Antilles, and crafted a ritual, forged through the use of sound, that evokes personal, national and cultural history. These shots or fragments of memory are bound together in movement. A "montage of moving, ascending feet" completes the shot. "Faces calmly straining under the weight. Descending feet. Their rhythm." The montage sequence here, then, would go like this: feet in movement, cut to faces, cut to feet. Then close up of faces. Close up of descending feet.

The rhythm refers to the beat of the shot, which, as in an early work of classical cinema such as *Symphony of a City*[2] uses rhythmic montage, thus synchronising that beat with the movement of the feet. But Walcott's script also includes smell or the simulation of smell, and while film cannot (yet) include scent, the narrator supplies the memory: "I remember the sharp smell of her sweat, the smell of the sea around the market, the sweet feeling that came over me, the women climbing the hill." Laura Marks concludes that the sense of smell, as well as the haptic, are important constituents of what she calls "intercultural cinema", or a cinema that emerges from filmmakers for whom the past is an empty hole or for whom there are only "ghosts of stories".[3]

Memory for migrant peoples, such as those who are descendants of the enslaved, becomes secreted into the body as smell and touch. Cinema seeks to release these memories through simulations. This is a potent idea in terms of how we view *Omeros* with its valorisation of all the senses and the privileging of smell in relation to Helen. In the film script, Helen bends to kiss the young boy through whose eyes this memory is being recounted. She does this as the narrator speaks, then, turns, smiles and departs. The point of view here is apparently that of the narrator who is a small boy, again reinforcing the fact that this is a memory, and a montage that brings the past into the space of the present. But it also points to the fact that it is a memory viewed from the perspective of an adult who is looking at himself in the past. It is therefore very much a reconstructed memory, but one that is ignited by sensuous images.

Montage editing acts here in the same way as memory, in that it breaks up the action into successive parts which are then collapsed into a unified whole by the mind's leap "to a conclusion".[4] These fragments are brought to the surface by a moment of recall that is of the body. The body is therefore the vehicle for undoing the fossilization of thought and allowing thought as a process of becoming to emerge.

Sound Systems

Memory is, in one of its manifestations, located in sound systems. We see the progression of this idea in "Cul de Sac Valley" of *The Arkansas Testament*.[5] Here, the "rivulets gravel" where the "light gutturals begin" (AT, p.10) provides the opening movement to the meditation on language unfurling itself and becoming repossessed. The harshness of sound here suggests the rawness of sound and the construction of Caribbean speech/dialect, and is achieved through end rhyme, consonantal sound and staccato rhythm. These approximate to the "devil-talk" of carnival "djab-djab" (diable).

This movement in sound leads to that inclusive stanza which links folk language, loss, memory and self-acceptance with sight and visibility:

> Like the lost idea
> of the visible soul
> still kindled here
> on illiterate soil ("Cul de Sac Valley", *Arkansas Testament*, pp. 10-11)

The "visible soul" is fused with the ghost of memory already contained in the photographic image of *Another Life*. But it is now, within the frame of this poem, and in the context of "The Lighthouse", given multiple meanings and accrues various associations, including the importance of visibility/invisibility; the association of thought with sight; illiteracy with a lack of soul and as a justification for genocide and subjugation, among other themes.[6]

Walcott's return to the "here" of St. Lucia is, as Edward Baugh has observed, more complex than it appears and in a "crucial sense, shows that 'here' is always 'there'. [...] The very act of defining it distances it"[7] and causes him to envision the landscape and people of home, as if in a hallucination, as if spectres. The images which accumulate are formed through a cinematic use of *pars pro toto*: close ups of "the minute hand of the luminous dial", a squint; a "hook of an eyebrow", and black hands; then there are the dismembered voices: a girl's laughter; a street lamp's echoes; "I laughed at the voice." Together these create an effect of a fractured reality. Time has created a distance, as has space. Memory growing dim, can romanticize, as in "The Light of the World", but it cannot make these images concrete.

But the use of fragmentation here is also the beginning of a new level of imagining or a pause before a leap occurs. The fragments that are released because of Walcott's identification with the black man of America will become the fragments that are edited together in montage to form the moving lines of *Omeros*.

The people of St. Lucia in *Arkansas Testament*, who have now become nostalgic echoes in the poet's mind, become associated in a significant way with the "invisible" black American. Through the hidden reference to Ralph Ellison's *Invisible Man*, (which becomes more pronounced as the work progresses), the word "visible" introduces the twin themes of *Arkansas Testament.* These themes are: Walcott's new identification with the plight of Black America and his own growing frustration at his inability to represent his people. This latter idea is given passionate expression in *Midsummer* where, again, the recognition of the role and function of the artist breeds a kind of despair:[8]

> Spectres multiply with age, the peopled head
> is crossed by impatient characters, the ears clamped shut;
> behind them I hear the actors mutter and shout –
> the lit stage is empty, the set prepared,
> and I cannot find the key to let them out. (*Midsummer*, XIII, p. 23.)

"The tongue they speak/ in, but cannot write" (*Arkansas Testament*, p. 10) gives the poet a paternalistic right to inscribe and speak for them. As Baugh has observed, Walcott tends to "embalm" the folk in the amber of nostalgia or pity.[9] "Cul de Sac Valley" and *Arkansas Testament*, as a whole, are seminal works because Walcott, in the act of "transfixing" and framing, steps outside the boundaries of his own art and looks at himself looking in. His characters can hiss:

> *What you wish*

from us will never be,
your words is English,
is a different tree. (*Arkansas Testament*, p. 10)

This, as an assertive voice, has already begun to "saw" the silence "in half".

This silence of those whose "leaves" are "unread" because they speak a language that they cannot write, becomes equated with the stitched silence of a people who have been blinded by the language of standard English taught by an imperial power through a colonial education. It "blinds" "like a page/ of glare on the road" (AT, p. 11). Illiteracy and the education and language of imperialism all create an inability to represent the self and lead to a "forced poetics" and what both Glissant and Brathwaite have called "the self in maroonage". The petrifying effect of the colonial education system is associated with the tears of the girl whose pain is a dawning awareness of her "difference"; the self-image of those blinded to their own beauty whose racial features are seen to be ugly in the light of a "superior" aesthetic or idea of beauty. The mother's words link the girl's physical being to a natural world; a world created in God's image: "Her swift hands/ plait the rivulet's braid."

This beauty of the natural "raw" world allows Walcott to suggest an affirmative movement through language. The "inner silence along/ a red track the forest/ swallows like a tongue" is not the silence of obliteration, but in its movement (both "swallows" and "track" signify active states) connotes an internalized, mole-like self-preservation similar to the withdrawal of the maroons of Jamaica or the Amerindians of Guyana who either fled to the hills or the bowels of the interior. The inner journey to the forest is, as speech (tongue), an index of the path which memory has taken. It is, in effect, the "lost" idea that is memory, and which is encapsulated in the very harshness of the sounds of Antillean rhythms, in its "gravelly" and "guttural" music. Language, and sound as part of that language, becomes both the index and passage through which memory can be retrieved and the idea of self, which is self-image, made visible.

The poet's "memory is small" (p.13); the girl's memory is silent, but internalized. She therefore becomes the means through which the poet, who wishes to name through inscription, can extend the boundaries of his own psychic recall. He crafts the frame of consonants which "scroll/ off my shaving plane" (p. 9), and which will contain "the black vowel barking" (p. 10). This signifies the mongrel nature of art and anticipates the resolution of this idea in the black mongrel at the close of *Tiepolo's Hound*. The girl therefore becomes the vowel in the valley's mouth, that sound which deepens the poet's understanding of himself, though she has no true voice of her own. She sounds his need to belong, retrieves the forgotten memory of his origins and the idea of himself. But in "Cul de Sac Valley" that girl remains virtually invisible, until she becomes the figure who "enters the stanza" and who "climbs straight/ up the steps of this verse"(p.14), though like the village, she remains a "closed text". This sense of estrangement is also there in his encounter with seen but scarcely knowable black women in "Oceana Nox", one of those women described in the line: "and her white disk moves like a camera's lens/ along the ebony of a high-boned cheek" (*AT*, p. 54). The woman's romanticised image in "The Light of the World" is an even more significant one. She actualizes the gulf that exists between the poet and people. She is an imagined lover and her presence marks a distance that makes that love intense, but it is a distance that will never be transcended.

The idea of voicelessness is repeated in different ways in *Omeros*. Plunkett's lust for Helen, which remains at a level of an illusion, leads him to speak for Helen and to seek to construct a history for her. This is given considerable emphasis in the 1995 film script.

Walcott gives the following lines to Plunkett in this script and this might serve as a clarification of his position on time, memory and history and what his later works seek to do.

> PLUNKETT
> It's a demonstration of coincidences.
> And it's not reincarnation, that's too naïve.
> ("Omeros", 1995 film script, p. 120).

Plunkett is speaking to his wife Maud, and explaining that history is "prophetic". His reading of Helen's history is that the Helen fought for in the Battle of the Saints is the same as the Helen of Paris and her appearance is a sign of return. This refers to the naval battle of 1782 between the British and the French, that resulted in the eventual handover of the island to Britain. For its beauty, St. Lucia was known as the "Helen of the West Indies". So Helen is an "incarnation" of a beauty and a battle that has existed and been repeated several times before. The continuing dialogue between Plunkett and the narrator in the film script gives weight to Plunkett's words.

Simultaneity

In the film script "Omeros", Walcott introduces the history of Hector, Achille and Helen through successive montage sequences that make time fluid, and give concrete expression to his concept of simultaneity. While in *Omeros*, the poem, time might appear to enter into a causal relationship with movement, in the sense, for example, that a particular event is derived from a particular movement, as in the movement of the boat, "In God We Troust" and the sea swift, which leads to Achille's return to Africa; or the impact of war on Plunkett's memory, or even the movement of the "comet," as it leads to Hector's death, in the film script a different kind of relationship becomes apparent. Time and space in the death of Hector, for example, are both collapsed. This, of course, is the rationale behind the use of montage in the poem. In the film script, the event becomes a space-time crystal.[10] Hector and the slaver become one and Hector's death IS the death of the slaver that occurs when Achille sojourns in Africa.

Film becomes a mechanism for the realisation of a concept of simultaneous events occurring as one identical action, or global image. The actions circle each other and do not lead to other actions in a causal chain but as a set of repeated images that is produced by the artistic manipulation of various lines of past and present made to exist in the here and now. The action of killing Hector the Greek by Achilles, or the African slaver is not motivated by any cause that exists as part of an on-going action in chronological time, but by an accumulation of sedimented relationships. So too Walcott suggests that the cause of the battle between Hector and Achille in St Lucia lies outside the time of present history.

Achille (V.O.)

I hold the oar in my hand, and that was my lance, I'd have to run like a panther, like a black wind.

CUT

(EXT. Day. ACHILLE races through the deserted village, past doors ajar with the white eyes of frightened WOMEN, past a smoking midden, past two dead FISHERMEN killed by the SLAVERS, then onto the low plain where he gathers speed to the sound of tribal chanting, then again to a camouflaging pattern of leaf and shade, then onto the bank of the river where he plunges in, startling crocodiles, then across to the other bank where he rests, panting in loud groans.)

CUT

Then later in the script:

CUT

(EXT. The same. The SLAVER turning around. When he turns to continue, ACHILLE is there. They face each other for a few seconds. Then ACHILLE silently charges, battering the SLAVER with the oar even when he is dead. ACHILLE looks at the dead man in horror.)

ACHILLE (V.O.)

I didn't want to kill him, but I had no choice. For the rage in our history, I smashed his head.

CUT

(EXT. Day. The dead SLAVER is HECTOR's double.)
(TS "Omeros", 1995 film script, pp. 165-166).

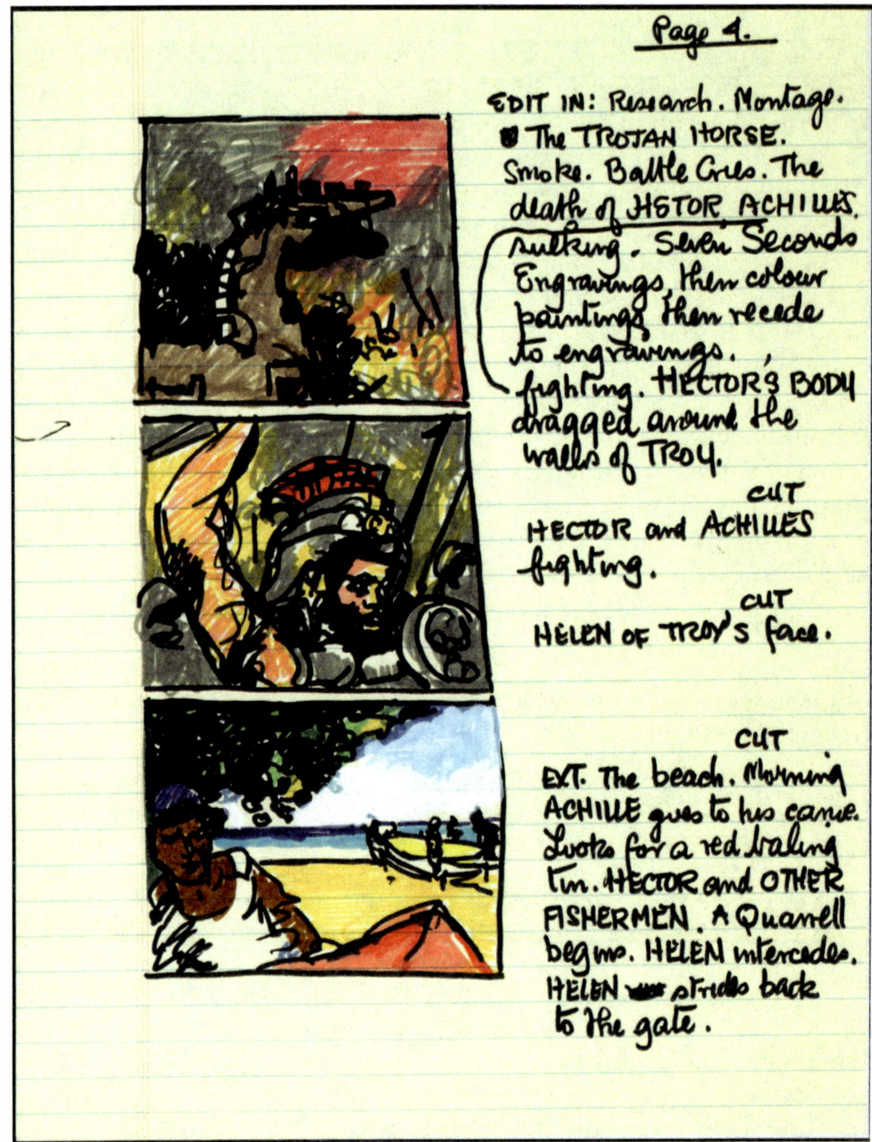

Storyboard for "Omeros", page 4. The Trojan Horse
The Thomas Fisher Library, University of Toronto
Ms. Coll. 136, Box 65, November 198?5 or 1986

Walcott also gives to Seven Seas the right to "see" Helen as Helen of Troy and Seven Seas becomes the poet for whom the past *is* the present.[11]

> SEVEN SEAS
> Great qualities, since the history of the world,
> will seek each other out in different races,
> if a cutlass is lifted or a lance is hurled.
> (inserted as p. 12a, "Omeros" film script)

Film provides the concretisation of these lived occasions, superimposing one event over the other, yet making of them distinct actions to show how history has evolved and yet remains the same. But Walcott is at pains to differentiate the three kinds of events that are being recorded in the work as representations of the past. As noted above, there is received memory in Helen's mirage, there is also traumatic memory and there is memory born of desire. There is then a return of events that are the same and that are linked to specific qualities identified in Seven Seas' words:

> CUT
> over generations, the same different places
> will produce heroes, breed quarrels, make one woman
> the vessel, the chalice of her tribe; the ocean
> CUT
> (HELEN'S face)
> brings voices to us, and all these voices are mixed,
> for what is the sea but memory in motion,
> the names return or change, but that change is fixed.
> CUT
> (MA KILMAN'S face)
> I hear the groans that travelled across the water
> from a far country, and yet I feel a calm joy
> like the sunlight on my eyes, after the slaughter
>
> and the ~~wrong~~ white History they taught me as a boy.
> CUT
> (PLUNKETT shifts, lowers his head.)
> I settle here on mornings sometimes in the shade
> of the almonds listening to your voices, the waves
> with their one language, and because I have shared
>
> blindness, which has no time, I hear heroes, not slaves!
> CUT
> ("Omeros", film script, inserted as p. 12a).

Blindness is associated with timelessness, in this way reinforcing a connection that lies beneath and beyond both physical appearance and chronological sequencing. Images conjure the past as actuality in the film script and frame the events as recollection in the present. Film in this instance is used to give these presences the potency of a haunting that serves to filter the present through the past and to show the recurrence of events as they unfold in the ensuing action. As poet, Walcott is setting up the past as the frame and the prism through which the present and future occur, as if already contained in that past. The father's voice in the film script instructs the poet to:

> Measure the days you have left. Do just that labour
> which marries your heart to your right hand; simplify
> your life to one emblem
> ("Omeros", 1995 film script, p. 3).

The emblem here is the feet of the women, translated from the poem *Omeros*. And the father's words, "Learn this after I die/ that just like them,/ your calling is keeping time", is a restatement of:

> O Thou, my Zero, is an impossible prayer,
> utter extinction is still a doubtful conceit.
> Though we pray to nothing, nothing cannot be there.
>
> Kneel to your load, then balance your staggering feet
> and walk up that coal ladder as they do in time,
> one bare foot after the next in ancestral rhyme. (p. 75)

The beat in the film script is to be found in the actual movement of the shot that approximates "one bare foot after the next in ancestral rhyme." Memory becomes here more than a child's memory, and accesses the ancestral rhythms of a people who will give the work its sonic unity and its pulsating entry into the communal history of those to whom both poem and film script are dedicated. The sound-track turns to that of a mechanical beat sounded by the whistle of the ship and the clanking machinery, which create a discordant break with the clamour and the argument of the women.

By page five, the metaphoric capabilities of montage are extended through juxtaposition, to further the effect of sound and sights from the past, and of land and sea as accumulative lines that continue the progressive act of creativity: "Ext. White paper. Foam. Fade from sepia monochrome into colour. White paper. White foam. A hand, the narrator's writes. Omeros". The imagination, as a creative force born of remembered familiar sights and sounds, now shapes new metaphors as the voices of the children filter through the background sounds. These metaphors are the accumulated layers of experience, but because this is a film script, Walcott can depict the actions and the source of the actions in successive layers of time that achieve a density of form while yet maintaining a clarity of meaning. He uses sepia to signify the past, in a familiar filmic technique, but also moves into colour utilising the transitional leap from black and white to colour that became a cornerstone of Eisensteinian montage theory. This signified a leap to colour and consciousness in the red flag of *Battleship Potemkin*.[12]

Both the time of imagination and causal time coalesce in this textured surface that is spatio-temporal in effect, in other words time made fluid remains located in a particular lived space, suggesting that place itself contains and sustains memory.

"Omeros" as film script also approaches the narratives of Helen, Achille, Hector, Plunkett, Maud and Seven Seas through a clear evocation of the power of childhood memory, in this way suggesting that both the education system, childhood reading and stories and events have an enduring effect on the adult psyche. Achille, Hector and Helen are depicted in a classroom learning about the myths of Homer. And at the key scene of Helen's mirage, seen in *Omeros* on page thirty-five, the film script adds a significant difference:

> (EXT. A freeze. Same time. The HORSE, in a gallop, the RIDER, HELEN in the yellow dress moving away. Battle-cries. Smoke. HELEN's startled face. Lances and WARRIORS, an instant of memory. The schoolbook illustration.
>
> CUT
>
> ("Omeros", 1995 film script, p. 74).

The past here participates in different movements. As frieze it represents the frozen or calcified result of memory that comes from outside, as in a "schoolbook illustration", and that bears no relation to the present lived reality. The recollection is, however, seen to be more than an event stored in memory. It is shaped by an imaginary and born of desire. This combination of desire and illusion is also present in the materialised figure of Walcott's father or his ghost. Walcott's father in fact cannot be a memory, since he died when Walcott was one year old. Yet the image of the father dominates the action. Memory is then more than recollection. It is retrospection shaped by desire that gives rise to a flight from reality or a simulation of reality. This sense of a simulacrum is attached to the idea of the cinematic or the potential of film to create illusions.

In this script, Walcott uses the freeze-frame to signify the ways in which the imagination and memory hold the individual in thrall. The freeze-frame simulates a still photograph and is thought to have been invented by Alfred Hitchcock, himself a master of montage, in 1928. The scene of Helen at the beach's end is perhaps the most significant in the poem *Omeros*, since it sounds the idea of "change" in different notes and is also the moment when change is associated most significantly with rebellion.

Helen, in *Omeros*, is no disembodied weakling. Nor is she silent as is evident in the narrator's smooth transition to her voice when she walks out of the hotel and recounts her tale stating that she does not intend to "take no shit/ from white people and some of them tourist – the men/ only out to touch local girls; every minute –/ was brushing their hand from her backside so one day/ she get fed up with all their nastiness so she tell/ the cashier that wasn't part of her focking pay" (pp. 33-34). She gains independence and her rage, which is associated with Achille's rage, suggests a root cause in ending disfranchisement. Her rage signifies the true movement to change and is noted in the sequence, which begins, "Change burns at the beach's end" (p. 34). Helen's rage evolves from the experiences internalized in *Arkansas Testament*, and which in its accumulated effect leads to Walcott's recognition of his own powerlessness as a writer.

This sense of internalised rage is epitomised in Olive Senior's "Penny Reel" from *Over the Roofs of the World* as a flight that releases the woman from her skin and turns her into a soucouyant.[13] In Walcott's *Omeros* a similar leap or transmutation occurs because of pent-up rage that bursts the bounds of habit and servitude. Here it is figured as emerging through two lines: "in that space between the lines of two lifted oars, / her shadow ambles"(p. 34, *Omeros*). There is no coincidence in the repetition of the word "ambling", which links her with the girl of "Cul de Sac Valley" and her lack of self-image. In the poem *Omeros* and in the film script and shooting script, the force engendered by the movement of two conflicting lines, shaped textually by the poem and imagistically by the film, generates first a pause that divides, and then an action or leap to a new dimension.

The shot on page 3 of the story-board is of the interior of the hotel with Helen serving tourists (see illustration, p. 154). The instruction reads: "Insolence." Then the camera cuts to the hotel bar where she is in conversation with the supervisor in medium shot when she quits. The cut is to Helen slamming the door and striding past the waitress and beginning to undress and passing tourists along the wall in Pigeon Point. Then there is a cut and a transition to a long shot of Helen walking on the beach swinging her sandals; there is a horse in the distance. The long shot here facilitates this idea of distance. Then the camera cuts to the horse galloping in medium shot. Then freeze-frame. Battle cries. The Fall of Troy. The Trojan Horse. All in quick succession. So that what is happening here is that the freeze-frame gives the idea of a moment of stasis that is then opposed to the quick movement of the mind as it recalls successive images of memory. Time becomes locked in past images. Walcott places a note on the top of the next page which reads:

Edit in: Research. Montage.
The Trojan Horse.
Smoke.

> Battle Cries. The death of Hstor (sic) ACHILLES.
> sulking. Seven Seconds
> Engravings, then colour
> paintings then recede
> to engravings.
> Fighting. HECTORS BODY
> dragged around the walls of TROY.
> Cut
> Hector and Achilles fighting.
> Cut
> Helen of Troy's face.

The montage sequence includes a direction of time. In other words Walcott is calculating the beat of the shot. The rhythm is calculated here for tension first created by Helen's rage, then her act of assertiveness, then the change in tempo that signifies the impact of the various pasts. The correct rhythm becomes essential to the build-up of images that will coalesce into a global idea/image, to which the whole sequence is directed. The visuals resound.

Storyboard for "Omeros", Helen in the Bar: Insolence, The Thomas Fisher Library, University of Toronto, Ms. Coll. 136, Box 65, November 188?5 or 1986.

Endnotes

1. Derek Walcott, Film script/ Screen play, "Omeros", MS COLL. 136. Box 14. Thomas Fisher Rare Book Library, dated in text, May 1995. Story-board, MS COLL 136, Box 65, Folders 1-42.
2. Walter Ruttman, *Symphony of a Great City* (Germany, 1927).
3. Laura Marks, *The Skin of the Film. Intercultural Cinema, Embodiment and the Senses* (Durham and London: Duke University Press, 2000), p. 29.
4. Sergei Eisenstein, *The Film Sense*, trans and ed. Jay Leyda ([1943] London: Faber and Faber, 1986).
5. Derek Walcott, *Arkansas Testament*, "Cul de Sac Valley", pp. 9-12).
6. See Martin Jay, *The Denigration of Vision in Twentieth Century French Thought* (University of California Press, 1994).
7. Edward Baugh, *Derek Walcott* (Cambridge: Cambridge University Press, 2006), p. 177.
8. Derek Walcott, *Midsummer* (London: Faber and Faber, 1984).
9. Edward Baugh, "The Arkansas Testament" in *The Art of Derek Walcott*, ed. Stewart Brown (Chester Springs, Pennsylvania: Seren Books / Dufour Editions, 1991), p. 128.
10. Deleuze, *Cinema 2*, pp. 68-97.
11. See "The Muse of History", *What the Twilight Says. Essays* (London: Faber and Faber, 1998), p. 36-64.
12. Sergei Eisenstein, *Film Sense* (London: Harcourt, 1942).
13. Olive Senior, "Penny Reel" in *Over the Roofs of the World* (Toronto: Insomniac Press, 2005), pp. 80-82.

CHAPTER 8

GHOSTLY ECHOES

Light and the space between two moving lines create a sense of a new way of seeing. A new form emerges. The desire to render the experience and existence of a people and their interaction with a particular landscape, which has been inextricably bound with their history in terms of plantation economies, and the transplantation or importation of both peoples and species, gives rise to a deliberate act of writing that seeks actively to usher in ghosts. Since New World history must be viewed simultaneously as a blank page and a history of multitudinous presences, that sense of writing as an act of intersection, the axis of "memory and prediction" is made more acute.[1] Memory is embedded in the myth, folklore, and the land itself.

Perhaps the most crucial use of film in Walcott's poetry is therefore as a way of giving concrete substance to the layers of existence or beliefs that people the Caribbean consciousness. Breiner notes Walcott's use of spectral presences and hallucinations.[2] He suggests that the figure of the apparition in *Dream on Monkey Mountain* derives specifically from Walcott's absorption of the influence of Japanese cinema, but also notes the important distinction between ghosts and hallucinations in Japanese drama and cinema:

> We need to be accurate about this, especially because Japanese film (like nô drama) frequently exploits precise distinctions between supernatural spirits, human ghosts, and hallucinatory projections. This kind of distinction is important in *Ugetsu*. After he sells his wares to the ghost, and as he is on his way to her castle, Genjuro stops at a kimono shop and considers purchasing one for the wife he has left behind. Thinking of her, he sees her come into the shop, and we see her touching the clothes and exclaiming over them (0:36:42); here she is certainly a hallucination or a kind of memory, rather than a ghost. Arguably it is by drawing attention in this way to the difference between a ghost and an imaginative projection that Mizoguchi prepares us for the final homecoming scene.[3]

What is important for Walcott is that these distinctions become crucial to *Dream on Monkey Mountain* and *Malcauchon*[4] and travel into *Omeros*, which derives much of its complexity from its conception as a form of hallucinatory projection that also summons ghostly presences and supernatural spirits. Film allows the materialisation of these presences that are both present and absent. It privileges a "sixth sense" of which Seven Seas is the avatar.

Ghostly presences and hallucinations abound throughout Walcott's work. In *Star Apple Kingdom*[5], a hallucination gives rise to a ship with its skeletal shapes remembering the Middle Passage. Helen in *Omeros* sees a mirage at the beach where "change burns" and this leads to one of the most filmic sequences in the work. Achille suffers sunstroke and returns to Africa, but he may also have died. These are hallucinations or products of a perhaps fevered imagination. In the last two instances they are the result of some traumatic event. The "change" that occurs suggests that a transformation of perception has occurred. Achille goes to sea after his rejection by Helen and his "death" sends him into a spiral of dual seeing and being that culminates in a recognition of his separation from his origins, but also of the residual presence of the past in cultural forms such as carnival. The hallucinations of both characters derive from a leap to new ways of seeing the self, in which the mirage itself signifies that which has been the cause of psychic nightmare. This is particularly suggestive of Deleuze's time-image, which emerges after trauma.[6]

In *Omeros*, there are also spectral presences or ghosts that rise like smoke to inhabit the earth, seeking retribution or reparation. These are the first peoples, but also the dead of the Middle Passage who are ultimately subsumed, like the dead leaves that Achille and Seven Seas burn, into the making of the poem. Maud returns as a spectral presence and so do the ghosts of Walcott's father and Homer, who become guides. There seems to be a distinction, then, between these different presences. Ghosts are the layers of the past that Harris evokes as central to the shaping of a cross-cultural aesthetic.

In *Tiepolo's Hound*, the spectre of Pissarro takes "possession" of the poet in St Thomas, in a move that suggests the need for atonement (p. 140). And certainly *The Prodigal* is a ghost story. Not only does the poet see Joseph Brodsky in Italy, but the ghosts of his mother and all the dead inhabit a white city in his head and become re-assembled into the fabric of the work, along with the spectral sounds of the atrocious acts hidden under the white beauty of the Alps and from which screams and sounds are emitted as constant reminders not only of the holocaust, but of Europe's sepulchral history as a whole. Film allows the passage of these ghosts and the dual idea of the hallucinations bred by double consciousness and continuing evil, as well as enabling Walcott to look again at the function of memory as it relates to the four hundred years of enslavement and the effects of colonialism.

Hauntology, if we widen its meaning to include all aspects of the supernatural and the spiritual, is, therefore, a constant theme of many of Walcott's works and the representation of this haunting, as Harris has maintained about Caribbean art in general, requires a new form. Walcott in *Omeros* uses superimposition, fragmentation and framing as mechanisms to bring to the present a sense of both an illusory past and a haunted present. For Deleuze, art and cinema generate the "unthought". Trauma breaks the relation with the past and leads to images that are discontinuous and governed by irrational cuts, where action does not lead to reaction, but to a sheet of time where past and present reside in capsule form in the direct image of time. The image becomes frozen through its lack of causal relation with the past, while still evoking the consequences of that traumatic past. Cinema in its new form, whether in its use of dissociation of sound and image, or in actions that seem to go nowhere, opens a fissure that allows time to flow. In the crystal image there is this mutual search, "blind and halting, of matter and spirit, beyond the movement image".[7]

Walcott's use of layers of the past, or spectral presences, may then be separated into two distinct ideas. On the one hand, he seeks to show how history or memory are medusas that hold the self in a vice of locked origins and power relationships. On the other hand, he seeks to demonstrate that while the writer must assume the role of Adam in giving things new names, he must always have that past at his back, remembering the shadows that have ushered in the Caribbean as a new world. The past is rupture and an open wound, but the very fact of that fissure allows newness or potential. The sense of a primal beginning or newness, or a refashioning of the past is, as he has said, a bitter-sweet conception which retains the taste,[8] the acidity of the past, while simultancously recognizing the vast potential of that history of exile, of void, of broken traditions, and of amnesia. The capacity to "rename the world" was, for Walcott, in direct antithesis to the ethos and the art of the old world, and his comments on Beckett serve to illustrate this:

> Beckett is a very honest writer. He is honest about what his tragic sense is, that everything is going to end in a final mute, inaudible 'O'.
>
> ...And I think that view, however true it may be for Beckett, is a dead end for language, which he himself could go down. He could only go down that cul-de-sac to the point where all that he had left was a mouth, an open mouth. But to me that is still a Baroque idea. That is still a Romantic idea. It is still an idea, quite justifiable, that has come out of Beckett's experiences of what Europe is, and the horror of modern civilization. But that is not a terminus for us. That is not a terminus for people who have not necessarily gone through it. It is certainly not a terminus for people who, tomorrow morning, might want to wake up and say more than just 'O', and might want to finish the line.[9]

But it is also significant that the "O" as opening and as frame or mouth acts as both mirror and vehicle of the residual traces of that broken connection with the past of several traditions, for a people born of the diaspora. The resemblance here to Harris's theorising of the "phantom limb" and a limbo aesthetic is uncanny. The limb cut off from its body (Africa) remembers at a subconscious level the place of its origin, and limbo as dance is a ritual enactment of that dismemberment. It is also a curative process through which the newly transplanted ex African forges new relationships through artistic re-enactment of the memory of the pain of being locked in a hold in the belly of a ship. The dance of limbo, then, spatialises the experience of the Middle Passage through its movement and its mapping of space. The architectural shape of limbo is also, in its form, a memory and a mimic of the many-limbed spider God Anansi. It is an "activation" of subconscious and "sleeping" resources in "the phantom limb of dismembered slave and god".[10] This mnemonic act I read as a crystalline image of trauma of origins, and one that informs a new creativity born out of the very spaces opened up by breaks in time and space.

Walcott's Nobel lecture remembers this limbo aesthetic, noting that the Ramleela had first been perceived in his eyes as a "severed limb of Asia remembering the body", but that he had misread the event through "a visual echo of history". What he later saw was "elation" and a "delight of conviction" and "not loss".[11] Here Walcott is playing with the two meanings of loss and also the meaning of echo; one meaning indicates unending potential, as in an echo in a cavern or an empty space, the other suggests emptiness. In a real sense the phantom limb holds both ideas simultaneously, since as loss it provides the rationale for the remaking of an identity through necessity, but as trace or vestige it also represents a continuing echo of lost traditions in the unconscious.

The "O" which, for the Caribbean, is the "O" of dawn becomes, in the novel/ epic poem *Omeros*, the figural opening or space that allows Walcott to meditate on a very complex theory of art based on the importance of echo and reverberation. The "O" is very specifically linked to the sounds of the original peoples; it exists as a repeated echo in the work. It is also, more significantly, inextricably linked to the light of dawn and the idea of repetition, which is to undergo several mutations between the publication of *Arkansas Testament* and *The Prodigal*.

The "monodic O" has an especial relevance to the articulation of a Caribbean aesthetic since it synthesizes the act of writing with the process to self-image in a graphic mode. Both true self-image and truthful representation in the act of writing are possible only when the monodic veneration of the past and the self-centredness of contemporary civilization are circumvented. In other words, this occurs when the subject "I" moves beyond its self-venerating subjectivity to become a communal, interactive individual. This is evident in a 1989 draft fragment from *Omeros* held at the University of the West Indies, St Augustine:

Thenceforth a man
became his own circle and sundial and with that pose
the gradual decline of Tragedy began.

In the monstrous shadows of a humanist's afternoon,
in the long shapes of statues on empty terraces,
in swifts hurtle like arrows from every noun

that tries to name them, heading for the sea-mists,
away from the architect's limits, the open-mouthed faces
perfectly reproduced, without vision without an iris.

Here the draft poem signals an elegy to the death of language. In the final version of *Omeros*, Walcott emphasises the role of the imagination in the act of image-making, and suggests the failure of imagination in the Old World.

The phrase "the monodic O" allows two images to merge: history as a gaping wound or an absence, and the self locked in its own self-veneration, which is an image of the isolation of contemporary existence. This "O", which Walcott has equated with the gaping hole of Beckett's *Not I*, is placed in antithesis to communal wholeness and freedom of expression, which is imaged as the "O" of invocation. This hole, as an opening, is distinct from the closed silence, which sees nothing other than itself. Nonetheless, in applying the schema of a dance of contrapuntal opposites in *Omeros*, this "O" of the void becomes an essential part of a system that includes reversals and that constitutes the process to transformation or the leap to a new dimension envisioned in the work as a whole. In the *attempt* to articulate, the "O" of loss and of void creates an inward movement into the unconscious. This inward movement becomes the passage into the "mer" of *Omeros*, figuratively the sea of history.

The use of montage in "Vangelo Nero" allowed Walcott to experiment with time; to take leaps beyond linear time. The flight of the swift in *Omeros* is the result of this experimentation and becomes equivalent to a movie projector and, in this sense, is a figural representation of the technique employed in the work, but it goes beyond this. The swift, as projector, actually carries Achille back through time and forward again. Achille's suffering in the past is, then, equivalent to the hallucination in the desert; they are both projections, fantasies born of the dalliance in the past and equivalent to the shadow shapes or illusions that the movie projects. But these illusionary shapes lead to the recognition of difference.

Achille's journey is conceived as a long drawn sound, which he follows. It repeats the journey down the "track" already figured in "Cul-de-Sac Valley", but in a form made concrete through cinematic projection. The swift's flight, as a simulation of exile from Africa, and as a re-enactment of that process, leads to a sense of loss:

Now he heard the griot muttering his prophetic song
of sorrow that would be the past. It was a note, long-drawn
and endless in its winding like the brown river's tongue:

"We were the colour of shadows when we came down
with tinkling leg-irons to join the chains of the sea,
for the silver coins multiplying on the sold horizon,

and these shadows are reprinted now on the white sand
of antipodal coasts, your ashen ancestors
from the Bight of Benin, from the margin of Guinea."
(*Omeros*, pp. 148-149)

Book Three as a whole explores the various elements of this "long-drawn and endless" note, perceived as an 'O" of loss and remembrance, and projects it as a series of shots which are recreations of the past, and which are, on one level, as in Harris's limbo aesthetic, the flight of the mind and its ability to create fictions or to re-make connections and narratives of the self. This flight of mind and imagination is linked to language and leads to a willing invitation to memory, as in the invocation which Ma Kilman utters as she undresses herself, loosens the trappings of civilizations and returns through the goat track, hearing the language of the ants, to that elemental self that finally howls with despair and its sense of loss.

The "monodic O", already containing the threads of black despair, of historic waste, or the decimation of the tribes and the breakdown of marriage, becomes, in one of its manifestations, the concrete reverberating sound of isolation:

... to Helen, stripping dried sheets along
the wire in Hector's yard, the monodic moan

came from the hole in her heart. It was not the song
that twittered from the veined mesh of Agamemnon,
but the low-fingered O of an Aruac flute.
(*Omeros*, p. 152)

The hollowness of this "O" is placed in antithesis to the communal wholeness of the "O" of invocation and parallels the "O" of sunset, which is placed in opposition to the "O" of dawn. The encircling "Os" are the accumulated echoes of the various losses and the loss of faith, which now reverberate within the empty space of St. Lucian history and Walcott's personal history. Helen's masturbation suggests the tendency of those who have suffered intense hurt, and whose pain has become unbearable, to become "in love with themselves", and to move inward or to become solipsistic. The girl's inner journey in "Cul de Sac Valley" of *Arkansas Testament* is here subsumed as a memory since it too is an act of inward looking. The moaning of the "O" in *Omeros* is, therefore, equated with a dynamic of its own. It is the pause that allows for contemplation, and an inward movement, which, placed against the need for progress or a movement outward, generates its own energy.

The compositional structure of the poem as film montage represents the culmination of Walcott's quest for a form through which this intersection of the past and the present becomes the cross between the real and the imagined. Therefore, the form itself is a transformation since it lends itself to this duality. In a real sense film becomes the means to an articulation of the loss and the potential of the Caribbean and emerges as a model for a Caribbean aesthetic. As such film as form constitutes the culmination of the on-going debate about the nature and validity of Caribbean art and culture and its place within world literature as a whole.

As outlined above, the echoing movements of *Omeros* and *The Prodigal* create concrete evocations. These emerge through oppositional lines and lead to the image of the tunnel at the start of *The Prodigal* through which the past echoes and which ultimately beckons to the ghosts that inhabit other enclosed spaces. Travel exposes an internalized sense of inferiority to other places, especially Europe, and references images of beauty and imagination linked to Western mythologies such as, "The Ice Maiden".[12] Idea/images of beauty and superiority that reside in the poetic imaginary therefore also constitute an echo. Movement in space, across continents, becomes a way of uncovering the layers of narratives and imported and untrue myths that have led to the poet's myopic vision. The past as encircling lines that lock in an individual psyche becomes the psychic terrain within which echoes reverberate, as ghosts or spectres that haunt the imaginary of both old and new worlds and that are repeated as echoes in time and space:

> I saw the walled city early in the morning
> with its sprinkled streets; under the arcades
> the beggars slept, unshifting as History.
> There was the city, then there was the magical
> echo of the city's name and the same sulphurous
> mirage of its double created by history,
> by the shade of the rusting almonds, by the galvanized sea
> whose ruts were left by the galleons, Cartagena
> and the ghost of Cartagena; (*The Prodigal*, p. 47).

This is a movement that also echoes Book Three of *Omeros* in its system of repetition generating further echoes. Book Three actually begins with a movie and memorialises the return to Africa as a place of origin and does so in strictly filmic terms:

then the horned river-horses rolling over themselves
could capsize the keel. It was like the African movies
he had yelped at in childhood. The endless river unreeled

those images that flickered into real mirages: (*Omeros*, p. 133)

Achille's journey is a retracing of the path of trauma and a re-charting of a narrative, through an imaginative flight. Achille is swept on to the shores of his ancestral home, but after the first shock of recognition and the initial joy of homecoming, he comes face to face with his reflection. His search for the gods of his ancestors has been met with silence: "He stood in the clearing/ and recited the gods' names. The trees within hearing/ ignored his incantation" (p.140). Achille is then presented "among those voluble leaves, his people,/ estranged from their chattering." Here the familiar theme of alienation, which has been at the heart of Walcott's early poetry, surfaces. He is estranged from their volubility, signifying both their loss of voice and his loss of connection to Africa, his ancestral place.

The word "volubility" has all the ramifications of a talkative people, a people in love with language, for whom rhetorical skill is equated with success and self-image. But of greater significance, this estrangement is perceived in terms of the opposition between past and present. This distance is conceived of as a worldview encased in language. Walcott's divided self (Achille as Walcott's alter-ego) is uppermost here. He is also estranged from himself because this past revisited is one side of himself, of his ancestral memory. The other follows the ancestral line traced by Plunkett and makes him, as poet, the descendant of the white colonizer. The past is therefore doubly divided from the present. The river is a reflective surface, crystalline in its effect, since it throws back an image that is divided or fragmented. Its "featurelessness" signifies both the impact of a lost history and self-enclosing effect of that loss, since it no longer has in its reflective apparatus the mimetic faculty or the representational attribute of the artistic image.

... but the shadow face

swayed by the ochre ripples seemed homesick
for the history ahead, as if its proper place
lay in unsettlement. So, to Achille, it appeared

they were not one reflection, but separate men –
(*Omeros*, pp. 140-41)

The word "reflection" permits various echoes to reverberate: philosophical thought or reflection, the reflected image (of lens or mirror) and self-image. In this sense it is similar to the echoes emitted from the tunnel of memory or the past, and becomes a new line in the progressive movement of the poem. More precisely, reflection is located as an act through which several lines of flight of imagination emerge: seeing the self through a surface that gives no stable or unified image back; thought as a way of seeing the Caribbean through the lens of European philosophy or ideas located in reason, as opposed to perceptions shaped by other ways of seeing, which the poem as a whole seeks to validate; the present as a place that is different from the past.

The idea of reflection in the context of this chapter is also aligned to photography and its reflective surface. The photographic image here becomes attached to the word, through which echoes or associations might be generated. The photograph also creates echoes, because while it is still or static in a visual sense, in reality its "idea" is not fixed in either time or space, because of its associations. It is both a past moment and a trope for the mind's creative process, and also a spur to memory. But it is also, as an image, separate from, though a reflection of, the subject.

Reflection connotes thought and self-image. The wound inflicted on the self, by both history and exile, leads to a double schism that causes a lack of positive self-image and a need to restore equality between thought and intuitive knowledge systems. Reflection (thought) has already in the poem been perceived as a divisive force. Plunkett's reflection on the island's history leads to a romantic desire to "improve" and dispel the ignorance of the natives, but Walcott's own absorption of Western thought has led to a different embellishment. They adopt different strategies that ultimately lead to the same process of transformation:

> like enemy ships of the line,
> we crossed on a parallel; he had been convinced
>
> that his course was right; I despised any design
> that kept to a chart, that calculated the winds.
> My inspiration was impulse, but the Major's zeal
>
> to make her the pride of the Battle of the Saints,
> [...]
> was an ideal
> no different from mine.
>
> (*Omeros*, p. 270)

The film script "Omeros" gives added space and emphasis to the fact that both Plunkett and Walcott as narrator are involved in a similar enterprise. Their desire to heal "wounds" leads to narratives that are essentially the remaking of myths.

Harris's writings foreground the intention, as he says in his essay,

"Creoleness: Civilization at the Crossroads", to "touch chords of deep-seated emotion and passion which lie within shared layers of experience in person and society; layers that are native to the embattled, philosophic core of universality, universal crisis, within creoleness".[13] He fastens on the universal crisis for which the Caribbean's history takes on the form of an image. The creole is wounded by the breaks in his lineage and the historic fissures that have shaped his relation to the space of Guyana and the Caribbean as a whole. Yet, beneath the layers of the psyche, unconscious interactions and shared experiences assume potent significance and beckon towards a shared sensibility.

What Harris suggests in this essay is that there are deep linkages within the "unconscious/subconscious/conscious" imagination that enable a cross-cultural dynamic and ethic. This "simultaneity" goes beyond the appropriations of sophisticated artists such as Picasso who co-opt the art of the African, for example. It recognises the cross-cultural similarities between gods of different civilisations, as in Legba's similarity to Hephaestus (p. 242) or, in the case of Walcott, Homer's associational image with that of Seven Seas, a blind fisherman. The key to such linkages, according to Harris, lies in "paradoxes of vulnerability" and Walcott's privileging of the wounds that manifest in all the key figures of his novel-epic provides a parallel to these ideas.

The vulnerabilities represented through the figure of Legba, god of the crossroads, signifies and creates a bridge across chasms, because it points to the need to see and read difference through the imagination and outside of what Harris calls "the prescriptions of political and cultural habit" (p.243). The capacity to see differently and to see difference, but yet also to see and recognise the "fossil" origins of culture and ethnicity, is very much part of the progressive logic of Walcott's work as a whole, and intrinsically knitted into the very tapestry of the weave that shapes and structures their interconnections. The question becomes:

> Why not see Helen
>
> as the sun saw her, with no Homeric shadow,
> swinging her plastic sandals on that beach alone,
> as fresh as the sea-wind? Why make the smoke a door? (*Omeros*, p. 271)

Why indeed use another myth or another culture to describe the Caribbean? All that "Greek manure" has in fact led to a form of myopia that sees with "one eye" rather than all the senses. But it is also the point where the echoes in Walcott's head were insistent. To enter the "light beyond metaphor" (p. 271) entails as he says in *The Prodigal*, a simultaneous apprehension of both sides of his past and the past of the Caribbean. The point is "not comparison".[14]

To go beyond metaphor is to enter into a realm beyond comparison. And for Walcott this is both existential and, to quote Homi Bhabha, "unhomely." It suggests a state of nonbeing, in the sense that all essential human attributes are elided and the individual is no longer distinct, but one with a world of spirit. This state is entered into through the passage into death in *Omeros.* In the film script for "The Haitian Earth",[15] Yvette is made a symbol of the Haitian earth itself: "This earth is the colour of your own flesh, Yvette. You will look after it and make it beautiful and healthy." Her death signifies the beginning of a new dawn in Haiti and she embraces it with song. The death of Hector and the death of Maud also signify forms of initiation into self-knowledge and new awakening linked to an idea of place and community.

The death of Hector leads to a purely filmic interlude, which is a synthesis of the primary thematic lines of the poem. The idea of death includes, at this point, the various deaths that are essential to the artistic and philosophic projects of the work and contains an idea of reversal or an unwinding of events. Death leads to reversals, in keeping with the idea of film. The action can now be wound back or reversed, perhaps signifying the desire to go back and change the past because the "woodsmoke smelt of a regret/ that men cannot name" (p. 234). But this regret leads to a simplicity where

> The rites of the islands were simplified by its elements,
> which changed places. The grooved sea was Achille's garden,
> the ridged plot of rattling plantains carried their sense
>
> of the sea … (*Omeros*, p. 234).

The idea of reversal is then used to point to the theme of death itself, since the poem now focuses on the impact of death as time rewinds "in slow motion" (p. 230), suggesting a slowing of time and psychic numbness and a pause or pit of numbness. The film script replaces the lines above with a chant of mourning, akin to the keening that Walcott would have noted in his close reading of John Millington Synge's *Riders to the Sea*, which signifies both communal grief and a confrontation with sublime forces.[16] But this moves toward a reversal of time so that the boundaries between death and life now become fluid.[17] When Maud dies, she apparently appears through Ma Kilman, who sees an image of the beautiful Glen-da-Lough and there follows a new awareness generated in her husband, Plunkett, who from that moment is "bound for good to another race" (p. 307). The result is the validation of a cross-cultural ethos and an echo of Deleuze's idea of "becoming imperceptible".

In another filmic reversal on pages 291 and 292, the image of the camera repeats the idea of the still shot as a mechanism for spiritual exploitation, here with obvious economic overtones. The poet is admonished by Seven

Seas, who as seer points out the spectral nature of life in the elsewhere of the narrator's travels. Life at the other side of the globe is now viewed as, "cities with shadowy spires stitched on a screen/ which the beak of a swift has ravelled and unravelled" (*Omeros*, p. 291). The narrator admits that he has been playing "tricks with time", though as author he is separate from his narrator, who is also a "phantom" presence. The filmic reversal is therefore a way of opening the door to spirit presences. These cities and the other life to which the poet has journeyed are no more and no less spectral than the ghost dance (p. 218) or figures that form in the flames of the hearth-fire. They are all both real and unreal. They exist as presences in the poet's imagination and are born of his own desire, as suggested in the first pages of the film script, "Omeros". His poetic flight gives substance to these phantoms:

> Helmets of mud-caked skulls. Out of the spectres
> that the forge of the Malebolge was bubbling with,
> a doubled shape stood up. Its grin was like Hector's.
>
> Hector in hell, shouldering the lance of an oar!
> In this place he had put himself in full belief
> of an afterlife; a shadow in the geyser
>
> that arched like a comet with its fountaining steam, (*Omeros*, p. 292).

Apart from the Dantesque overtones, this is almost like a carnival masquerade, with the poet losing faith in himself, religion and myth, but following the path of ghostly presences that unite Hector with his Greek counterpart and with the two young Englishmen. The quest turns to a question, which becomes whether the poet has learnt to see with other eyes. So, ultimately, the idea of the visual evolves into a question of how one is seen and how one sees. The poet is a "seer", in that through reversals of sight and of sense, he has developed a sixth sense like Seven Seas and now sees ghosts.

These presences emerge at the crossroads or point of intersection. The journey to home, which is also a journey to a re-appropriation of names, can only be undertaken with two "oars'" and two "oars men". The image of interlocking oars now replaces the parallel oars of the preceding pages. This is the image of the supporting and interlocking positions of the twin components of Antillean history and culture, of that which can be seen and that which is not visible, and of the power of the audiovisual image.

Through the "X" of this intersection, or the conflict of two lines, a new dynamic that leads to a new aesthetic is engendered. The demi gods who are film producers are now no longer the manipulators of the Caribbean text, nor do they choose the script. The Aegean, as more chimera than camera, marks a distinction between an image of fixity (as in the first verses of the poem) and moving image. Since change and movement have been struck through several notes in the text and are repeated refrains, the movement is here seen to be part of the overall design. But this is movement that remembers, that allows time to issue forth and that sees in a glacial image the simultaneous existence of several pasts and the creative potential of this production.

The Prodigal also creates concrete images of the accretions of history and the horror beneath them in terms of sound and visual, setting up an audiovisual movement throughout the poem as a whole. One particular sequence of images sums this up: The "Chasms and fissures of the vertiginous Alps" set up the dizzying movement experienced by someone who suffered, like Walcott, with vertigo.[18] The continuous flow of the movement in space, as the aeroplane flies over the Alps, then assumes a plummeting spin that simulates the spiralling descent of a beautiful and fallen angel, Lucifer. The fissures and chasms then become the cracks through which the sounds of violation emerge. These operate in counterpoise to the "paradise of ice" that is also a "camouflage". The "white-knuckled horror" is both the poet's fear and the terror of those who have died and whose deaths are also a "violation of that pre-primal silence". The theme of whiteness here suggests a racial hubris that leads to genocide and explains the loss of faith, which is now connected to Lucifer's hubris, and his loss of faith, which led to his fall from heaven. Lucifer, as representative of light and beauty that hides evil, is then, as the poem progresses, connected to a mythic idea of beauty that leads to "Hans Christian Andersen's 'The Ice Maiden'/ with its snow-locked horror" (p. 15). The image of being frozen or enthralled by a myth of beauty is seen to originate in books read as a child. The lines contain contradictions that reveal the conflict between what a child learns of white beauty and the reality of racism. That contradiction is heard in the "grumbling" and the "gasping" as well as made visible in the play of colour and motion that is set up in the structure of the poem on page nine. What these oppositional movements evoke is the ghostly absence of the dead, who have been exterminated.

The poem therefore deals with the atrocity of death and the presences that still inhabit the present landscapes of the world in a very concrete sense. It summarises Walcott's concern with ghosts and distinguishes the ghosts of history from personal illusions or desires, his ambition and his own fears. The descent of the aeroplane generates an illusion of falling born of physical and psychological fear. This colours his imagination and breeds a connection with myths that he has internalised since childhood. But the ghostly sounds and buried bodies of the holocaust are real. They are not illusions and they are not fictions. However, they have been the subjects of a fiction, which is the myth of Europe as civilised, authoritative and rational. The poem releases the poet, the reader and the Caribbean from the veneration of such monodic ideas and rooted histories. It allows for the circulation of counter-narratives and the small histories of those who have been marginalised and rendered silent because of their difference and their perpetual flows and movements.

It is in *White Egrets* that the ghosts of past, present and to come surface in their full terror, a terror that leads to the sublime. This collection of 2010 brings the idea of death to its aesthetic and philosophical conclusion. As a poet, Walcott's mind has been peopled with presences, and it is a truth that people mattered to him. Here he summons up memories of those many who have died or who, like himself, are nearing the end.[19]

The very image of the egret is spectral since it is white and it also signifies the possibility of something beyond the grave, since the egrets "stalk through the rain/ as if nothing mortal can affect them, or they lift/ like abrupt angels, sail, then settle again" (p. 9). They, like the poet's hand, teach "selection", and a "language beyond speech". As figures within the text they take their hue from the first usage, which summons figures of a corpse in the image of rigid chessmen who have lost both voice and echo. In this sense, they are the opposite of the "O" or the echoing systems of his previous poetry, which sought to give voice to the region. But in saying this, we need also to note that there is a system of reversals available to the filmmaker and to the poet who uses a montage method. The immediate follow-up to a failure of sound is the provision of a montage list or a series of objects that would be, or should be, shot sequentially, one shot following the other, but with the eye, through eidetics, collapsing all, so that we have a sense of movement and continuity. The sentence quoted from *White Egrets* is long and flowing, utilising a method from *The Prodigal* to give the effect of multiple senses orchestrated in movement, with the eye supplying the movement. For example, in *The Prodigal* on page 60, the greyness of sunrise, the wet trees, the waterlogged pathways, the misty landscape, the absence of birds, the moving combers peeping through the light rain add up to a significant idea not only of a change in climate and in landscape, but of an obscuring of self. The use of sibilants and c sounds here adds a sonic dimension that is both an echo and an idea of a succession of images that overwhelm the individual. We might say that the use of consonance builds a line of penetrating silence or the echoing of a grave. The shaft that might be light does not illuminate. It then redefines what "historic echoes" mean, since these are abruptly closed in the unfinished line, "Sometimes a shaft..." that leads to a reassessment of what that light and knowledge and those echoes might signify. The verses are followed by the crucial image of the "visionary" wood, that has already been discussed, and which leads to a moment of holy reconciliation and spiritual acceptance, oddly enough of a Christian communion. Here the spirits that rise are of the bread of Christ and the hope of resurrection.

White Egrets repeats this method of layered sounds and images to summon another epiphanic moment. This is heralded by "astonishment" (p. 8). Here the moment is made more intense by the use of a film frame. The egret sails into the frame as a result of the carefully chosen images that build the line, as in a film. There is a shot of a cool green lawn, quiet trees, a forest on the hill and these all fuse into an emblem. As with *The Rig*, *Steel* and *Omeros* we have a whole medley of different lines. Together, they create an intense leap that signifies a leap beyond death, or what Monsignor Patrick Anthony has called, the "after death".[20] These are ecstatic creative moments and they "shoot to heaven". Death as a companion, "like Eumaeus" (p. 10), signposts the primary project of the collection, which is to play with the terror and the anticipation of dying. But in the Greek reference, it also indicates that death treats all impartially, like Odysseus's swineherd and friend. Technically, it should be the figure of Brodsky or Walcott who do not recognise death as a companion, but here it is death who is the third companion, like Eumaeus, and is the "unutterable word" that is "always with us". The reference to the impartiality and fairness of death also gives a sense that there is an almost paternal feeling towards both men, one at that point in time, near death, the other now contemplating death. The egret is above all else a "seraphic soul" as "Joseph was" and its flight to the heavens is "noiseless".

The sound of the word "Eumaeus", however, also conjures another companion, this time on the road to Emmaus, so Walcott is playing with several meanings through the layers of sound and their resonance. Jesus, on the day of his resurrection, appeared to two companions as they were walking and they did not recognise him until they broke bread together. And that play gives added meaning to his dalliance with those other companions who have died. These include Brodsky, August Wilson, Oliver Jackman, even the sighting of his first love in a wheelchair, like himself, and the loss of lust.

White Egrets does more than create lists that leap to new dimensions. It incorporates, very specifically, the echoes of Walcott's film influences, in particular the source of his technique. In this instance, the reference is to Eisenstein, which is one of the reasons that this book signals and singles out this aesthetician.

> I watch the high trees tossing at the edge of the lawn
> like a heaving sea without crests, the bamboos plunge
> their necks like roped horses as yellow leaves, torn
> from the whipping branches, turn to an avalanche;
> all this before the rain scarily pours from the burst,
> sodden canvas of the sky like a hopeless sail,

gusting in sheets and hazing the hills completely
as if the whole valley were a hull outriding the gale
and the woods were not trees but waves of a running sea.(p. 7)

This is a direct reference to Eisenstein's Odessa mist sequence. It is one of the most famous emotive build-up of images in all of film history. Eisenstein calls this method "the music of landscape".

In retrospect, we recognise that the image of the corpse wrapped in sails in *Omeros* also evolved from Eisenstein's *Battleship Potemkin* in the scene where those sailors who rebelled at being given rotten meat are covered in tarpaulin and their comrades told to shoot them. But they do not. The image becomes associated with defiance and revolution, a leap to a new dimension. The spectre of death strikes a similar note in *White Egrets*. There is a call to revolt against that corpse-like image that has no echoes, with which the book began. Instead the poem recites the various repetitions of "no" that become a "sunlit surprise". Despite all the negatives, there is nonetheless, still the possibility of "an unfolding letter", to Aimé Cesairé, the founder of the Negritude movement, that remains like a haze on the mind, "beyond the lines of blindingly white breakers" (p. 87).

There is a further echo of *Potemkin*, and in order to elucidate it I want to describe the process of editing for a film documentary, using one small section of Walcott's reading of this poem. This is the verse that begins: "I watch the huge trees tossing at the edge of the lawn/ like a heaving sea without crests, the bamboos plunge/ their necks like roped horses…" The huge trees at the edge of the lawn set up a frame within which there is movement in the necks of roped horses, which is an image of contained movement that is then juxtaposed with frenzied unrestrained movement in the yellow leaves that are torn from the trees. The images we used here in editing are of the sea as a framing device, then the bamboos swaying, then the horses that are fettered; then cut to branches in frenzy which, through editing software, enables these leaves to whirl; then cut to the rain in sheets; then cut to sheets of canvas; then cut to a sail, with its canvas sodden; then cut to sheets of sails gusting in the wind; then cut to the hills in mist; then cut to a hull that suddenly protrudes like the hull of a battleship. The whole is synchronised in a rhythm that keeps the beat of a funeral procession and Walcott's voice.

As points of intensification in this verse we move towards a series of contrasts that build up the tension. We have, in particular, a counterpoint between the soft and the rigid at intervals, which then climax in the opposition between the sea and the sodden sail and the hull penetrating the frame, with all its phallic symbolism that includes the image of "outriding" here, and the "gusting" in sheets that gives rise to a haze.

The rhythm is identical to the movement of the Odessa mist sequence, and in fact, in editing, I used a section from *Potemkin* at the point where the line goes "sodden canvas of the sky like a hopeless sail…" The most important lesson that Walcott learnt from film was in finding the "inner necessity" of the whole, or in exploring and discovering how to unite different parts through a single idea that infuses the whole. This inner necessity equals finding the rhythm. *Potemkin* uses "visual rhyme". So does this sequence from *White Egrets*. The Odessa mist sequence goes like this according to *Nonindifferent Nature* (p. 228):

> And here the black mass of the hulks of ships swallows the whole expanse of the screen and slowly floats past the camera…
>
> The general combination of motifs moves from the airiness of the mist through the barely perceptible outline of objects – through the lead-gray surface of the water and gray sails – the velvety black hulks of the ships and the hard rock of the embankment.
>
> The dynamic combination of separate lines of these elements flows together into a final static chord.
>
> They merge together into a motionless shot, where the gray sail becomes a tent, the black hulks of the ship –the crêpe of the mourning bow, the water – the tears of women's bowed heads, the mist – the softness of the outlines of the – out of focus – shot; and the hard rock becomes the corpse lying prostrate on the paved, cobblestone embankment.
>
> And now – almost inaudibly – the theme of fire enters.
>
> It enters as the flickering candle in the hands of Vakulinchuk; so it may grow into the flaming wrath of the meeting held over the corpse, and it flares up with the scarlet flame of the red flag on the mast of the mutinying battleship.[21]

The effect is tonal and melodic and through the interplay of fluid and hard, and the slow introduction of colour that intensifies, leads to a transformative action. It also creates an intense emotional effect. In *Potemkin* it is the scene of mourning after Vakulinchuk's death.

In "White Egrets" the inner necessity of these images emerge in Walcott's final lines:

> Now when at noon or evening on the lawn
> the egrets soar together in noiseless flight
> or tack, like a regatta, the sea-green grass,
> they are seraphic souls, as Joseph was. (p. 10)

The leap is to a new dimension, that of the angelic state. It is achieved by getting as close as a poet can to a textured image that moves with accumulating force, dips, only to rise again into a new concept.

Endnotes

1. See Kenneth Ramchand, "Walcott and Ramlila", in *Interlocking Basins of a Globe. Essays on Derek Walcott*, ed. Jean Antoine-Dunne (Leeds: Peepal Tree Press, 2013), pp. 197-2017.
2. Laurence Breiner, "The Impact of Japan on Derek Walcott's Early Plays", *Comparative Theater Review*, Vol.13 (English Issue) March 2014.
3. Breiner, p.14.
4. Derek Walcott, *Dream on Monkey Mountain and Other Plays* (New York: Farrar, Straus and Giroux, 1970).
5. Derek Walcott, *Star Apple Kingdom* (London: Jonathan Cape, 1980).
6. Gilles Deleuze, *Cinema 2. The Time-Image*, trans. Hugh Tomlinson and Robert Galeta (Minneapolis: University of Minnesota Press, 1989).
7. Deleuze, *Cinema 2*, p. 75.
8. Derek Walcott, "The Muse of History", published in *Is Massa Day Done?* Orde Coombs ed. (New York: Anchor / Doubleday, 1974) 1-27. See also *What the Twilight Says. Essays*.
9. "Derek Walcott in conversation with Jean Antoine", *Poetry Ireland Review 34* (Spring 1992), p. 81.
10. Wilson Harris, *History Fable and Myth in the Caribbean and Guianas* ([1970] Callaloo Publications, 1995), p. 20.
11. Derek Walcott, *The Antilles: Fragments of Epic Memory* (London: Faber and Faber, 1993).
12. Walcott, *The Prodigal*, (New York: Farrar, Straus and Giroux, 2003), p. 15.
13. *Selected Essays of Wilson Harris: The Unfinished Genesis of the Imagination*, ed. Andrew Bundy (London: Routledge, 1999), p. 237.
14. *The Prodigal*, p. 75.
15. "The Haitian Earth", Derek Walcott Collection, Alma Jordan Library, The University of the West Indies, St. Augustine, (1972).
16. John Millington Synge, *Riders to the Sea*, 1902, WEB.
17. See Jean-Pierre Durix, Mimesis, *Genres and Post-Colonial Discourse. Deconstructing Magical Realism* (London: Macmillan Press, 1998).
18. Walcott, *The Prodigal*, p. 9.
19. Derek Walcott, *White Egrets* (New York: Farrar, Straus and Giroux, 2010).
20. Patrick Anthony, *Interlocking Basins of a Globe*, pp. 244-58.
21. Sergei Eisenstein, *Nonindifferent Nature*, ed., and trans., Herbert Marshall, (Cambridge: Cambridge University Press, 1987), p. 228.

CHAPTER 9

MAKING NEW

Walcott's work demonstrates a fascination with the movement of the Caribbean body and the Caribbean voice. The theatre that he sought to create, that is a "theatre where everything was possible", of necessity involved experimentation in how that body could be brought into dramatic play to provide an intense emotional experience for the audience. The potential of art was for him connected to the atomic in its release of quantum energies.[1] In this sense he drew close to Wilson Harris.

Art for Harris entails both images and forms that leap beyond the confines of human limitations and trigger explosive and constantly burgeoning new images. These explosions open portals through which the latent memories of the collective unconscious emerge. These vestiges or traces of myth and memory are forced to the surface through the dynamism of language itself. For him, language is a form of play that enables a plastic enactment of "the perpetually altering circuit of decision and production, of action and responsibility [...] of decay and confusion."[2] The word "plastic" is an interesting one and is traditionally used to describe the capacity of film, since, through montage, an image or a sequence of images can be moulded into new ideas or concepts through conflict or juxtaposition. It is also not perhaps coincidental that Harris used a quotation from Herbert Eagle's introduction to Eisenstein's *Nonindifferent Nature* as an epigraph to *The Mask of the Beggar*:

> Sergei Eisenstein (*The Battleship Potemkin*) emphasized the collision of disparate and conflicting elements in montage in order to produce in the synthesis, new concepts and emotions. He coined such phrases as "overtonal montage" to describe collisions produced by the juxtaposition of objects with rich cultural implications (thus in *October* he seeks to discredit Orthodoxy by juxtaposing the religious icons and idols with Asian and African statues, which for his European audience would connote the primitive and superstitious.)

The Visual in Caribbean Literature: Walcott and Harris

It is interesting that Mary Lou Emery in discussing the use of visual art in writers of the Caribbean sees this kind of dynamic in Harris's work, but suggests that Walcott's concerns and his use of the visual remain on the level of the socio-political, aesthetic and ideological. In her reading, Walcott's use of painting allows an "unsettling" of ideas of masculinity and colonial possession, in particular in its examination of the marginalisation of the black in a painting. She argues that *Tiepolo's Hound*, for example, does not enter into what we might call spiritual relationships. His use of the visual – in this instance painting – instead leads to: "A mournful resignation, in the realization that the sublime moment that he seeks depends on his own inscription as a man of African descent, in the modern aesthetics that require blackness as its constitutive Other."[3]

One might, however, read Walcott's meditation on light in *Tiepolo's Hound* as a prelude to the ecstatic state, akin to the sublime, that he enters into towards the end of *The Prodigal*. But this leap is already implicit in the conflictual movement of *Tiepolo's Hound*, in its opposing of spaces and perceptions, of present time and the past of memory. These seek actively to force an image of difference to emerge. Pissarro hears the "same noise in the chuckling bilge/ of anchored schooners. No, no, not the same!" and is then pursued by "the eye / of a crazed duke" up the stairs to the Louvre (*Tiepolo*, p. 34). Sounds and sights are like visual and sonic weapons that attack his sensibility, enacting an oppositional movement that leaves him depressed and bewildered. The use of conflict, first in terms of conflict of sound and visual, generates in *Tiepolo's Hound* the idea that Pissarro's vision and his distance from home, led to something new, a kind of creolisation of European art. Essentially, the use of conflict, as Harris recognises in his reflection on contrapuntal montage, generates a flight or leap to a new state.

Emery also makes the strange statement that while the figure of Achille in *Omeros* is "at heart ekphrastic", it does not "directly or centrally focus on visual art".[4] She focuses, of course, on the visual art of painting. But her interest is primarily in art's capacity to create portals, and she sees Harris's use of painting as a way of approaching what he calls *timehri* after the Amerindian name for drawings or paintings on rocks and that Brathwaite has associated with soul and inner self in his use of this word and of what he calls the *nam*. In *Omeros*, the visual is not figural, nor is it the use or copy of a painting for purposes of description, or as an entry into new states of being or feeling. Instead visuality hinges on the creation of cinematic audiovisuality, which has movement and time as first principles. Unlike *Tiepolo's Hound*, *Another Life* and *O Starry Starry Night*, where Walcott confronts actual paintings and photographs or uses the act of painting as a way of describing a particular state of the artist at a particular phase,

Design for "O Starry Starry Night".
Courtesy Sigrid Nama.

Omeros does not explore the confrontation of painting, nor does it see the museum as a viable entry into art's relation to reality for the Caribbean artist, as Emery suggests. In fact the museum in *Omeros* is a mausoleum connected to a dying culture.

Omeros is the poem most clearly concerned with the ways in which a visual art can bring the subject closer to hidden layers of self and of time. More specifically, it is the poem that in its use of the conflictual lines of montage, identified in Harris's quotation, enables Walcott to arrive at an internalised idea of being buried deep in the unconscious and to a sense of Caribbean difference. In fact, in *Omeros* the filmic works in a way that is not so different from the way in which Emery reads the portal as created in works by Harris.

Harris, in his examination of American Literature can see no "distinctive movement in the arts... to cope with the divided heritage of the world, since one may only point to the symbol of an overwhelming ordeal without release".[5] Walcott and Harris attempt as artists to generate the energy released through conflict: "Whatever happens – art will always be – since life in its essential contradiction is art; it is the deep unconscious humour or carnival".[6]

This "carnival", explored repeatedly by the Guyanese writer as an act of imagination, leads to the dramatization and concretisation of layers of experience. This exteriorisation of self entails at a very deep level an examination of the human's relationship to earth and sea and the whole of the natural environment.[7] Harris concludes:

> Man will never pass beyond prehistoric conditions until all his gods have failed, and their failure, which puts him on the rack, opens up the necessity for self-knowledge and for the scientific understanding of his environment.[8]

Reshaping the Architecture

The reversal to an elemental power may of course be seen as a continuation of that belief or advocacy of the primal elemental need to survive and the reliance on instinct and pure common sense, already evident in *Ti-Jean*. It is found in the establishing image of an early screenplay for "Ti-Jean and his Brothers" written as an animated film with songs and music by Andre Tanker. The opening sequence reads:

> Image. Opening Shot:
>
> The Universe. Night. A Mandala or prayer wheel representing the Universe. It turns slowly. The sky revolves through morning, noon and night. A painting by William Blake. Music. The overture begins.

The theme of this overture is Moonchild and the Voice-over sings:

> Moonchild, come live with me
> Sunchild come live with me
> Earth child come live with me
> God's child we all can see.[9]

The theme is cosmic harmony, and in citing Blake, also involves a mysticism not often seen in Walcott's drama. In *Moon-Child*, the reworked musical of this early play, Walcott retains the critique of strength and intellect that is at the heart of *Ti-Jean and His Brothers*, and also incorporates the folk figures of the loupgarou and *gens-gagé*, for example.[10] He also includes the themes of incest within the white creole community, already present in earlier stage plays. *Moon-Child* also vehemently condemns the nefarious practices of politicians and the corruption that leads to the sale of land owned by the poor St Lucian who has no deeds and inherits only through "oral and never inked,/ family inheritances, based on/ an aunt or an uncle's word" (p. 64).

The planter is also beautiful, suggesting the appeal of evil and its seductive presence: he was, "young, supple, eager, / both serpentine and bold" but he is also a necromancer and in him the forces of the black arts come to fruition. He has studied magic in "Haiti and Tibet (p. 66) and can now "buy men's souls for money" (p. 67). These are the forces that Ti-Jean aligns himself against and the evil of power and politics comes to a head in this representation. Set at Christmas time, the musical weaves a tapestry of beauty around the planter and links it to his intense pride that can brook no disagreement.

Ti-Jean is a David against this Goliath. His person also combines all the senses, for as he speeds down the path to get kerosene, he sees the African violet's exuberant bouquets, hears the *topis tambour's* drum and recalls the taste of fruit of his boyhood, and the smell of *moubain* and *pomme-aracs*. As such, he is "the child of nature" and the island is his to protect (p. 82). The crux of the matter lies in the words:

> LET US TAKE A LESSON FROM
> TI-JEAN AND HIS BROTHERS
> HOW HIGH-RISES GOING TO COME
> FROM LAND THAT WAS HIS MOTHER'S
>
> MORE AND MORE NEGOTIATION
> LEAVING POOR PEOPLE STRANDED
> THEY GO SELL OUT MY POOR NATION
> UNLESS JUSTICE IS DEMANDED (pp. 92-93).

Furthermore, the planter is constructed as a Catholic, in fact he plays a priest (p. 44), so the play also serves as cutting critique of Catholic bigotry remembered from his youth, when a priest in St Lucia wrote and published a poem condemning Walcott's "heresy". In *Moon-Child*, Ti-Jean lives within a Catholic community, but does not share their idea of communal salvation, and instead depends on his own individual will and action to defeat the devil/ planter. This does not separate him from community, nor does it make him solipsistic and self-centred. His service is to community and he is at one with the natural world.

Ti-Jean's character is one grounded in disobedience and in this sense he is a parallel to the Lucifer figure, but he is also a deeply protestant figure, in the truest sense of the word "protestant", since he rejects Catholic obedience and dares to say "no" and to seek his individual truth. His actions border on anarchy and are in keeping with an art that is asymmetrical and that refuses classical conformity. His revolutionary resistance also echoes Walcott's obsession with the Haitian revolution, in particular since there is a reprise of Toussaint in the words "L'Ouverte" (p. 83).

Art as the product of elemental power closes the text in the recalling of the creatures of the folk imagination: the *gens-gajé*, maman de l'eau, the little bolom and the loupgarou who are in their "usual" places. Art or song is no longer derived from the structures of power and dominance and perceived as derived from extra-terrestrial or transcendental presence, but is instead aligned to an elemental power in the face of the global greed and destructiveness of the human self. Beauty is not an imposed idea or ideal, but the energy released in the face of conflict.

Just as the life experiences, the relation to land and natural environment and common sense, as well as sheer wit and resilience, are the traits that mark the folk hero Ti-Jean as a living legend for Walcott, and one to which he returned over and over again, so too in *Arkansas Testament* and *Omeros* he reiterates the value of the ordinary.

Caribbean filmmakers speak very often of making films that will tell "our own stories", since notoriously cinema has been the greatest creator of exoticism that the Caribbean has encountered. Films such as *I Walked with a Zombie* or *Fire Down Below*[11] have immortalised the Caribbean islands as "any place whatevers" without identity or personality, but only as sites of pleasure, savagery or sexual release. Any island is a Caribbean resort and can be used interchangeably. But the poet, Walcott, sought to invent a new narrative and a new visibility.

In *Omeros*, this emerges as an answer to various questions: "Why was he down here?" "Why? asked the glass sea-horses,/ curling like questions. What on earth had he come for,/ when he had a good life up there?" The sea-mosses continue the questioning: "Wasn't love worth more/ than the coins of light pouring from the galleon's doors?" (p. 45). The series of questions that assail Achille as he dives for gold and lobsters beneath the

WILLOUGHBY (laughs then turns)
(4)
(Sound of Harmonica)
WILLOUGHBY (turns right)
Who's that coming through
the coconuts,Fagette?
FRANKLIN
Fagette. Coming to ~~light~~ six
the ~~lamps~~ lanterns.
Camera pulls back:
Fagette enters frame
Cut to Camera pan
from F8s POV or
Repeat
shot 3. Credit.
Lantern swinging in hand.
FAGETTE (off)
Goodevening,Major,
Goodevening Captain Franklin,
Bon soir,bon soir.
"all his sad captains"
Cut to
CLOSE UP; FRANKLIN
FRANKLIN
All his sad captains.
(louder)
Bon,soir,Fagette.
– 30 Secs.
music
hold:
TIME :3 mins :30 secs

Storyboard for "Franklin".
The Derek Walcott Collection, The Alma Jordan Library, UWI, St Augustine. Box 10, folder 4.

Page from "Ti Jean Notebook".
Derek Walcott Collection, The Alma Jordan Library, UWI, St Augustine.
Box 10, folder 13.

sea are versions of questions that the poet asked himself. These questions are concerned with the motivations that govern the making of art: money, fame and even love. In one sense these are pointless questions just as the quest is described in the word "bubble", which is here dream or illusion or fiction, as in "every bubble englobed a biography" (p. 46). It corresponds to Achille's dreaming return to Africa or Helen's fantasy of assertive self-sufficiency. Brathwaite and Walcott both use this image to signify a dream reality and it is this sense of an imaginary creation that the poem now valorises. The poem recalls the spectral presences and terror of the sea, which is a "world without sound", where the "brain-coral gurgled their words" (*Omeros,* pp. 45-46). These silent images of memory, retained in a dream "bubble" under the water, are associated with fictions aligned to material values where men are objects and become reduced, because the "skin calcifies" and the soul turns to stone. This is the effect of wars of conquest that make men into objects and cargo.

The references here suggest similarities with Brathwaite's *Mother Poem*, and *Sun Poem* of *Ancestors*. The "bubble" as dream, recalls the poem "Bubbles" and the waging of a war of language by this poet, for whom nation language contains the history of a people. The third book in this trilogy, *X/Self* and the poem, "X/Self xth letter from the thirteenth provinces",[12] as an expression of this, is a Caliban like re-appropriation of language and a use of montage to "tief" power from the technocrats and those others of a "missile culture".[13] The use of technology and montage makes the later Brathwaite a candidate for film theorising, in particular in his use of gaps, silences and the visual iconography and composition of the poems. Technology represents for both writers, then, a material vehicle for making new fictions.

Telling the Small Stories

Walcott's reconstruction of the idea of the Antilles in *Moon-Child* and *Omeros* is enabled by his creative use of cinematography and his adaptation of the visual and sonic to a re-telling of the small histories of the Antilles. These narratives are also reinventions so that he becomes, like the filmmaker and the bard, a maker of myths. His adaptation of contrapuntal montage to the act of writing also enables the graphing of Caribbean psychic reality, while maintaining a focus on the landscape, seascape and the present experiences of the Caribbean and its situation within increasing globalisation and the greed of big business cartels.

The image of the drifter in *Omeros* brings together the movement of film and the idea that Walcott, as poet, is always, like Ulysses, on the move or travelling. "The Aegean's chimera/ is a camera, you get my drift, a drifter/ is the hero of my book" (pp. 282-283); this serves a dual function: to tighten the connections between the Homeric act of creation and the act of Caribbean creativity, and to focus on movement and on the simultaneity of time that bring great art into one circuit. The chimera as goat and fancy or illusion, also connects the body and its drives to the power of the imagination or flight of fancy. These are the sources of great art. The origins of stage tragedy and of the Caribbean are seen to be similar. The connection with the plays *Ti-Jean* and *Moon-Child*, both of which have the goat as a symbol of Ti-Jean's cunning triumph over the devil, becomes acute.

The question of illusion, or the Caribbean mind's susceptibility to illusion, as in the cinema, is further associated with the dream of a return to origins, as in Achille's return, in a mirage, to Africa. By bringing these various facets together, Walcott, through cinematography, responds to a question posed by Wilson Harris in "Tradition and the West Indian Novel":

> how can one begin to reconcile the broken parts of such an enormous heritage, especially when those broken parts appear very often like a grotesque series of adventures, volcanic in its precipitate effects as well as human in its vulnerable settlement?[14]

The creation of a formal structure, which mirrors the multifaceted, polyglot, moving life of the Caribbean, transforms that ferment of contradictory existence into a source of creativity that leads to self-renewal. In Walcott's insistence that the cracks and discontinuities of Antillean history are in themselves constitutive of the present reality of that existence, and that the form of the work of art should reflect this truth, he substitutes an image of human reality as a series of negotiations and realignments for an idea of identity as finished or complete in itself.

The idea generated by the projected image of *Omeros* is that culture, to quote Raymond Williams, is "a description of a particular way of life which expresses certain meanings and values and not only in art and learning, but in institutions and ordinary behaviour".[15] That, moreover, this "description" is never fixed or immutable but rather susceptible to transformation over time through the adjustments made by the individual and by society as a whole, in the process of interacting with others who are also engaged in the attempt to clarify their particular meanings and values. Culture is therefore to be perceived as a communicative network that engenders new meanings and ideas of self and society over time.

The Prodigal also revokes the dominance of a particular hegemonic culture and does so by destroying the internalised idea of inferiority engendered by the established equivalence of white with beauty and goodness. Both poems accomplish this through movement and motion and through the release of time. They actively enter into the "gulf" (*Omeros*, p. 283) and make creative use of this emptiness.

Walcott's ambitious project in his poems also echoes Harris's concern with the need for the fulfilment within the person of that instinct for self-hood and self-realisation which is nullified by a landscape of denigration, humiliation and historical void. Viewed from this perspective, Eisenstein's statements on film's potential for harmony and its unification of art and ethos seem prophetic and justify in no small measure Walcott's attempt to transform the social and political climate through an artistic vision informed by theories of film montage.

Endnotes

1. See *Mask of the Beggar* (London: Faber and Faber, 2003).
2. C.L.R. James, quoting Heidegger, afterword, *Tradition, the Writer and Society*, by Wilson Harris, (London: New Beacon, 1967), p. 70.
3. Mary Lou Emery, *Modernism, the Visual, and Caribbean Literature* (Cambridge: Cambridge University Press, 2007), p. 186.
4. Emery, p. 188.
5. Harris, Tradition, p. 10.
6. Harris, Tradition, p. 12.
7. See for example Wilson Harris's "Carnival of Psyche" and *Carnival*.
8. Harris, *Tradition*, p. 17.
9. "Ti-Jean and His Brothers. Animated Film", Box 6, Folder 27, Derek Walcott Collection, Alma Jordan Library, The University of the West Indies, St Augustine. Undated.
10. Derek Walcott, *Moon-Child* (New York: Farrar, Straus and Giroux, 2012).
11. *I Walked with a Zombie*, Jacques Tourneur, 1943; *Fire Down Below*, Robert Parrish, 1957.
12. Kamau Brathwaite, *Ancestors. A Reinvention of Mother Poem, Sun Poem and X/Self* (New York: New Directions, 2001), pp. 444-456.
13. Kamau Brathwaite. See "Titan" and "the fapal state machine" of *Ancestors* as examples, pp. 406-12 and 435-39.
14. Wilson Harris, *Tradition the Writer and Society* (London: New Beacon, 1967), p. 31.
15. Quoted by Stuart Hall in "Culture, Community, Nation", *Cultural Studies 7.3* (October, 1993), p. 351.

CONCLUSION

It is my hope that this conclusion is a beginning. We cannot ignore the importance of the filmic, nor of the incursion of the digital into our everyday lives. The infiltration of mechanical and technological images seems virtually complete in our present day. If art is relevant, then of necessity it must be affected by this new art and by the progressive use of font, and of fragment and by the fact that we live in a world without borders in a very real sense.

Time and space now mean something different. Our interactions no longer require presence. Virtual archives now make the past a living and active present. The visual has become a way of transmitting knowledge and information, either through television or through the Internet.

That Walcott's last work was a collaboration between himself and the painter Peter Doig gives credence to the idea of the value of the visual in poetry. The work *Morning, Paramin* sets up a dialogue with the visual work of art. The poems are not interpretations but responses to the impact of the eye on the mind.[1] This idea in itself is no longer new.

But it does bring Walcott's work full circle. He here records the fact that the visual is a trigger for specific responses and also notes the value of movement and the sonic dimension of the visual as in:

> We imagine that we can hear what certain painters
> heard as they worked: Pollock the cacophony of
> traffic, O'Keefe the engines of certain lilies, Bearden
> cornets muffled in velvet, Peter Doig the
> brooding, breeding silence of deep bush, (p. 77)

Images of the eye also entail an assault on other senses. Film and the cinema acknowledge that art is never an isolated attack but rather an ensemble. The true lesson of cinema philosophy or aesthetics is that we feel in concert and that how we see is orchestrated through arrangements that impact in ways similar to sound.

What I have argued in this book is that Walcott sought to remain faithful to poetry while seeking to include the ideas that he derived from film. He sought, as have other writers, to produce the impact of the filmic in writing through the use of cinematic techniques, in the main theorised by early film theoreticians such as Eisenstein. These lessons he learnt because of his own, almost obsessive, interest in film-making, and from a belief, which is a very modernist one, that the word can be stretched and made elastic.

His works demand that the reader and the viewer see language as more than words. It is not simply that the writer must take account of tonality, and the arrangement of words, but must also understand that structures of language operate in non-cerebral ways. Language in its many forms can convey directly into the mind of an audience through the generation of affect. This, I have argued, is because of the effect of the cinematic and the filmic in general, on the body and because, as Deleuze has argued, cinema or film already contain movement and thus enable the movement of thought. It is for this reason that a revolutionary poet, or one who seeks to transform the consciousness of his audience, attempts to introduce the visceral effect of film on body and mind.

Walcott's study of classical film montage, as is evident in particular from scripts such as 'To Die for Grenada", introduced him to the aesthetic principles of montage and its philosophies, in particular the concept of the attraction and the value of affect and the capacity of film to transform human consciousness.

Omeros and *The Prodigal* are the two works of poetry that demonstrate these principles most precisely. I have therefore devoted some time to their analyses. In order to examine the effect of film on the poetry and to show how extensive was Walcott's interest in film, I have gone into detail in analysing some of the film scripts, of which there are many.

I have concentrated on those scripts, such as "Vangelo Nero", which bear a direct relationship to the poetry either in terms of imagery, as in the image of the corpse wrapped in sails in both works, or in the use of particular rhythms or a specific technique such as the close up, or superimposition.

One of the emerging ideas in this work is that Walcott is not alone in his use of cinema, or in his sense of the filmic. Both Kamau Brathwaite, in an overt way, and Wilson Harris, in an indirect way, share his concerns and his intuitions about the impact and potential use of the filmic. The impact of the filmic goes well beyond this and we can point to the work of Shani Mootoo, Dionne Brand, NourbeSe Phillip among many others, including the recent work of Jennifer Rahim. This work therefore opens out onto a discussion of Caribbean modernism and contemporary Caribbean literature.

Through this method of analysis and the introduction of film theory and aesthetics, I hope to have provided a new way of looking at Walcott's art and its effect on modern literature.

Endnote.

1. Derek Walcott and Peter Doig, *Morning, Paramin* (London: Faber & Faber, 2016).

WORKS CITED

Antoine-Dunne, Jean. "Moving Beyond Poetry into the Heart of Time". *Film and Film Culture* 4 (2007): 84-90.

"Derek Walcott and Jean Antoine in Conversation". *Poetry Ireland review* 34 (Spring 1992): 72-85.

Antoine-Dunne, Jean. Ed., *Interlocking Basins of a Globe. Essays on Derek Walcott*. Leeds: Peepal Tree Press, 2013.

Åkervall, Lisa. "Cinema, Affect and Vision". *Rhizomes* Issue 16 (Summer 2008) http://www.rhizomes.net/issue16/akervall.html

Balaev, Michelle. Ed., *Contemporary Approaches in Literary Trauma Theory*. London: Palgrave Macmillan, 2014.

Bakhtin, Mikhail. *The Dialogic Imagination. Four Essays*. Trans. Caryl Emerson and Michael Holquist. Austin: University of Texas Press, 1981.

Baudrillard, Jean. *The Evil Demon of Images*. Sidney: Power Institute Publications, 1987.

Baugh, Edward. *Derek Walcott. Memory as Vision. Another Life*. London: Longman, 1978.

——. "*The Arkansas Testament*". *The Art of Derek Walcott*. Ed. Stewart Brown. Chester Springs, Pennsylvania: Seren Books / Dufour Editions, 1991: 123-136.

——. *Derek Walcott*. Cambridge: Cambridge University Press, 2006.

Beckett, Samuel. *Not I. The Complete Dramatic Works*. London: Faber and Faber, 2005.

Bhabha, Homi. *The Location of Culture*. London & New York: Routledge, 1994.

Burnett, Paula. *Derek Walcott. Politics and Poetics*. Florida: University Press of Florida, 2001.

Brathwaite, Edward Kamau. *Rights of Passage*. London: Oxford University Press, 1967.

——. *Masks*. London: Oxford University Press, 1968.

——. *Islands*. London: Oxford University Press, 1969.

——. *Contradictory Omens. Cultural Diversity and Integration in the Caribbean*. Mona: Savacou Publications, 1974.

——. *Mother Poem*. Oxford and New York: Oxford University Press, 1977.

——. *The Arrivants. A New World Trilogy*. London: Oxford University Press, 1981.

——. *Sun Poem*. Oxford: Oxford University Press, 1982.

——. *History of the Voice. Development of Nation Language in Anglophone Caribbean Poetry*. London: New Beacon, 1984.

——. X/Self. Oxford: Oxford University Press, 1987

——. *Ancestors. A Reinvention of Mother Poem, Sun Poem* and *X/Self*. New York: New Directions, 2001.

——. *Born to Slow Horses*. Middletown: Wesleyan University Press, 2005.

Breiner, Laurence. "The Impact of Japan on Derek Walcott's Early Plays". *Comparative Theater Review* Vol.13 (English Issue) March 2014.

Brodber, Erna. *Jane and Louisa Will Soon Come Home*. London: New Beacon, 1980.

Camps, Helen. Telephone interview. 22 June 1993. Republic of Ireland.

Ciccarelli, Sharon. "Reflections Before and After Carnival: An interview with Derek Walcott". *Chant of Saints*. Ed., Michael Harper and Robert Stepto. Chicago: University of Illinois Press, 1979: 296-97. Reproduced in *Conversations with Derek Walcott*. William Baer. Ed. Jackson: University Press of Mississippi, 1996: 34-49.

Cobham-Sander, Rhonda. "'An Enemy So Was a Compliment': Walcott, Brathwaite and the Formal Possibilities of Creole". *Interlocking Basins of a Globe*. Ed. Jean Antoine-Dunne. Leeds: Peepal Tree Press, 2013: pp. 100 – 122.

——. *I and I. Epitaphs for the Self in the Work of V. S. Naipaul, Kamau Brathwaite and Derek Walcott*. Mona: The University of the West Indies Press, 2016.

Collier, George. Ed. *Derek Walcott. The Journeyman Years: Occasional Prose 1957-1974*. Vols. 1 &2, Cross/Cultures 171 &172 Amsterdam: Rodopi, 2013.

D'Aguiar, Fred. "Anansi". Martin Munro. Ed. *The Haunted Tropics. Caribbean Ghost Stories*. Mona: The University of the West Indies Press, 2015.

Docherty, Thomas. *After Theory*. Edinburgh: Edinburgh University Press, 1996.

Dash, J Michael. *The Other America. Caribbean Literature in a New World Context*. Charlottesville: UP of Virginia, 1998.

Deleuze, Gilles. *Cinema 1. The Movement-Image*. Trans. Tomlinson and Habberjam. London: Athlone Press, 1992.

——. *Cinema 2. The Time-Image*. Trans. Tomlinson and Galeta. London: Athlone Press, 1989.

Deleuze, Gilles and Felix Guattari. *A Thousand Plateaus: Capitalism and Schizophrenia*. Trans. Brian Massumi. Minneapolis: University of Minnesota Press, 1987.

Derrida, Jacques. *Specters of Marx. The State of the Debt, The Work of Mourning & the New International*. Routledge Classics [1993] New York: Routledge 1994.

Durix, Jean-Pierre. *Mimesis, Genres and Post-Colonial Discourse. Deconstructing Magical Realism*. London: Macmillan Press, 1998.

Eisenstein, Sergei. *Film Essays and a Lecture*. Ed. Jay Leyda. [1982] Princeton: Princeton University Press, 2016.

——. *The Film Sense*. Ed. and trans. Jay Leyda [1942], London: Faber and Faber, 1986.

——. *Film Form. Essays in Film Theory*. Ed. and trans. Jay Leyda. New York and London: Harcourt Brace, 1977.

——. *Nonindifferent Nature*. Ed. and trans. Herbert Marshall. Cambridge: Cambridge University Press, 1987.

——. *S. M. Eisenstein. Selected Works. Vol.1. Writings, 1922-34*. Ed. and trans. Richard Taylor. London: BFI, 1988.

——. *Towards a Theory of Montage. S. M. Eisenstein. Selected Works. Vol. 2.* Eds. Michael Glenny and Richard Taylor. Trans. Michael Glenny. London: BFI, 1991.

——. *Eisenstein. Writings.1934-1947. Vol. 3*. Ed. Richard Taylor. Trans. William Powell. London: BFI, 1996.

Emery, Mary Lou. *Modernism, the Visual, and Caribbean Literature*. Cambridge: Cambridge University Press, 2007.

Flaxman, Gregory. Ed. *The Brain is the Screen. Deleuze and the Philosophy of Cinema.* Minneapolis and London: University of Minnesota Press, 2000.

Gardner, Colin. *Beckett, Deleuze and the Televisual Event. Peephole Art.* London: Palgrave Macmillan, 2012.

Glissant, Édouard. *Poetics of Relation*. Trans. Betsy Wing. Michigan: University of Michigan Press, 1997.

——. *Caribbean Discourse. Selected Essays*. Trans. J. Michael Dash. Charlottesville: University Press of Virginia, 1989.

Goldstraw, Irma. *Derek Walcott. An Annotated Bibliography of his Works*. New York and London: Garland Publications, 1984.

Hall, Stuart. "Culture, Community, Nation". *Cultural Studies* 7.3 (October, 1993): 351.

——. "Culture and Identity". Mbye Cham, *Ex-Isles. Essays on Caribbean Cinema*. Trenton, New Jersey: Africa World Press, 1992.

Harris, Wilson. *Palace of the Peacock*. London: Faber and Faber, 1960.

——. *Tradition the Writer and Society*. London: New Beacon, 1967.

——. *History, Fable and Myth in the Caribbean and Guianas*. Massachusetts: Calalloo Publications, 1970.

——. *Selected Essays of Wilson Harris. The Unfinished Genesis of the Imagination*. Ed. Andrew Bundy. London: Routledge, 1999.

——. *The Mask of the Beggar*. London: Faber and Faber, 2003.

Ismond, Pat. "Naming and Homecoming", *ACLALS Bulletin* 7th ser. 2 (1985): 27.

——. *Abandoning Dead Metaphors. The Caribbean Phase of Derek Walcott's Poetry*. Kingston: University of the West Indies Press, 2001.

Ivanov, V. "Functions and Categories of Film Language", Trans. Stephen Rudy. *Film Theory and General Semiotics*. Ed. L.M. O'Toole and Ann Shukman. Oxford: RPT Publications, 1981.

Jay, Martin. *The Denigration of Vision in Twentieth Century French Thought*. California: University of California Press, 1994.

James, C.L.R. *Wilson Harris. A Philosophical Approach*. General Public Lecture Series. Gen. ed. E.D. Ramesar. St. Augustine: University of the West Indies, Extra-Mural Department, 1965.

——. Introduction. *Tradition, the Writer and Society*. By Wilson Harris. London: New Beacon, 1967: 69-75.

Joyce, James. *Ulysses*. London: Penguin, 2000.

King, Bruce. *Derek Walcott. A Caribbean life*. Oxford: Oxford University Press, 2000.

Kristeva, Julia. *Desire in Language. A Semiotic Approach to literature and Art*, ed. Leon S. Roudiez. Trans. Thomas Gora , Alice Jardine, and Leon S. Roudiez. New York: Columbia University Press, 1980.

La Capra, Dominick. *Representing the Holocaust: History, Theory, Trauma.* [1994] New York: Cornell University Press, 1996.

Lambert, Gregg. "Cinema and the Outside". *The Brain is the Screen. Deleuze and the Philosophy of Cinema.* Ed. Gregory Flaxman. Minneapolis and London: University of Minnesota Press, 2000.

Lamming, George. *Of Age and Innocence.* London: Michael Joseph, 1958.

——. *Pleasures of Exile.* MI: Ann Arbor, 1960.

——. *Water with Berries.* [1971]. Leeds: Peepal Tree Press, 2016.

Loreto, Paola. *The Crowning of a Poet's Quest. Derek Walcott's Tiepolo's Hound.* Amsterdam: Rodopi, 2009.

Lovelace, Earl. *The Dragon Can't Dance.* ([1979] London: Faber and Faber, 2003.

Macedo, Lynne. *Fiction and Film: The Influence of Cinema on Writers from Jamaica and Trinidad.* Chichester: Dido Press, 2003.

Marks, Laura. *The Skin of the Film. Intercultural Cinema, Embodiment and the Senses.* Durham and London: Duke University Press, 2000.

Munro, Martin. *The Haunted Tropics.* Caribbean Ghost Stories. University of the West Indies Press 2015.

Naipaul, Vidia. *The Middle Passage.* London: Andre Deutsch, 1962.

——. *The Mimic Men.* London: Andre Deutsch, 1967.

Naylor, Paul. *Poetic Investigations. Singing in the Holes of History.* Evanston: North Western University Press, 1999.

Otto, Melanie. *A Creole Experiment. Utopian Space in Kamau Brathwaite's "video-style" Works.* Trenton NJ: Africa World Press, 2009.

Rambaran, Irma. "Reel Text: a comparative analysis of the filmic works of Derek Walcott". MPhil Thesis presented to the University of the West Indies, St. Augustine, 2011.

Ramchand, Kenneth. "Walcott and Ramlila", *Interlocking Basins of a Globe. Essays on Derek Walcott.* Ed. Jean Antoine-Dunne. Leeds, Peepal Tree Press, 2013: 197-2017.

Reckin, Anne. "Tidalectic Lecture. Kamau Brathwaite's Prose / Poetry as Sound Space."http://scholarlyrepository.miami.edu/cgi/viewcontent.cgi?article=1048&context=anthurium

Rohlehr, Gordon. *The Shape of that Hurt and Other Essays.* Port of Spain: Longman, 1992.

Skeet, Jason. "Woolf plus Deleuze: Cinema, Literature and Time Travel". (http://www.rhizomes.net/issue16/skeet.html). RhizomesIssue 16 (Summer 2008).

Sontag, Susan. *On Photography*. New York: Farrar, Straus and Giroux, 1977.

Synge, John Millington. *Riders to the Sea*. 1902. WEB.

Tarkovsky, Andrey. *Sculpting in Time. Reflections on the Cinema*. Trans. Kitty Hunter-Blair. Texas: University of Texas Press, 1987.

Todorov, Tzvetan. *The Conquest of America*. Trans. Richard Howard. New York: Harper Perennial-Collins, 1987.

Taussig, Michael. *The Nervous System*. New York and London: Routledge, 1992.

Walcott, Derek. *Dream on Monkey Mountain and Other Plays*. New York: Farrar, Straus and Giroux, 1970.

——. *Another Life,* Fully annotated by Edward Baugh and Colbert Nepaulsingh. ([1973] London and Boulder: Lynne Rieiner Publishers, 2004.

——. *Sea Grapes*. London: Jonathan Cape, 1976.

——. *Joker of Seville* and *O Babylon*. New York: Farrar, Straus and Giroux, 1978.

——. *Midsummer*. London: Faber and Faber, 1984.

——. *Remembrance and Pantomime*. New York: Farrar, Straus and Giroux, 1980.

——. *Star Apple Kingdom* (London: Jonathan Cape, 1980).

——. *The Fortunate Traveller*. New York: Farrar, Straus and Giroux, 1982.

——. *Three Plays. The Last Carnival. Beef, No Chicken. A Branch of the Blue Nile*. New York: Farrar, Straus and Giroux, 1986.

——. *The Arkansas Testament*. London: Faber and Faber, 1987.

——. "Caligula's Horse", *After Europe*, Critical Theory and Post-Colonial Writing. Eds. Stephen Slemon and Helen Tiffin. Sydney: Dangaroo Press, 1989: 138.

——. *Omeros*. London: Faber and Faber, 1990.

——. *The Antilles: Fragments of Epic Memory*. London: Faber and Faber; New York: Farrar, Straus and Giroux, 1993.

——. *Conversations with Derek Walcott*. Ed. William Baer. Jackson: University Press of Mississippi, 1996.

——. *What the Twilight Says. Essays*. London: Faber and Faber, 1998.

——. *Tiepolo's Hound*. New York: Farrar, Straus and Giroux, 2000.

——. *The Haitian Trilogy*. New York: Farrar, Straus and Giroux, 2002.

——. *The Prodigal*. New York: Farrar, Straus and Giroux, 2003.

——. "Down the Coast". *ep;phany. A literary journal* (Fall/ winter 2007-2008). Ed. Willard Cook

——. *White Egrets*. London: Faber and Faber, 2010.

——. *Moon-Child*. New York: Farrar, Straus and Giroux, 2012.

——. *Derek Walcott, The Journeyman Years. Occasional Prose 1957-1974*. Ed. George Collier. Amsterdam: Rodopi, 2013.

——. *O Starry Starry Night*. New York: Farrar, Straus and Giroux, 2014.

——. With Peter Doig. *Morning, Paramin*. London: Faber and Faber, 2016.

MS and TS

——. "Malcauchon (Malcauchon), or Six In The Rain: A Play In 1 Act". Written in 1958. Box 6, Folder 6, Derek Walcott Collection, Alma Jordan Library. The University of the West Indies, St Augustine. A copy of the play was published by The U.W.I. Extra Mural Department in 1966. However the cover and pages one to four are missing. The copy is marked throughout with pencil insertions and revisions. Included also are fragments of pages nine to twelve and fourteen. There are also duplicate copies of those pages.

——. "The Haitian Earth". TS. Box 5. Folder 3, 1972. Derek Walcott Collection. Alma Jordan Library, The University of the West Indies, St. Augustine. The Haitian Earth. The Black Emperor. T.V. Epic. Crysalite productions. A television mini series. Nine episodes.

——. "The Haytian Earth". TV Epic. TS. Box 5, Folder 4, Derek Walcott Collection. Alma Jordan Library, The University of the West Indies, St. Augustine. Outline, cast list, treatment for nine episodes. Dated 24 June 1978.

Walcott has reworked the theme of the Haitian revolution many times. The earliest record, according to Irma Goldstraw, is to be found in the mimeograph, *Henri Christophe: A Chronicle in Seven Scenes*, Kingston, Jamaica: Extra-Mural Department, U.W.I., c.1949. This was written in 1949 for Roderick Walcott.

——. "Un Voyage a Cythère". A Play for Television. Scenario. Draft Project for Film. Seven page typescript with illustrations by the author. Box 6. Folder 6. Derek Walcott Collection. The Alma Jordan Library. The University of the West Indies, St Augustine. c.1965; this has never been produced, but is very similar in theme and characterization to the play-script *In a Fine Castle*, [1963] 1970, (there is also an undated fragment of a radio-script of this play in the archives) which is also called Conscience of a Revolutionary. Both bear a family resemblance to the film and stage-scripts of *The Last Carnival* (see below).

——. "Steel". There are several versions of *Steel* both as film script and as stage play. I am using a personal copy of the stage play used in the World Premiere, September, 2005 production in Queen's Hall. My copy of the film script was given to me by Nigel Scott and is dedicated "for Roddy and for Turks Steel Band".

——. "The Loupgarou". Film scenario. Box 6. Folder 8. Derek Walcott Collection, The Alma Jordan Library, The University of the West Indies, St Augustine. Circa 1972.

——. "Vangelo Nero". Film scenario. Box 6, Folder 5; Box 6, Folder 9. Derek Walcott Collection, The Alma Jordan Library, The University of the West Indies, St Augustine. 1972.

——. Letters and telegrams between Walcott and Dino deLaurentiis concerning "Vangelo Nero". Temporary Flat Box 1, Derek Walcott Collection. Alma Jordan Library, The University of the West Indies, St Augustine. Final telegram 6 June 1972.

——. "O Babylon". Original Screenplay by Derek Walcott | Music Galt Macdermot. Box 6. Folder 12. Derek Walcott Collection, Alma Jordan Library, The University of the West Indies, St Augustine. This is an undated ts. fragment of fifteen loose leaves. The stage version was published in 1979.

——. "Ti-Jean and his Brothers". Animated Film. Screen Play by Derek Walcott. Songs and music by Andre Tanker. Box 6, Folder 27, Derek Walcott Collection, Alma Jordan Library, The University of the West Indies, St Augustine. This is exists in published form (see list of stage plays above) and in various other versions, including a film fragment (c.1980), and video versions. Undated.

——. Ti-Jean Filmscript with revisions. MS Coll. 136. Thomas Fisher Library, University of Toronto. Box comprising 149 pages, dated Feb 14, 2008.

——. "The Last Carnival". Walcott's production script. Box 6, Folder 11, Derek Walcott Collection, Alma Jordan Library, The University of the West Indies, St Augustine. c. 1982.

——. "The Last Carnival". A four-page outline for a film script. Derek Walcott Collection. Box 6, Folder 11, Alma Jordan Library, The University of the West Indies, St. Augustine, dated June 6th '78. This was re-written as play-script, 1982 (see bibliography above).

——. "Pantomime". A Tele Play. Box 7, Folder 6. Derek Walcott Collection, Alma Jordan Library, The University of the West Indies, St. Augustine. Filmed for Television in 1978.

——. "The Rig". An early ts. draft with slight ms. emendations. Box 6, Folder 11, Derek Walcott Collection. Alma Jordan Library, The University of the West Indies, St Augustine. Only Act 1 and part of Act 2 are available in the archives.

——. "Upon This Rock". A seventy-eight page typescript of an unpublished four act stage drama. Box 5, Folder 8, Derek Walcott Collection. Alma Jordan Library, The University of the West Indies, St Augustine. The Isle Is Full of Noises. c. 1986.

——. "Omeros". Draft. Box 25, Folder 10. Derek Walcott Collection, Alma Jordan Library. The University of the West Indies, St Augustine. 1989- ?. There is no clear indication in the University of the West Indies archives as to which draft this page belongs.

——. "Afterword. Animals, Elemental Tales, and the Theatre". COLL.136. Box 1. Folder 1. Thomas Fisher Rare Book Library. Transcript of speech delivered at the University of Virginia. Dated 3 September, 1993.

——. Film script/ Screen play "Omeros". MS COLL. 136. Box 13. Folders 1-30; Box 14. Folders 1-32. Thomas Fisher Rare Book Library. 1995 dated in text.

——, "Omeros". Screen play and storyboards. MS COLL. 136. Box 67. Folders 1-103. Thomas Fisher Rare Book Library. MS COLL. 136. Box 65. Visual Arts Folders 1-42. Dated by the Fisher as 1985? or 1986.

——. "Monos" and "To Die for Grenada". MS COLL. 136. Box 67. Folders 1-103. Thomas Fisher Rare Book Library. [Draft 7. Dated May 10, 1988.] "To Die For Grenada" storyboard. MS COLL 136. Box 67, The Thomas Fisher Rare Book Library.

——. "American History X". Film Script. MS COLL. 348. Box 27. Folders 1-8. Thomas Fisher Rare Book Library. 1998.

——. "Good Old Heart of Darkness". MS COLL. 136. Box 1. Folders 19-31. Thomas Fisher Rare Book Library.

——. "Hart Crane". Screenplay. Storyboard. Watercolours (photocopies) notes. MS. COLL. 136. Folders 20-26. Thomas Fisher Rare Book Library.

——. "The Haytian Earth". Screenplay and storyboards. MS. COLL. 136. Box 21. Folders 1-24. Thomas Fisher Rare Book Library.

——. "Pantomime". Screenplay, scenario and storyboards. "A Film Scenario". MS COLL. 136. Box 27. Folders 18-27. Thomas Fisher Rare Book Library. Dated May 23, 1985.

——. "To Die for Grenada" or "Monos". Screenplay and research notes. MS COLL. 136. Boxes 38-41. Thomas Fisher Rare Book Library.

——. "To Die for Grenada". "Urgent Fury" (alternate title). MS COLL. 136. Box 39. Folders 1-5. Thomas Fisher Rare Book Library. Dated March 3, 1987.

——. "The Last Carnival". Sketches and watercolours, some in storyboard format. MS COLL. 136. Box 65. Folders 63-75. Thomas Fisher Rare Book Library.

——. "Marie Laveau". Thomas Fisher Rare Book Library. MS COLL. 136. Box 65. Folders 76-79. Sketches and watercolours.

——. "Pantomime". Storyboards. Sketches and watercolours. MS COLL. 136. Box 65. Folders 80-92. Thomas Fisher Rare Book Library.

——. Walcott at Bowling Green University. Derek Walcott's contribution to a symposium "Imagining the Caribbean, Identity and Aesthetics" at Bowling Green in March1999. Video recording supplied by Christopher Laird.

——. Gayelle Series Two 1986. Programme #4 147X U-Matic 02-Oct-86 00:26:56 QuickTime (.mov) 720×480 Edited Feature on Derek Walcott's involvement in a film on Hart Crane, interviewed by Tony hall who also interviews the Director, Lawrence Pitkethly. An extract from the film is shown featuring Nigel Scott as Hart Crane 00:08:27 Derek Walcott, Lawrence Pitkethly, Tony Hall, Nigel Scott Queen's Park Hotel bar, Queen's Park West, Port of Spain.

——. "A Branch of the Blue Nile". Film script. Personal copy.

——. Derek Walcott in conversation with Jean Antoine-Dunne. Filmed 14 October 2015, at his home in Cap in St Lucia.

Derek Walcott films

——. *THE RIG* colour corrected 749B U-Matic 1981 01:33:58 QuickTime (.mov) 720×480 Edited Programme. Feature length movie written & directed by Derek Walcott. Produced by Bruce Paddington. Editor Christopher Laird. Cinematographer Cast: Maurice Brash, Joanne Kilgour, John Isaacs, Charles Applewhaite Nigel Scott, Glenn Davis, Lawrence Goldstraw, Joy Ryan , Gerry Llewellyn, Natalie Rogers, Brenda Baden Semper, Carol La Chapelle, Adele Bynoe, Elizabeth prince, Helen Camps, John Smith, A.J. Milner, Lauretta Lezama, Radin Mayoro, Muriel Redhead, Tony Allsop, Hayden Bernard, Lisa Ann Pierre, Garthleen Richardson, Wayne Gould, Cheryl Prince, Arlene Chung, Natasha Gould, Victor Gould, Carol Redhead, Angela Williams, Beverly Ann Williams, Leonard Stuart, Parry Redhead, Gary Gould, Doretta Lezama, Renrick Gray, Quintin Gray, Nigel Augustus, Learie Joseph, Eric Charles, Evelyn Fleming, Farhad Shageen, Felix Boyce, Rodney Collin, Angus Warren, Claude Lucas Mayaro beach. One Hour (Television Movie) Banyan Productions. 1983. The play was transmitted on Trinidad and Tobago Television on Dec. 31, 1984. Filmed in Mayaro and St. Augustine 1981-1983. This is Walcott's only completed full length film.

Lawrence Pitkethly. 1985. *Hart Crane* (Walcott as script writer).

Filmed versions of stage plays and poems cited.

——. *The Haytian Earth*. Film. Warwick Productions. 1984. This production based on the stage version was commissioned by the Ministry of Education and Culture with the National research Development foundation of St. Lucia in 1984. Shot on location in St Lucia.

——. *The Saddhu of Couva*. 2001. Film. Directed by Derek Walcott. Filmed by Yao Ramesar.

——. *Marie Laveau*. Video production. Banyan Productions. Written by Derek Walcott 63V & 64V U-Matic 1979 01:42:21 QuickTime (.mov) 720×480 unedited A production of Derek Walcott's MARIE LAVEAU in a world premiere workshop production at the College of the Virgin Islands, St. Thomas, with music by Galt MacDermot and choreography by Norline Metiver. Members of the Caribbean Chorale College of the Virgin Islands, St. Thomas Theatre.

Yeats, W.B.. *Collected Poems*. Wordsworth Poetry Library, 1994.

Wilmer, S. E. and Audrone Žukauskaite. Eds. *Deleuze and Beckett*. London: Palgrave Macmillan, 2015.

Films

Sergei Eisenstein. 1925. *The Battleship Potemkin*
Sergei Eisenstein. 1929. *The General Line* or *The Old and the New*.
Walter Ruttman. 1927. *Symphony of a Great City*.
Jacques Tourneur. 1943. *I Walked with a Zombie*
Akira Kurosowa. 1950. *Rashomon*.
Robert Parrish. 1957. *Fire Down Below*.
Perry Henzell. 1972. *The Harder They Come*.
Francis Ford Coppola. 1979. *Apocalypse Now*.
Jean Antoine-Dunne. 2015. *Walcott as Poet and Seer*.

God Speed

INDEX

A Branch of the Blue Nile (Walcott), 13, 50; film script, 50-51
affect (in film theory), 12, 17, 25, 26, 27, 31, 42, 48, 50, 51, 58, 63, 80, 81, 90, 97 n. 19, 105, 124, 140, 190
Åkervall, Lisa, cinema as endurance, 30
allusion in Walcott's poetry: in general, 34, 68, 87; language as carrier of history, 68, 91ff; to Samuel Beckett, 42, 163; the Bible, 172-173; Joseph Conrad (*Heart of Darkness*), 70; Francis Ford Coppola (*Apocalypse Now*), 68; Daniel Defoe (Robinson Crusoe, 42, 43, 66; Dante, 167; Eisenstein (*Battleship Potemkin*), 134-136, 174-175; Perry Henzell (*The Harder They Come*), 55; Homer, 42, 91, 107, 108, 168; Kurosawa (*Rashomon*), 64, 65; George Lamming (*Of Age and Innocence*), 120; Mizoguchi (*Ugetsu*), 159; Shakespeare, *The Tempest*, 41; P.B. Shelley, 85; Susan Sontag, 69; Jean-Jacques Watteau, 44-45; W.B. Yeats, 69, 70, 93;
Anansi, 20, 162
Ancestors (Brathwaite), 82, 185
Andersen, Hans Christian, 91, "The Ice Maiden", 171
Another Life (Walcott), 33, 44, 63, 72, 73, 178; theme of light in, 72; folklore in, 118
Anthony, Msgr. Patrick, on "the after-death", 173
Antillianité, (Glissant), 32
Apocalypse Now (Coppola), 68, 131-132, 133
Arkansas Testament (Walcott), 15, 20, 63, 181; "The Light of the World", 64, 150; "Cul de Sac Valley", 65; "White Magic", 72; "Oceana Nox", 150
Aruacs, 74, 87
attraction, the (in film theory), 17, 26, 27, 36 n. 10, 80, 139, 141 n. 6, 190
Auden, W.H., 67
Bakhtin, Mikhail, on the carnivalesque, 85; on laughter and the circus, 139
Banyan Productions, 13, 14, 142
Baudrillard, Jean, "demonic image", 18, 132
Baugh, Edward, 7, 34, 44, 73, 76, 77 n. 12, 147, 148
Beckett, Samuel, *Krapp's Last Tape*, 42, *Not I*, 50, 163; Walcott on Beckett's "honesty" and the monodic "O", 161, 162
Beef, No Chicken (Walcott), 13
Bergson, Henri, on Deleuze's reading of, 114
Bhabha, Homi, 37, n. 21, 169
Bishop, Elizabeth, 67
Bishop, Maurice, 128, 132
Black/white relations, Walcott on, 46, 132; identification with Black America, 148; black and white as images of racism and their reversal, 171
Blake, William, 179, 180
Braidotti, Rosa, on ethics, activism and community, 32
Brand, Dionne, 190
Brathwaite, Kamau, poetry and the cinematic, 18; tidalectics, 32-33; "Ogun", 75; Sycorax Video Text (as montage of sound and graphics: making sound concrete), 81-83; "missile culture", 185; *History of the Voice,* 81; on the performative, 82; on nation-language and "dialect", 93; *Contradictory Omens*, 102-103; *X-Self*, "Julia", 103, "Letter from Roma", 103-104; *Mother Poem*, 104, 185
Breiner, Laurence, 64, 159
Brodber, Erna, *Jane and Louisa Will Soon Come Home* and kumbla metaphor, 20
Brodsky, Joseph, 89, 173
Burnett, Paula, 68-69, 85

Burroughs, William, 112
Calypsos and calypsonians, 34, 40, 41, 42, 43, 53, 59, 60
Camps, Helen, 20
Caribbean history, as trauma, as discontinuity, see, in particular, Chapters Five and Eight, and 25, 29, 30, 33, 37 n. 21, 40, 46, 49, 52, 56, 60, 66, 67, 74, 87, 104, 107-108, 112, 113, 114, 118, 124-125, 132, 137, 146, 150, 153, 159, 161, 163, 166, 168, 186.
Carnival (Trinidad), 44, 45, ("white people carnival), 46, 50, 51, 60, 85, 138, 139, 140, 147, 160, 170, 179; carnival and revolution, 44
Carnivalesque, the, and performance, 41
Castro, Fidel, 68
Cesairé, Aimé, 174
Cezanne, Paul, 75
Chamoiseau, Patrick, 87
Christophe, Henri, 117, 122
Ciccarelli, Sharon, 83
Conrad, Joseph, Walcott's interest in, 87; *Heart of Darkness*, 68, 70
Contradictory Omens (Brathwaite), 102-103
Coppola, Francis Ford, *Apocalypse Now*, 68, 128-132, Walcott's critique of as aestheticizing evil, 133
"Creoleness: Civilization at the Crossroads" (Harris), 167-168
Crusoe and castaway, motif of in Walcott's writing, 42, 43, 66
"Cul de Sac Valley" (Walcott) *The Arkansas Testament*, 65; sound in, 147, 149-150, 156
cummings, e.e., 67
Deleuze, Gilles and Guattari, Felix, theory of the rhizome, 15, 26-27; on the "affect" as movement to community, 31-32
Deleuze, Gilles, as revisioner of Eisenstein and influence on writing of the book, 12, 15, 24, 27, 34, 189; movement-image and time-image and thinking differently, 17-18; movement into thought, 18; montage and the penetration of the senses/ body, 25; on post-1945 cinema as cinema of fissures and disjunction, 25-26, 28; critique of Eisenstein's organicism, 26, 28; deterritorialism, 26, 34; the overtone and relevance to Walcott's poetry and film, 26; film as associative thinking, 27; on his use of Eisenstein's theory of the overtone, 28; on the interstitial and relevance to later Walcott, 29, 37, n. 21, 80, 114; on cinema as "brain", 31; on the crystalline image and its relevance to Walcott's writing, 33; dramatic images and the shock of thought, 49, 125; generating the "unthought", 161
deLaurentiis, Dino, 14
Dessalines, Jean-Jacques, 118, 123
Dickens, Charles, 70
Docherty, Thomas, on "the possibility of enchantment", 46
Doig, Peter, *Morning, Paramin*, 189
"Down the Coast" (Walcott), 24-25
Dream on Monkey Mountain (film, Walcott), 13; *Dream on Monkey Mountain* (TV), 14
Eagle, Herbert, 177
Eisenstein, Sergei, as influence on Walcott, 12, 15, 190; influence on writing of the book, 12, 95, 187; on montage,16; on affect, 24, 27; on pathos structure, 39-40; on penetration of the body through montage, 46-47; on Japanese art as montage and cross-sensory perception, 47-48; the overtone, 80-81; on the shooting script, 120; on the "attraction" and the close-up, 139-140; on the overtone, 20, **26**, 36 n. 10, 47, 50, 80, **81**

Ellison, Ralph, 87, *Invisible Man*, 148
Emery, Mary Lou, on Harris and Walcott's concerns with art, 178-179
Film Sense, Film Form (Eisenstein), 26, 27, 95, 97 n.19,
Film theory: see affect, montage, movement in time, the poetic, light.
Film, as a means of apprehending the Caribbean, 14-15
Fire Down Below (Parrish), 14, 182
Flaxman, Gregory, on Deleuze and brain as screen, 18
"folk", the, Walcott's relationship to, speaking on behalf of, embalming in nostalgia, 148-149; voicelessness, 149-150; in *Omeros*, 150
folk figures, 181; see also ja gage, loup-garou.
French Creole world, Walcott on, 44-46
Gardner, Colin, on Eisenstein and Deleuze, 136
Gauguin, Paul, 75
Gilkes, Michael, 13
Glissant, Édouard, 15, 16, 24, 91, 123, 127 n. 33; on the rhizome as a cross-cultural poetics, 26-27; Walcott's interest in, 87; *Poetics of Relation*, 15, 26-27
Greece and the Caribbean, 42, 83, 124, 133, 151, 168, 170, 173; in "To Die for Grenada", 133; "all that Greek manure", and simultaneous apprehension, 168;
Grenadian revolution and its fate, Walcott's pessimism over, 132
Harris, Wilson, 16, 70, 185, 186, 190; *Palace of the Peacock*, 30, 32; *The Mask of the Beggar*, 32, 75, 177; ; "Creoleness: Civilization at the Crossroads", 167-168; "Tradition and the West Indian novel", 186; history and the limbo imagination, 16, 30; quantum images, 31, 74; on Jean Rhys, 68; Walcott's interest in Harris, 87; on the cross-cultural aesthetic, 112, 114; the phantom limb and sleeping resources, 162; on shared layers of experience within Creoleness, paradoxes of vulnerability, 168; on Eisenstein, 177; on knowing and respecting the environment, 179
Hart Crane (film, Walcott), 14
Henzell, Perry, 55
Hinkson, Jackie, 60
History of the Voice (Brathwaite), 81; on the performative, 82; on nation-language versus "dialect", 93
Holocaust, images of in Walcott's writing, 70, 90, 160, 171
Homer (as character in *Omeros*) and the Homeric, 42, 71, 83, 85, 91, 107, 108, 109, 155, 160, 168, 173, 186
Hurricane, as a trope in Walcott's poetry, 67, 123, 124, 125, 138-139
I walked with a Zombie (Tourneur), 14, 181
Jã gajè/ gens gage (see also folk figures), 118, 127 n. 27, 180, 181
Japanese cinema, Walcott's interest in, 64, 159
Japanese theatre, Kabuki and Noh, Walcott's interest in, 47
Jones, Errol, 14
King, Bruce, 122
Kristeva, Julia, *Desire in Language, Revolution in Poetic Language*, 110
Kuleshov, Lev, 36, *The Great Consoler*, 65
Kurosowa, Akira, as influence on Walcott, 12, (*Rashomon*) 64, use of light, 65, 66;
L'Ouverture, Toussaint, 117, 122
Laird, Christopher, 14
Lambert, Gregg, on Deleuze and cinema as "brain", 31, 48; on freeing the image from inertia, 49-50

Lamming, George, on Prospero and Caliban, 41; *The Pleasures of Exile*, 41; *Water with Berries*, 41; *Of Age and Innocence*, 117
"Laocoön" (Eisenstein), 81
Larkin, Philip, 67
Laveau, Albert, 11, 122
"Laventille", *The Castaway and Other Poems* (Walcott), 60
Lawrence, D.H., "The Man Who Loved Islands", 65
light, as language of affect, 63; as trope, 63-66, in Christianity, 63
Loreto, Paola, 75
Lovelace, Earl, *The Dragon Can't Dance*, 104
Lowell, Robert, Walcott's interest in, 112
Lucifer, 171
Mailer, Norman, 112
Malcauchon (Walcott), 13, 30, influenced by *Rashomon* (Kurosowa), 65; 159
Man with a Movie Camera (Vertov)
Marie LaVeau (Walcott), 12, 14
Marks, Laura, on affect, sensuousness and memory, 25, 27, 51; on the sense of smell, 146
Maroonage, the self in, 107, 123, 149
McBurnie, Beryl, Little Carib Folk Group, 83
Midsummer (Walcott), 148
Mizoguchi, Kenji, influence on Walcott's use of ghostly echoes, 159
Monet, *Les Nympheas*, 105
montage: as organising trope for the book, 11, 16-17, 25, 30, 64, 108, 136, 165, 172; montage theory in general, 68, 81; in Eisenstein, 20, 26, 28, 35, 39-40, 46, (on Japanese theatre), 47-48, 81, 133, 154; in Deleuze, 25, 27, 28, 30, 33, 48; in Kuleshov, 65; Walcott's explorations of montage, in general, 40, 49, 80, 143, 147, 185, 187; in *Pantomime*, 42-43, *The Last Carnival*, 46; *A Branch of the Blue Nile*, 50; *Steel*, 57; "The Man who Loved Islands", 66-67; "The Fortunate Traveller", 69-70; *The Prodigal*, 88; *Omeros*, 71, 103, 104, 107, 108, 136, 137, 151, 156, 157, 179; "Omeros" (filmscript), 146, 147, 148, 154; "Vangelo Nero", 122, 163; "To Die for Grenada", 134-135; *The Rig*, 144, 145; in work of Kamau Brathwaite, 81, 103-104, 185; in Wilson Harris's ideas, 177, 178
Moon-Child (Walcott), 11, 71, 88, folklore figures in, 180-181, 185, 186
Mootoo, Shani, 190
Morning, Paramin (Walcott and Doig), as a dialogue with the visual, 189
Mother Poem (Brathwaite), 185
movement in time (in film theory), 12, 13, 15-18, 25, **26**, 28, 41, 43, 45, 46, 47, **48-49**, 50, 51, 53, 57, 60, 64, 66, 67, 68, 69, 70, 71, 74, 80, 81, 83, 85, 88, 89, 92, 123, 134, 142, 146, 156, 163, 165, 171, 172, 185, 186, 189, 190
movement-image (Deleuze), 25, 26, 80, 114, 125, 136, 161
Munch, Edvard, *The Scream*, 137
Muslimeen attempted coup in Trinidad, 128
Myth of Europe in Walcott's writing, 53, 70, 91, 93, 112, 160, 161, 171
Naipaul. V.S., on Caribbean futility, 40; on mimicry, 40, 123; Walcott's dialogue with, 86, 123; *The Mimic Men*, 42; *The Middle Passage*, 40
Naylor, Paul, 103
Nonindifferent Nature (Eisenstein), 26, 27, 177
O Babylon (Walcott), 12
O Starry Starry Night (Walcott), 72, 178
Of Age and Innocence (Lamming), connections to *The Haytian Earth*, 117
Omeros (Walcott), 15, 17, 20; as

film script, 20, 167; theme of endurance, 30, and crystalline image, 33; the Caribbean as difference and process, 39; theme of light in, 63, 64, 71; light and memory, 73-74; candlelight in stage production, 75; light in film script, 75; as a multi-voiced dialogue, 86; lines of sight and sound, 102-125; the theme of enslavement, 102-103; the poem as a sound-visual system, 104; the transplantation of language systems, 104-105; as the rewriting of history, 105, 107; the camera and the cinematic in the poem, 107-108, reflective surfaces, 167, image of camera, 169, 170; on the ambivalence to the classical tradition, 108-109; Ma Kilman and the evocation of the past, 110; reconciliation with the psyche of differences, 112, 186; as film, 145-147; montage sequences in, 150-157; the monodic "O" in, 163-164; theme of language and divisions of history, 166; theme of healing wounds of history, 167-168; phantoms in, 170; the filmic as portal, 179

Orishas: Legba, 34, 168; Ogun, 75, 124; Shango, 60, 124

overtone, the (in film theory), 20, 26, 36 n. 10, 47, 50, 80, 81, 169

Paddington, Bruce, 14

Palace of the Peacock (Harris), as a circuit of relations, 30; on journey beyond the self, 32

Pantomime (TV, Walcott), 13, 14, film script and stage play, 18; mimicry, survival and subversion, 40-41; montage editing in, 43

"Papa's Flying Machines" (Walcott review), 16

Phillip, NourbeSe, 190

Picasso, Pablo, 168

Pirates of the Caribbean, 14

Pissarro, Camille, 72, 75-76, 178

Pitkethly, Lawrence, 14

Pocomania, 135

poetic, the (in film theory), 12, 20, 24, 51, 134, 144

Poetics of Relation (Glissant), 15, 26-27

Pound, Ezra, 67

Rahim, Jennifer, 190

Rambaran, Irma, 14

Ramleela, in "The Antilles Fragments of Memory" (Walcott), 162

Rashomon (Kurosowa), 64

Reckin, Ann, on Glissant and Brathwaite, 87

Rhys, Jean, *Wide Sargasso Sea*, 68, 87

Robertson, Hugh, 14

Rohlehr, Gordon, on "aesthetic code-switching", 34, 96 n. 13

Roman Catholicism, in Walcott's work, 88, 180-181

Scamander, in *Omeros*, 137

Senior, Olive, "Penny Reel", 156

Serengeti, in *Omeros*, 137

Sesenne (Descartes, folk-singer), 93

Shelley, P.B., 85

Sidone (D.W.'s Aunt as storyteller), 25

Skeet, Jason, on Deleuze and time-images, 29-30

Slavery as shaper of present, Walcott on, 132

Solipsism, attempts to move beyond, (Deleuze, Harris, Glissant), 31-32

Sontag, Susan, 69

Spottiswoode, Roger, *Under Fire*, 133

St Omer, Dunstan, 72

Steel (Walcott), 11, 35; film script, excavation and fabulation, **51-60**, multiple narratives in, 53; Europe vs Creole in, 53-55; resemblances to *The Harder they Come* (Henzell), 55; film as an image of desire in the play, 56; filmic devices in the play, flashback and fluidity of time, 57-59; affective strategies, 60

steelband, Walcott on, 51, and violence, 52; in *The Rig*, 142

sublime, the, and terror in Walcott,16,

46, 64, 90, 102, 169, 172, 178
Sun Poem (Brathwaite), 185
Symphony of a City (Walter Ruttman), 146
Synge, John Millington, *Riders to the Sea*, 169
Tanker, Andre, 179
Taussig, Michael, 81
The Battleship Potemkin (Eisenstein), 12, 133, 154, 174, 176, 177; Walcott's allusions to in "To Die for Grenada", 133-135; and in *Omeros*, 135-136; in *White Egrets*, 173-175
"The Figure of Crusoe" (Walcott), 66
The Fortunate Traveller (Walcott), 20, 122, as a collection that interrogates the filmic and the play of light, 68; "The Fortunate Traveller", 14, and montage theory, 68-69, 70; theme of light in, 70; "The Spoiler's Return", 34, 41, 85; "The Man Who Loved Islands", 65-66, 67, 68; "Old New England", 69; "The Season of Phantasmal Peace", 71, 91
The General Line (Eisenstein), 39-40
The Harder They Come (Henzell), 55
The Haytian Earth (Walcott), as TV, play and film, 14, 112, **114-118**, 169; Walcott's recurring concern with Haitian revolution, 181
"The Isle is Full of Noises" (Walcott), 44, 78 n. 18
"The Last Carnival" (Walcott), 12, 45, 46, 128
"The Loupgarou" (film script, Walcott), theme of light in, 72; 112, **118**
"The Muse of History" (Walcott), 15, on history as void (qv Deleuze), 29; on the past as acidic, 33; history as Medusa, 108; on creating history as mythic tapestry, 115
"The Poet in the Theatre" (Walcott), on the voice in poetry, 67
"The Walking Fish", *Sea Grapes* (Walcott), 124
The Last Carnival (Walcott), 13
The Mask of the Beggar (Harris), 32, 75, 177
The Middle Passage (Naipaul), 40
The Mimic Men (Naipaul), 40, 42
The Pleasures of Exile (Lamming), 41
The Prodigal (Walcott), 15, 16, 20, 63, 175; theme of light in, 76, 169; montage techniques in, **88-90**; montages of place and language, **90-95**; reconciliation of difference in, 112, 168; ghostly echoes of the past in, 165; "The Ice Maiden", 165; themes of history in, 171; revoking the hegemony of European culture, 186
The Rig (film, Walcott), 14, 16, **142-145;** intercutting techniques in, 144; failings of technique in, 145; connections to *Omeros* and *Steel*, 145
The Star-Apple Kingdom (Walcott), and the "double" of Shabine, 34; the past in, 44; trope of light in, 70
Thomas, Dylan, 67
Ti-Jean and His Brothers (film, Walcott), 13, filmscript, 179; play, 186
Ti-Jean, as recurring folk figure, 11, 181
timehri, in Brathwaite, 87 and Harris, 178
"To Die for Grenada" (Walcott), 12, 14, 128-135, 190, connections with the filmic in *Omeros*, 135
Tourism as neo-colonialism in Walcott, 43
Tourneur, Jacques, *I Walked with a Zombie*, 14, 181
Towards a Theory of Montage (Eisenstein), 27
"Tradition and the West Indian novel" (Harris), 186
Ugetsu (Mizoguchi), 64, 159
"Un Voyage a Cythère" (Walcott), 12, 14, 44, 46; mutation into "The

Isle is Full of Noises", 44, and then to "The Last Carnival", 45
"Vangelo Nero" (Walcott), 112, **118-122,** 190; use of montage in, 163
Vertov, Dziga, 12
Viva Detroit (Walcott), 12
Walcott, Derek, works discussed: *A Branch of the Blue Nile*, 13, 50; film script, 50-51; *Arkansas Testament*, 15, 20, 63, 181; "The Light of the World", 64, 150; "Cul de Sac Valley", 65, ; sound in, 147, 149-150, 156; "White Magic", 72; "Oceana Nox", 150; *Beef, No Chicken*, 13; "Down the Coast", 2; *Dream on Monkey Mountain* (film), 13, (TV), 14; *Hart Crane* (film), 14; *Malcauchon*, 13, 30, 159; *Marie LaVeau*, 14; *Midsummer*, 148; *Moon-Child*, 11, 71, 87, 180-181, 185, 186; *Morning, Paramin*, 189; *O Babylon*, 12; *Omeros* (Walcott), 15, 17, 20; as film script, 20, 167; theme of endurance, 30, and crystalline image, 33; the Caribbean as difference and process, 39; theme of light in, 63, 64, 71; light and memory, 73-74; candlelight in stage production, 75; light in film script, 75; as a multi-voiced dialogue, 87; lines of sight and sound, 102-125; the theme of enslavement, 102-103; the poem as a sound-visual system, 104; the transplantation of language systems, 104-105; as the rewriting of history, 105, 107; the camera and the cinematic in the poem, 107-108, reflective surfaces, 167, image of camera, 169,170; on the ambivalence to the classical tradition, 108-109; Ma Kilman and evocation of the past, 110; reconciliation with the psyche of differences, 112, 186; as film, 145-147; montage sequences in, 150-157; the monodic "O" in, 161-164; theme of language and divisions of history, 166; theme of healing wounds of history, 167-168; phantoms in, 170; the filmic as portal, 179; *Pantomime* (TV), 13, 14, film script and stage play, 18; mimicry, survival and subversion, 40-41; montage editing in, 43; *Sea Grapes*, 123; *Steel*, 11, 35; film script, excavation and fabulation, **51-60**, multiple narratives in, 53; Europe vs Creole in, 53-55; resemblances to *The Harder they Come* (Henzell), 55; film as an image of desire in the play, 56; filmic devices in the play, flashback and fluidity of time, 57-59; affective strategies, 60; "The Antilles Fragments of Memory", 162; *The Fortunate Traveller*, 20, 122, as a collection that interrogates the filmic and the play of light, 68; "The Fortunate Traveller", 14, and montage theory, 68-69, 70; theme of light in, 70; "The Spoiler's Return", 34, 41, 85; "The Man Who Loved Islands", 65-66, 67, 68; "Old New England", 69; "The Season of Phantasmal Peace", 71, 91; *The Haytian Earth*, as TV, play and film, 14, 112, **114-118,** 169; *The Last Carnival*, 13; "The Last Carnival", 45, 46, 128; "The Poet in the Theatre" (Walcott), on the voice in poetry, 67; *The Rig* (film), 14, 16, **142-145**; intercutting techniques in, 144; failings of technique in, 145; connections to *Omeros* and *Steel*, 145; "The Walking Fish", *Tiepolo's Hound*, 15, 20, 178; and theme of light, 63, 72, 75-76; sound in, 149; ghostly presences in, 160; "To Die for Grenada", 14, **128-135**, 190, connections with the filmic in *Omeros*, 135;

"Un Voyage a Cythère", 14, 44, 46; mutation into "The Isle is Full of Noises", 44, and then to "The Last Carnival", 45; "Vangelo Nero", 112, **118-122**, 190; use of montage in, 163; *Viva Detroit*, 12; *White Egrets*, 63

Walcott, Derek, desire to make films, 12, 24; influences in ideas about film, 12; as film-maker, 13, on desire for control, 13; on lack of funding, 14; on over-dependence on words, 20; on film and metaphor and simile, 24; exploration of possibilities of contrapuntal montage, 40, 80; on the oral and the scribal, 83; the filmic as a means of synthesis, 83-84; the visual in his poetry, image of the postcard, 15; use of own paintings, 15; motif of camera and photograph, 17, 44, 68, 117; of filmic improvisation, 18; poetics of sense and body, 20, 40, 42, 50; motif of light, 21, **63-66, 67-73**; on light and language, 75, as an image of the borderland between life and death, 76; film as an aesthetic of fragments, 34, 148; on the close-up, 117, 136-138, 148; freeze frame, 155; on freeing the image from the accretions of time, 49; on film as the medium for responding to Caribbean conflict and displacement and generating the new, 49-50; montage and interstices, 80, 85; "doubling" as the creation of space between meanings, 85, in *Omeros*, 85-86, 110, 112; sound and sight in, 122-123, 147-150; colour imagery in, 140; spectral presences and film; the filmic in *The Prodigal*, 89-95, of the holocaust, 171; on the Caribbean as a place constructed through external media images, 128; spectral presences and film in *Dream on Monkey Mountain*, 159; the influence of *Ugetsu* (Mizoguchi), 159, in *Malcauchon*, 159; in *Omeros*, 159-160, 166, 170; in *The Star Apple Kingdom*, 160; in *Tiepolo's Hound*, 160; in *The Prodigal*, 165

Walcott: theme of home and home-coming in, 58, 73, 105, 109, 138, 148, in *Omeros*, 166, 170, 178; death as a trope, in Omeros, 136-138, 139, 169; rebirth as a trope in *Omeros*, 138, 140; trope of drifting and travel, 185-186; folklore and myth in, 11, 55, 83, 92, 123, **124**, 125, 144, 147, 148, 159, 180, 181; "The Loupgarou", 118; "Vangelo Nero", 118; in *Moon-Child*, 181; Ti-Jean, as recurring folk figure, 11, 181; Christian imagery in, 63, 69, 70, 71, 89, 92, 118, 120, 122, 138, the road to Emmaus, 173

Walcott and the natural world: the motif of the goat and sensuality, 20, 41-42, 107-108, 110, 164, 186; the lizard as a motif of memory and time, 17, 124; the swift as motif in Omeros, 163; the egret as a symbol of the pen and writing, 93, 122, as spectral and existing beyond the grave, 172, 175; hurricane, as a trope, 67, 123, 124, 125, 138-139

Walcott and the Trinidad Theatre Company, 83;

Walcott on Brathwaite, admiration and condemnation, 82; evidence of moving closer in aesthetics, 82, 86, 93, 96, n. 8, 123, 185; on carnival, 50; on history and art, 15; on language, 92-93; Rohlehr critique on movement between search for organic unity and the creative void, 33, 34

Walcott, Roderick, 25, 76

Walton, Dean, 12

Water with Berries (Lamming), 41

Watteau, Jean-Antoine, *The Embarkation to Cythera*, 44-45
"What the Twilight Says, an Overture" (Walcott), 42, 64, 73
White Egrets (Walcott), 63, **172-175**; themes of death and spectral presences, 172; the filmic in 173, 173-175; "Forty Acres", 90
Williams, Raymond, 186
X-Self (Brathwaite), "Julia", 103, "Letter from Roma", 103-104, "X/self's xth letter from the thirteenth provinces", 185
Yeats, W.B. "The Fisherman", 69; "September 1913", 70; "Among School Children", 73; Walcott's interest in, 86; "Easter 1916", 93, Cuchulain, 122

ABOUT THE AUTHOR

Dr Jean Antoine-Dunne is a former Senior Lecturer in Literatures in English at the University of the West Indies, St Augustine. She delivered the Walcott Nobel Lecture in 2006, and the Walcott Lecture at Carifesta UWI Symposium, Cave Hill, in 2017. She has published widely on contemporary Irish and Caribbean writing. She divides her time between Ireland and Trinidad.

She has been awarded a BA from UWI St Augustine, an MA by Major thesis from Maynooth College Ireland, a PhD from University College Dublin, and was Unilever Newman Fellow in Film and Modern Literature at University College Dublin from 1997-2000. She also holds a Diploma in European Human Rights Law from University College Dublin. She worked as a freelance arts reviewer in Ireland (provincial papers), and has written innumerable reviews of contemporary Irish and Caribbean writing. She is a Beckett scholar and worked on the Beckett archives in Dublin, Reading, Texas at Austin, and Syracuse, and also is a Walcott specialist.

She taught Film and Modern Literature at University College Dublin, and taught on the Race and Ethnic Studies Programme at Trinity College Dublin. She also taught Modernism and the Advanced seminar in West Indian Literature (comparative studies) at The University of the West Indies, St Augustine, where she also lectured on postcolonial Literatures and film and literature on MA programme, and gave extensive graduate supervision. She designed the BA in Film at the University of the West Indies, St Augustine with the assistance of Bruce Paddington in 2006, and was the first Coordinator of the Film Programme at The University of the West Indies, St Augustine (2006 -2009). She also was the Coordinator of Graduate Programme in Literatures in English (2009 -2012) and introduced courses in Film and Literature.

Her documentary on Derek Walcott, *Walcott as Poet and Seer*, premiered at the Bocas Lit Festival in 2015.

INTERLOCKING BASINS OF A GLOBE: ESSAYS ON DEREK WALCOTT
EDITED BY JEAN ANTOINE DUNNE

An essential addition to the understanding and appreciation of Walcott's work, these essays range from discussion of Walcott's earliest poetry in *Twenty-Five Poems* (1948) to his most recent collections that explore encroaching old age, *The Prodigal* (2004) and *White Egrets* (2010).

The contributors to this collection are predominantly, but not wholly, Caribbean-based, which ensures that, whilst his position as poet of the world is celebrated, the Caribbean, and more specifically St Lucia, is seen as the source to which Derek Walcott's writing constantly returns.

Gordon Rohlehr offers a powerfully contextualised political and aesthetic reading of the whole range of Walcott's poetry; Harold McDermott surveys the "mulatto" aesthetics of Walcott's critical writing; Rachel Friedman, a Homer scholar, notes how Walcott's work in *Omeros* and *The Odyssey: A Stage Version* challenges a rereading of the original epics; Edward Baugh, perhaps the most distinguished of all Walcott critics, explores how Walcott's poetry crosses local and international spaces; Rhonda Cobham-Sander revisits the old story of the alleged competitive relationship between Walcott and Kamau Brathwaite and finds a flow of influence from the latter to the former; Louis Regis documents Walcott's writing on calypso as part of Walcott's ambivalent relationship to the popular; Jean Antoine-Dunne explores the visual/filmic imagination in Walcott's work; Edward Chamberlin, and Jennifer Toews write about the Walcott archive at the Thomas Fisher Rare Book Library, University of Toronto and make available eighteen reproductions of Derek Walcott's theatre sketches, most in full colour; Kenneth Ramchand looks closely at Walcott's approach to the Indo-Caribbean Ramlila in his Nobel speech, "The Antilles: Fragments of Epic Memory"; Antonia MacDonald, who grew up in St Lucia, confronts the problems of how to teach the real complexity of Walcott's work to young people in St Lucia; George B. Handley uses an ecocritical focus on Walcott's poems of nature to chart a persistent element of spirituality in his work; and finally, there is Patrick Anthony's essay on the ambivalent religious impulse in Walcott's later work and his focus on death and after death.

Price £17.99 • ISBN: 9781845232207